From Crisis to Calm®

Achieving Safer Outcomes in Difficult Encounters

By Jeffrey G. Scholz

From Crisis to Calm

Achieving Safer Outcomes in Difficult Encounters

By Jeffrey G. Scholz

Copyright Notice

Published by 886 Consulting, LLC

ISBN 979-8-9950775-0-3
eBook ISBN 979-8-9950775-1-0
Library of Congress Control Number: 2026905664
First Edition, 2026
Published by 886 Consulting, LLC
Ballston Spa, New York
Printed in the United States of America

GENERAL DISCLAIMER

This book is intended for educational and informational purposes only.

The concepts, frameworks, and techniques described herein are designed to support safer communication, decision-making, and professional conduct during difficult or emotionally charged encounters. They are not a substitute for organizational policy, professional judgment, legal advice, medical advice, mental health treatment, or formal certification programs.

Readers are responsible for complying with all applicable laws, regulations, organizational policies, and professional standards governing their specific roles and environments. Situations involving imminent danger may require immediate protective action beyond the scope of communication-based strategies.

While de-escalation can reduce risk and improve outcomes in many situations, no method can guarantee safety or prevent escalation in every encounter. Human behavior is complex and unpredictable, and outcomes may be influenced by factors beyond any individual's control.

Professional Liability and Assumption of Responsibility

The author provides professional education and training in communication, situational awareness, and de-escalation strategies. The material presented in this book reflects professional experience, established principles of crisis communication, and applied training practices, but it does not constitute legal advice, medical advice, mental health treatment, or operational directives.

By purchasing, accessing, or reading this book, the reader acknowledges that decisions made during real-world encounters involve variables beyond the author's control, including the reader's behavior, the behavior of others, environmental conditions, organizational policies, and legal constraints. The author does not control how the information in this book is interpreted or applied and does not assume responsibility for the actions or decisions of readers.

The reader assumes full responsibility for their conduct, choices, outcomes, and consequences when applying or misapplying any information or material contained in this book. To the extent permitted by law, the author and publisher disclaim liability for any injury, loss, damage, or legal consequence arising from the use or misuse of the material, including but not limited to physical harm, property damage, emotional distress, or legal claims.

Nothing in this book is intended to encourage readers to exceed their authority, violate laws or policies, or place themselves or others in danger. Readers are responsible for acting within the scope of their training, personal limitations, professional role, and applicable regulations at all times. Readers are encouraged to seek additional training, supervision, or professional guidance, as appropriate to their role and environment, when applying the concepts discussed in this book.

Use-of-Force and Safety Statement

From Crisis to Calm emphasizes communication, situational awareness, and ethical influence as primary tools for managing difficult encounters. It does not promote avoidance, passivity, or the abandonment of lawful authority or safety responsibilities.

For professionals whose roles include enforcement, protective, or security duties, the techniques described in this book are intended to complement (not replace) existing safety training, defensive tactics, use-of-force decision-making frameworks, or emergency response procedures. Physical intervention, disengagement, or emergency response (in accordance with federal, state, and local laws and applicable organizational or agency policies) may be necessary when an immediate threat exists.

The author and publisher do not advocate or authorize any specific use-of-force response and do not provide operational directives. Decisions involving physical intervention, disengagement, or emergency response must be made by the individual professional based on their training, authority, organizational policy, and the totality of the circumstances present at the time of the encounter.

For civilians and non-enforcement professionals, personal safety should always take priority. When feasible, removing oneself from a dangerous situation and seeking assistance from appropriate authorities is the preferred response.

Fictitious Names and Scenarios

Unless explicitly stated otherwise, the names, characters, organizations, locations, and identifying details used in this book are fictitious. Any resemblance to actual persons, living or deceased, or to real organizations or events is purely coincidental.

Scenarios presented in this book are composites drawn from recurring patterns observed across many training environments, and/or the author's personal experiences throughout his career and after. They are intended to illustrate common dynamics and learning points, not to describe or reference any specific individual, agency, organization, or incident, unless specified otherwise.

About the Author

Jeffrey G. Scholz is a retired New York State Trooper who worked nearly three decades in law enforcement including almost 25 years with the New York State Police. He is an IADLEST National Certified Instructor and a New York State Division of Criminal Justice Services Master Instructor, and he is the recipient of the prestigious George M. Searle Award for Excellence in Police Training, an honor recognizing exceptional impact in professional instruction.

Upon his retirement in 2022, Jeff was serving as the Senior Investigator for BCI Training at the New York State Police Academy, where he was responsible for the development, facilitation, and delivery of training to more than 1,100 Investigators and thousands of uniformed members, recruits, civilians, and outside agencies statewide. Earlier in his career, he completed crisis negotiation training and went on to serve as the Division Coordinator for the NYSP Crisis Negotiation Program, overseeing statewide standards, training, and reporting.

Jeff's operational background includes a wide range of investigative and field assignments in addition to uniformed patrol to plainclothes investigations. He served as a Field Training Officer providing on-the-job training to new troopers, worked undercover narcotics investigations, conducted computer crime investigations, and served as a Major Crimes Investigator specializing in homicides, missing persons, suspicious deaths, and complex, high-profile cases. This phase of his career was distinguished by his ability to conduct sensitive interviews with both suspects and survivors, integrating trauma-informed practices with investigative interviewing techniques to uncover critical information while minimizing harm. He was also a responder to the September 11, 2001 terrorist attacks in New York City.

With more than a decade of dedicated instructional experience (both during his public service career and through his company, 886 Consulting, LLC), Jeff has delivered high-impact training to thousands of professionals in 17 states. While his foundation is rooted in law enforcement instruction, a significant portion of his work has focused on social services, human services, community agencies, healthcare, and other public-facing professions. His programs cover crisis negotiation, de-escalation, crisis intervention, behavioral observation, situational awareness, interviewing, implicit bias, procedural justice, and staff wellness, drawing directly from crisis negotiation and investigative principles and applying them to the real-world challenges faced by professionals who routinely engage with vulnerable individuals or emotionally dysregulated clients. His From Crisis to Calm program and Professional Sincerity concept emphasize outcome-driven communication, emotional regulation, and interpersonal safety, helping organizations reduce risk, strengthen engagement, and improve the likelihood of constructive outcomes during high-stress encounters.

Jeff continues to serve as a training consultant for the New York State Office of Mental Health and as a cold case consultant for the New York State Division of Criminal Justice Services. His work remains grounded in practical experience, nationally recognized credentials, and a commitment to equipping professionals across disciplines with the communication skills necessary to navigate complex human behavior safely and effectively.

From Crisis to Calm

Achieving Safer Outcomes in Difficult Encounters

CONTENTS

PREFACE

For 16 years of my law enforcement career, I served as a crisis negotiator. That role sharpened my understanding of conflict, stress, and human behavior under pressure. Negotiators are called when emotion has begun to overpower reason and interactions are moving toward outcomes no one wants. By the time we arrived, stress had reached a breaking point, communication had broken down, and choices felt increasingly limited. In those moments, true success rarely came from authority or force, but rather from influencing behavior by managing emotions, restoring clarity, and guiding interactions toward safer outcomes.

You can see that understanding reflected in the cover image.

The dominoes represent the way a crisis develops. A sequence of moments that build on one another. A misunderstanding becomes frustration. Frustration turns into resistance. Resistance increases emotional intensity. As emotion rises, perception narrows, and the range of available responses shrinks. At some point, the outcome begins to feel inevitable, even when it is not. Each domino tips the next, and the trajectory seems impossible to change.

The knight represents a different way of engaging with that process. In chess, the knight moves differently from other pieces. It does not rely on linear paths or direct confrontation. Instead, it influences the board by approaching problems from angles others cannot. In the context of a crisis, the knight is not about stopping motion, but about shaping it. Affecting how events unfold by influencing behavior earlier in the interaction. That capacity to influence outcomes without direct confrontation is precisely why the knight has become the defining symbol of the crisis negotiator.

For a long time, I believed this way of thinking applied primarily to law enforcement. Over time, working with professionals across public and private sectors, I learned that my assumption was incorrect. The same patterns appear everywhere professionals interact with people under stress: the hospital nurse managing a family member's panic in the ER, the retail employee facing an irate customer, the social worker conducting a tense home visit, the government clerk helping someone who's overwhelmed by bureaucracy, the loss prevention specialist addressing suspected theft. Crisis follows the same human trajectory regardless of setting. *Emotional* escalation almost always happens before *behavioral* escalation. Communication, good or bad, plays a central role in determining what happens next. And the way one person manages themselves in the interaction often has more influence on the outcome than any single policy, rule, or authority.

The knight, then, represents something broader than just the negotiator. It represents anyone who learns to recognize escalation early, manage their own responses effectively, and shape interactions toward safer outcomes. The knight is not defined by a title, a uniform, or a specific professional role. It's a skill set and a mindset that anyone can develop. One that allows you to step into a crisis from an angle others might miss, and change what happens next.

Why I Do This Work

Over nearly 30 years in law enforcement, I sometimes watched ordinary interactions turn into critical incidents. Not always because people intend harm, but because stress, emotion, and miscommunication go unrecognized or unmanaged. I have also seen the opposite: how calm, intentional communication can slow situations down, reduce emotional intensity, and change outcomes entirely.

I have watched poor communication contribute to tragic results, including serious injury and loss of life. I have also seen effective communication save lives, prevent violence, and bring resolution, sometimes through voluntary compliance, sometimes through critical admissions or confessions that allowed justice to move forward without further harm. The difference between these outcomes often had less to do with authority or tactics. It had far more to do with timing, tone, distance, and the ability to recognize what was happening beneath the surface of a person's behavior. Too often, I have seen well-intentioned professionals placed in impossible positions by systems that expect calm, clarity, and control without providing the tools to achieve them.

Those experiences led me to focus on a central question: What happens earlier in the encounter? Not in the final moments, when options are already limited and decisions are compressed by urgency, but in the minutes before that, during initial contact, early communication, and the first decisions about positioning, boundaries, and direction.

That question drove my deeper study of crisis communication, negotiation, and human behavior under stress. I pursued advanced training and education in crisis negotiation, behavioral assessment, emotional regulation, influence and persuasion, and the neuroscience of crisis. I read extensively, trained broadly, and sought out perspectives beyond any single discipline.

Eventually, I began teaching: first to other law enforcement professionals, then to social services, mental health practitioners, and later to healthcare, education, and other public-facing professions. What became clear is that while environments differ, the underlying principles do not. The neuroscience of emotional arousal does not change based on job title. Ethical influence works whether someone is wearing a uniform, a suit, business casual, or scrubs. How and whether that influence is applied, however, is always constrained by role, authority, safety thresholds, and legal responsibility. And the skills that reduce escalation and improve safety are transferable across settings.

But "transferable" does not mean identical. The principles travel well: validation, tone, timing, collaboration, options, and boundary-setting, but the application must match the role and the moment. A nurse, a social worker, a retail associate, and a police officer may use the same communication principles, but they do not share the same authority, the same legal obligations, or the same ability to safely stay engaged. In helping professions, the goal is often stabilization and voluntary cooperation. In enforcement or protective roles, the goal may include lawful compliance and immediate protection of others. And for civilians, the safest and most appropriate choice may be disengagement. Same principles, different permissions, different responsibilities, different thresholds for staying in the conversation.

I also discovered a widespread frustration among professionals. Not a lack of concern or effort, but a lack of preparation. Time and again, participants described difficult encounters: the aggressive client, the distressed patient, the threatening parent, the emotionally dysregulated customer, and asked why these skills were never part of their foundational training.

I wrote this book because many of these moments may have been preventable. Not through perfection, scripts, or unrealistic expectations. Through earlier recognition, better communication, and a clearer understanding of how people behave under pressure.

A Note on Scope and Application

This book is written from the perspective of a practitioner, not a laboratory researcher or policy theorist. It is grounded in years of observing how people actually behave under stress, and in directly encountering and navigating those moments firsthand. Sometimes with good outcomes, sometimes with outcomes that fell short, and often with lessons that only become clear in hindsight. The insights here don't come from idealized scenarios, but from real interactions where decisions and words sometimes carried life-or-death consequences.

Some of the concepts discussed here, such as validation, tone, timing, collaboration, and boundary-setting, will be familiar to readers with backgrounds in crisis negotiation, counseling, motivational interviewing, trauma-informed care, or behavioral psychology. Nothing in this book claims to invent those ideas. The focus is on how they show up in real interactions, under pressure, and how they are applied, or misapplied, when stakes are high and time is limited.

Throughout the book, neuroscience is discussed in plain language. That choice is intentional, and appropriate. I don't claim to be a scientific expert or anything as such. When terms like "amygdala hijack" or references to executive functioning appear, they are used as functional shorthand to describe observable shifts in attention, emotional regulation, and cognitive flexibility under perceived threat. These descriptions are not meant as literal or exhaustive accounts of brain activity, but as practical explanations for why certain communication approaches consistently fail or succeed in real-world encounters, practical explanations that back up what I have seen and done in real life.

The examples in this book span many professional environments, including healthcare, social services, education, retail, security, and law enforcement. The principles of human behavior under stress are broadly consistent across these settings. The permissions, responsibilities, and thresholds for action are not. Communication skills influence encounters, but they do not override legal authority, organizational policy, safety considerations, or the duty to protect others. Whether a conversation continues, shifts, or ends is always determined by role, context, and safety.

This book does not suggest that communication alone can prevent violence, resolve every crisis, or compensate for systemic failures. De-escalation, as discussed here, is an outcome. It's not a guarantee, not a mandate, and not always the appropriate goal in every moment. What the book does argue, based on repeated observation across sectors, is that unnecessary escalation is often driven by timing, tone, and perceived intent, and that professionals are frequently expected to manage these dynamics without having been taught how.

The pages that follow are intended as a narrative, experience-informed guide to recognizing those patterns and responding to them more deliberately, with greater awareness of how human beings process stress, and how our own behavior shapes what happens next.

What This Book Offers

Since retiring from the New York State Police in 2022, I've taught From Crisis to Calm (FC2C) hundreds of times to thousands of professionals, both civilian and law enforcement, in 17 states. This book exists because I wanted to reach beyond the classroom.

The principles that guide effective crisis negotiation are not negotiator skills. They are human skills, such as listening in a way that lowers emotional intensity, regulating your own response when someone else is overwhelmed, and recognizing rising stress before it turns into confrontation. Offering clarity and options that preserve dignity and setting boundaries in ways that reduce resistance rather than provoke it. These behaviors influence how people respond, which in turn influences how situations are resolved.

I'll say this numerous times throughout this book: De-escalation is an outcome, not a single tactic. This book walks through the skills, behaviors, and frameworks that can influence that outcome, from understanding how to read behavior and recognize escalation, to managing your own responses, to communicating in ways that preserve safety and dignity. Each chapter builds on the last, creating an approach you can adapt to your specific professional context.

How we reach that outcome depends heavily on the person in front of us. The skills in this book are effective in many situations, but we cannot talk to everyone, and sometimes the situation demands immediate action. For law enforcement professionals, that may mean the use of objectively reasonable force, applied in accordance with law and policy, as one pathway to a de-escalated outcome. For civilians and non-enforcement professionals, it means recognizing when the best option is to remove yourself from the encounter entirely. Either way, the goal remains the same: safer encounters.

From Crisis to Calm is not designed to turn anyone into a negotiator, nor does it ask you to step outside your role, training, or organizational policies. It is designed to help you understand how behavior shapes outcomes and how your communication, presence, and decision-making can either increase risk or move interactions toward greater safety. The goal is to help you recognize escalation earlier, communicate with greater intention, and make decisions that preserve dignity, enhance professionalism, and improve safety for everyone involved, not to promise perfect results or eliminate all conflict.

Some situations will still require firm boundaries, disengagement, or decisive action to protect people from harm. I would like you to be able to manage your own emotional responses and use influence to guide interactions before choices narrow to the point where harm feels unavoidable.

At its core, this work is about helping professionals show up consistently, communicate effectively, and navigate difficult human behavior in ways that protect safety without sacrificing dignity. Anyone can learn to increase awareness, influence behavior, understand how their actions affect outcomes, and, within their own responsibilities, move difficult encounters From Crisis to Calm.

The encounters that test professionals most rarely announce themselves in advance. They unfold in offices, classrooms, hospital rooms, store aisles, parking lots, and public spaces, often without warning and with little margin for error. This book aims to help close the gap between the responsibilities placed on public-facing professionals and the preparation they receive.

If your work involves interacting with people who may be stressed, angry, frightened, or in crisis, this book is for you. Read it as a training manual. Return to it as a reference. Practice from it. Discuss it with colleagues. The skills described here improve outcomes not because they are complicated, in fact some are so simple that they may seem cliché, but because they are applied early, deliberately, and with professional intent.

This book also asks something else of you: self-awareness. Working around crisis, conflict, and emotionally charged behavior takes a cumulative toll. Exposure to anger, trauma, fear, and volatility, especially if it becomes routine, can quietly erode patience, judgment, and emotional resilience. Your ability to communicate clearly, regulate your emotions, and make sound decisions is directly tied to your own mental and emotional health.

Part of professional safety is recognizing when stress, fatigue, frustration, or burnout are influencing how you show up in an interaction. It's understanding when you need to slow down, ask for support, take a break, or step away. It's also about being attentive to the signs in the people you work alongside and looking out for one another before problems arise during an encounter.

Taking care of yourself and your coworkers is not separate from de-escalation, it's foundational to it. Healthy teams communicate better, recognize risk sooner, and respond more effectively under pressure. This book is written with that reality in mind.

It's important to know what support systems are available to you before stress becomes overwhelming. Many organizations provide Employee Assistance Programs (EAPs), peer support teams, or other confidential resources designed to support mental and emotional well-being. Familiarity with these options before you need them removes hesitation in the moment and reinforces that seeking support is a professional decision, not a personal failing.

If you or someone you work with is experiencing significant emotional distress or crisis, national resources such as the 988 Suicide & Crisis Lifeline are available 24/7 by call or text. Knowing where help exists, even if you never use it, is part of responsible preparation in high-stress professions.

I hope this book gives you tools you can use immediately, concepts that make sense of experiences you've already had, and the confidence to influence difficult moments for the better. Not through force or authority alone, but through understanding, awareness, and genuine skill in managing what happens between people when stress is high and stakes matter.

Finally, if you're reading this work, I like to believe that you are invested in your work and the people that you serve. That is who this book is dedicated to, those on the front lines of crisis looking to help others. I hope that you love your work and put one hundred percent into it. But as I said, please don't forget to take care of yourself and your loved ones and your coworkers. If you find meaning in your job, you're doing work that matters. But just remember at the end of the day, it's a job. And as much as you love the job, it will never love you back.

CHAPTER 1:

WHY DE-ESCALATION MATTERS NOW

The Encounters We Face

It's a Tuesday afternoon when Susan Dickinson realizes her master's degree in social work hasn't quite prepared her for this moment.

The man across the desk is shouting. Not at her, exactly, but at the system, at his circumstances, at the universe that has placed him in a position where he needs to beg strangers for help feeding his children. His voice grows louder. His hands clench. Susan feels her own heart racing, and her mouth is dry. She'd been trained to assess eligibility for benefits, to navigate complex regulations, and to document cases thoroughly. No one had taught her what to do when someone is three seconds away from flipping her desk.

Susan isn't the only one right now struggling with how to act, what to say, and what to do if she has to protect herself.

Alice Strauss, a nurse at the hospital's emergency department, watches a family member's frustration escalate as he explains for the third time why their loved one can't be discharged yet. The family member steps closer, jaw clenched, finger jabbing the air near Alice's face.

In a suburban department store, a college student who's a part-time sales associate approaches a customer who's been asked to leave. The customer's voice rises. Other shoppers stop and stare. The associate's training covered inventory management and customer service recovery. It never covered this.

In a corporate HR office, a benefits specialist tries to explain why a claim was denied. The employee across from her isn't hearing explanations anymore. Instead, they're cataloging grievances, their tone shifting from disappointed to angry to something darker.

Over at the Knolls, a community church, Pastor Brian attempts to mediate a conflict between members of the congregation. What started as a discussion about worship music styles has devolved into personal attacks. Voices echo off the sanctuary walls. Someone stands up abruptly, knocking over a chair.

And in a rural county Sheriff's office, a deputy stands face-to-face with a man in crisis who has stopped responding to verbal commands and whose hand keeps drifting toward his waistband. Everything she learned in the academy feels simultaneously critical and completely inadequate.

As outlined earlier, the communication principles at play here are consistent across roles, but the decision to stay engaged, disengage, or intervene physically depends entirely on authority, policy, and safety. These scenarios illustrate the types of encounters that professionals in my training sessions face with troubling frequency. They share three things in common:

First, most professionals receive inadequate preparation for these moments. They have excellent training for the technical aspects of their roles, but when it comes to managing another human being in emotional crisis, they're operating on instinct, improvisation, and hope.

Second, in every one of these scenarios, there is a reason behind the other person's behavior. The father who can't feed his kids, the family member watching a loved one suffer, the employee whose claim was denied... they are not operating from a calm, fully regulated state. They are responding the way many people do under significant stress. You don't have to agree with how someone expresses their emotions to recognize that the emotions themselves are valid.

But here's the reality: you don't always know what's driving the behavior in front of you. In the moment of an encounter like this, the deputy isn't trying to diagnose emotion in the abstract. She has to assess behavior and possible intent in context, with limited information and real safety stakes. Situations like this require the same foundational skill as every other difficult encounter in this book: the ability to accurately read what is unfolding without defaulting to assumption. Sometimes that assessment points to legitimate distress. Sometimes it points to a credible threat. The difference matters, and this book addresses both.

Third, these encounters don't always have to escalate. With the right skills, framework, and mindset, they may be guided toward safer, calmer resolutions.

The consequences are real. But so is the evidence that proper training works: when the Louisville Metro Police Department implemented comprehensive de-escalation training, they saw a 28% reduction in use-of-force incidents, a 26% reduction in citizen injuries, and a 36% reduction in officer injuries.[1]

Based on my training and experience across law enforcement and civilian settings, those results are consistent with what I have observed more broadly: when people are trained to recognize escalation earlier, regulate their own responses, and communicate with greater intention, encounters are less likely to deteriorate, even in civilian and non-enforcement roles where authority, force, and legal thresholds differ.

Who This Book Is For

If you're reading this, you likely recognize yourself or your colleagues in the scenarios we just covered:

Healthcare workers: Physicians, nurses, emergency department staff, mental health professionals, patient services representatives

Social services professionals: Eligibility workers, case managers, child protective investigators, housing counselors, benefits specialists

Educators: Teachers, administrators, school counselors, support staff

Retail and customer service workers: Sales associates, managers, customer service representatives

Security and loss prevention professionals: Security officers, asset protection and loss prevention specialists, campus and event safety personnel

Human resources professionals: Benefits specialists, employee relations staff, workplace investigators

Faith community leaders: Clergy, pastors, rabbis, ministers, gurus, elders, staff, counselors, volunteers

Law enforcement: Police officers, troopers, sheriffs' deputies, corrections officers, probation and parole officers

Anyone who regularly faces the public: Court clerks, DMV employees, library staff, transit workers, government agency frontline personnel, insurance industry, and so on

In short: if your job involves interacting with people who might be stressed, angry, scared, or in crisis, and if you've ever felt underprepared for those moments, this book is for you, because the gap between what professionals need and what they receive has reached crisis proportions.

The Growing Crisis in Crisis Management

Let's start with some uncomfortable numbers.

Federal surveys and safety agencies estimate that nearly 2 million American workers report being victims of workplace violence each year, with many additional incidents likely going unreported.2 The Occupational Safety and Health Administration (OSHA) and various industry analyses estimate that the national economic impact of workplace violence reaches into the tens and potentially hundreds of billions of dollars annually when accounting for both direct and indirect costs including lost productivity, increased security measures, workers' compensation claims, and employee turnover.3

And while these numbers focus on incidents reported by workers, workplace violence doesn't stay contained to one side of the interaction. Patients, clients, customers, visitors, and bystanders are all part of the picture. When a situation escalates in a hospital lobby, a government office, or a retail floor, everyone present is affected, and everyone could be at risk.

But the real story isn't in the aggregate statistics. It's in the sector-specific data that reveals just how pervasive this problem has become.

Healthcare: The Front Lines of Crisis

Healthcare workers experience workplace violence at rates far exceeding those in other industries. Data from the Bureau of Labor Statistics (BLS) show that workers in the healthcare and social assistance sector account for roughly 70 to 75 percent of all nonfatal workplace injuries and illnesses due to violence, despite representing a much smaller share of the workforce.[4] OSHA and related federal guidance report that healthcare workers are approximately five times more likely to experience workplace violence than workers in other industries.[5]

These aren't just statistics. They represent experienced nurses leaving the profession, physicians experiencing trauma, and healthcare organizations struggling with staffing crises driven in part by workplace safety concerns. The Joint Commission (the independent nonprofit organization that accredits and certifies more than 22,000 healthcare organizations and programs in the United States) now includes workplace violence prevention elements in its accreditation standards.[6] Yet healthcare workers often report receiving little more than a brief video module and instructions to call security.

The financial impact is substantial. While comprehensive cost data varies, healthcare organizations face significant expenses related to workplace violence incidents, including medical care for injured staff, workers' compensation claims, increased security measures, legal costs, and the considerable expense of replacing experienced healthcare workers who leave due to safety concerns.

That doesn't account for the broader organizational impacts: decreased morale, increased sick leave usage, the reluctance of experienced staff to work in high-risk areas, and the ripple effect on patient care quality when experienced professionals leave or avoid certain assignments.

Retail: When Customer Service Becomes Survival

Retail workers increasingly report hostile encounters with customers. Research from the National Retail Federation (NRF) indicates that violent incidents and organized retail crime have increased substantially in recent years, with both theft-related confrontations and customer aggression becoming more common.[7]

Store associates, often part-time employees, are expected to enforce store policies, prevent theft, manage returns, and handle customer complaints, all while maintaining a friendly demeanor. Their training in difficult encounters is often simply, "We tell them to comply with customer demands" or "We train them to call security or management."

In other words: give in, retreat, or escalate to someone else. None of these responses actually equip workers with the skills to reduce emotional intensity or guide an encounter toward a safer resolution.

The numbers bear this out. A 2024 survey of 600 in-store retail workers conducted by Theatro, a Motorola Solutions company, found that 80 percent don't feel protected by their employer while on the job. Eighty percent of those workers have considered purchasing personal safety devices like pepper spray or personal alarms because of safety concerns at their store. When asked what's driving the stress, 33 percent cited increases in shoplifting and in-store crime, 27 percent pointed to staffing shortages, and 23 percent said unreasonable customers. Sixteen percent said they simply don't feel safe at work.[8]

The human cost is measured in injuries, trauma, and turnover. Turnover among hourly, frontline retail workers routinely exceeds 60 percent annually in many settings.[9] Workplace safety concerns are frequently cited as a contributing factor. When employees don't feel safe, they leave. When they leave, stores lose institutional knowledge, spend enormous sums on recruiting and training, and create service gaps that frustrate customers, which leads to more conflict. The cycle happens over and over.

The Theatro survey quantifies this flight risk: 73 percent of in-store workers are considering leaving their jobs, with the combination of safety concerns and staffing shortages cited as the top reason. Among those contemplating departure, 25 percent attributed it to both safety and staffing issues combined, while another 18 percent cited safety alone. Perhaps more alarming for retailers, 64 percent said they would consider suing their employer over an injury or safety issue from a store crime incident. The cycle is self-reinforcing: understaffing creates safety gaps, safety gaps drive turnover, and turnover deepens the understaffing.

Social Services: Helping Under Pressure

Social services workers occupy one of the most challenging spaces in public-facing work. They encounter individuals at their most vulnerable, most desperate, and sometimes most volatile moments. County eligibility workers, child protective services investigators, housing counselors, benefits specialists, and many other job titles regularly face clients experiencing mental health crises, substance use disorders, trauma, housing instability, and profound financial stress, often simultaneously.

Research consistently documents that social workers experience workplace violence at concerning rates. A national study of NASW members found that 62 percent reported experiencing physical or psychological assault by a client, with verbal aggression representing the most common form of violence.[10] In my training sessions with social services departments across New York State over the past decade, these concerns have been universally expressed.

Yet most social services agencies provide minimal crisis de-escalation training beyond a brief orientation session. When I work with county DSS offices, case managers and eligibility workers consistently report that, while they encounter aggressive or threatening behavior regularly, often multiple times per week and sometimes per day, their initial training in managing these situations typically consists of a short video or lecture with no opportunity to practice these skills.

The consequences extend beyond worker safety. When social services professionals don't have effective de-escalation skills, they're more likely to disengage from clients who need help the most, more likely to experience burnout and compassion fatigue, and more likely to leave the profession entirely. Workforce retention in child welfare and social services has been a persistent challenge,[11] and while the inherent difficulty of the work contributes to turnover, inadequate preparation for managing hostile encounters is a factor that participants in my training sessions frequently identify as contributing to their stress and their colleagues' decisions to leave.

Education: Classrooms in Crisis

The National Center for Education Statistics (NCES) reports that during the 2020–21 school year (the most recent year for which this series is available) about 6 percent of public school teachers reported being threatened with injury by a student from their school, and about 4 percent reported being physically attacked by a student from their school.[12] Using conservative estimates of the number of public school teachers in the United States, these percentages translate to well over 100,000 teachers who report having been threatened with injury or physically attacked by a student in a single school year. Educators consistently describe an environment where hostile interactions, with both students and parents, have become more frequent and more intense.

But the challenge isn't just student behavior. Teachers and administrators also describe increasingly hostile interactions with parents. Issues ranging from curriculum decisions to discipline policies to pandemic-related requirements have generated confrontations that sometimes feel threatening. School board meetings, once quiet affairs attended by a handful of community members, now sometimes require law enforcement presence in response to documented threats and safety concerns.[13]

What training do educators receive for managing these encounters? In most cases, minimal preparation at best. Teacher preparation programs focus on pedagogy, classroom management strategies for typical student behavior, and subject matter expertise. Crisis communication, if addressed at all, might receive only an hour or two during in-service training, often delivered through a lecture or video presentation without an opportunity for practice.

The impact on teacher retention is significant. We're losing talented, dedicated educators not because they don't love teaching, but because they don't feel safe or adequately supported in managing the non-instructional challenges they face daily.[14]

Corporate Environments: HR and Beyond

Even traditional office environments face workplace violence challenges. Human resources professionals, corporate security teams, and managers increasingly encounter employees in crisis, dealing with denied benefits claims, terminations, disciplinary actions, or the accumulated stress of modern work life.

Data on workplace homicides from the Bureau of Labor Statistics and other federal sources show that these rare but severe incidents arise from a range of circumstances, including robberies, customer interactions, coworker disputes, domestic violence that spills into the workplace, and employment-related conflicts such as disciplinary actions or terminations.[15]

Now, as we'll discuss later, if you're faced with that kind of violence, you're not going to stick around and try to talk to someone. Your best bet to stay safe is to get out. But what about the much more common disputes, arguments, and misunderstandings that occur? Those are the encounters that while difficult, may be influenced toward a better, safer outcome through awareness and communication. Yet organizational investment in de-escalation training for HR professionals and managers remains limited. I've found that while some organizations may provide active shooter awareness training, specific skill-building in de-escalation and crisis communication is uncommon.

The consequences of mishandling these encounters may be severe: wrongful termination lawsuits, workplace violence incidents, damage to employee morale, and in extreme cases, targeted violence. The financial risk alone should compel organizations to invest in proper training.

Security and Loss Prevention: The Training Desert

Perhaps nowhere is the gap between responsibility and preparation more apparent than in the private security industry. Estimates suggest that there are well over one million private security officers in the United States, a workforce that outnumbers sworn law enforcement officers.[16] Private security personnel are often the first point of contact when situations become tense or volatile.

But the training requirements for security officers remain minimal in most jurisdictions. Requirements vary substantially by state. As of this writing, California requires 8 hours of initial training for security guards, New York requires 24 hours total (8 hours pre-assignment plus 16 hours on-the-job training), Florida mandates 40 hours for Class D licensure, and Texas requires 6 hours for Level II non-commissioned security officers.[17] De-escalation and crisis communication, when included at all, typically receive minimal attention within these already brief training programs, often taught through lecture with no practical application, or even through remote video training.

Ongoing training requirements are even more limited. Many states require only minimal annual refresher training covering all mandatory topics, not specifically focused on de-escalation, but addressing all required subject areas in just a few hours per year.[18]

Compare this to law enforcement training. While police training certainly has gaps, even basic police academies typically provide substantially more instruction dedicated to interpersonal communication and crisis intervention. The Bureau of Justice Statistics reports that state and local law enforcement training academies provide an average of 806 total training hours for basic recruit training.[19] Security officers, who often work in hospitals, retail environments, and public spaces where they routinely encounter individuals in crisis, receive a fraction of that preparation.

In my training sessions with security teams, this disparity is a source of consistent frustration. These professionals recognize the importance of communication and de-escalation skills but report receiving minimal preparation beyond their basic licensing requirements.

This isn't a criticism of security professionals themselves. Most security officers are dedicated, skilled, and doing their best with inadequate preparation. It's an observation about an industry and regulatory system that assign enormous responsibility without commensurate investment in training.

Houses of Worship: Sacred Spaces, Human Conflict

Religious leaders and faith community staff face unique challenges. Pastors, priests, rabbis, imams, elders, staff and volunteers regularly counsel or encounter individuals and families experiencing profound stress: financial crises, relationship dissolution, grief, mental health struggles, spiritual doubt. They may mediate conflicts between congregation members, deliver difficult messages, and occasionally need to enforce boundaries with individuals whose behavior has become disruptive or concerning.

Yet theological education rarely includes practical training in crisis de-escalation. Seminary students learn scripture, theology, homiletics, and pastoral care theory. They don't typically learn how to respond when someone experiencing a mental health crisis becomes agitated during a counseling session, or how to manage a congregant whose anger feels threatening.

The Federal Bureau of Investigation has documented persistent concerns about threats against faith-based organizations, including houses of worship, through its hate crime statistics and public safety advisories.[20] Armed guards are becoming more common at places of worship, but when in place, they are there for the worst-case scenario. In an active lethal-force situation, armed intervention may be required to stop immediate harm. Thankfully, most encounters in houses of worship never reach that threshold. Many begin with conflict, distress, or disruption long before violence becomes imminent. While much attention focuses on external existential threats, these other conflicts can also escalate to concerning levels. Those spreading the word face these challenges with minimal formal preparation, relying primarily on intuition and pastoral presence rather than specific crisis communication skills.

Law Enforcement: My Starting Point

I came to this work through law enforcement, starting in 1994 with the Schenectady County (NY) District Attorney's office as an investigator and then spending nearly twenty-five years with the New York State Police, including service as a major crimes investigator, a crisis negotiator and, eventually, as Division Coordinator for the entire NYSP Crisis Negotiation Program. Law enforcement taught me that communication is the most powerful tool we carry. It can be more effective than any physical intervention in the vast majority of encounters, more versatile than any technology, and more lasting in its impact than any display of authority.

In law enforcement, where use-of-force considerations receive enormous attention and where many agencies now mandate crisis intervention training, significant gaps remain between the skills police need and the training they receive.

Police academies provide substantial preparation compared to many other public-facing professions, especially compared to the security field, yet the allocation of police academy training reveals priorities. Defensive tactics, firearms, and other physical skills typically receive more extensive training time than communication and de-escalation techniques, despite the fact that communication skills are used in virtually every police encounter, while physical force is used rarely by comparison.

The good news is that many agencies are recognizing this gap. Crisis Intervention Team (CIT) programs, which provide roughly 40 hours of specialized training in mental health crisis response, have expanded to more than 2,700 communities nationwide, according to the National Alliance on Mental Illness (NAMI).[21] This represents real progress. But these programs typically train only a subset of officers, often a specialized team, while the majority of officers, who handle most crisis calls, receive only the basic academy preparation in crisis communication and de-escalation.

The Cost of Getting It Wrong

When professionals lack effective de-escalation skills, the consequences ripple outward, physically and financially.

The Human Cost

First and most important: people get hurt. Workers experience physical injuries, psychological trauma, and lasting fear that affects their ability to do their jobs and their quality of life outside work. Individuals in crisis, who might have been helped, may instead experience physical confrontation, arrest, injury, or, in the worst cases, death.

The difference between escalation and a de-escalated outcome often comes down to a few critical choices made in the first moments of an encounter: the words chosen, the tone used, the patience shown, the space given. When someone responds to an individual in crisis with commands and urgency rather than communication and patience, they can inadvertently transform a manageable situation into a dangerous one, considering safety first, of course. That's why From Crisis to Calm focuses on awareness and recognition of threats, and how (and why) to respond after things have gone wrong.

The Financial Cost

Beyond the immeasurable human cost, there's a significant financial burden. Estimates vary by methodology, data source, and whether indirect costs are included, but multiple federal and industry analyses converge on aggregate annual costs in the tens to hundreds of billions of dollars.

- Direct medical costs: emergency treatment, hospitalization, ongoing care for physical injuries, and psychological trauma
- Workers' compensation claims: medical benefits and wage replacement for injured workers
- Legal costs: defense costs for liability claims, settlements, and judgments
- Increased insurance premiums: particularly for organizations with multiple incidents
- Security enhancements: additional guards, surveillance systems, and access controls implemented after incidents
- Lost productivity: time away from work for injured employees, reduced efficiency among traumatized staff, distraction of witnesses and colleagues

But a significant cost category is often overlooked: turnover.

When employees don't feel safe, they leave. Replacing experienced professionals is expensive across every sector. Replacing teachers involves substantial costs, including recruiting, hiring, onboarding, and productivity loss during vacancy periods.[22] Replacing social workers and other human services professionals likewise involves considerable expense.[23] These costs accumulate quickly, particularly in organizations experiencing chronic workplace safety challenges.

Organizations experiencing ongoing workplace violence often find themselves in a vicious cycle: incidents lead to turnover, turnover leads to understaffing, understaffing leads to longer wait times and higher stress, which leads to more incidents.

The Organizational Cost

Perhaps less quantifiable but equally important is the impact on organizational culture and effectiveness.

When employees don't feel safe, they:

- Avoid certain clients, patients, or customers who seem potentially volatile
- Become more rigid and less empathetic in their interactions, creating a self-fulfilling prophecy of conflict
- Spend mental energy worrying about their safety rather than focusing on their work
- Experience increased stress, burnout, and compassion fatigue
- Become less willing to go "above and beyond" in their roles
- Warn others considering the profession about the dangers, which could affect recruitment

When organizations experience repeated workplace violence incidents without adequate response, they send a message, whether intended or not, that worker safety is not a priority. This erodes trust, damages morale, and ultimately affects the quality of service the organization can provide.

The Societal Cost

Zoom out further, and the consequences of unmanaged crisis extend well beyond individual encounters or single workplaces. There is a broader societal cost to environments where professionals routinely feel unsafe, unsupported, or unprepared to manage high-stress interactions.

The following discussion is descriptive rather than prescriptive and is intended to highlight observed patterns rather than assign blame to individual professionals or institutions.

When social workers leave child protective services because they no longer feel safe, the impact does not end with staffing shortages. Vulnerable children face delayed investigations, caseloads grow heavier for those who remain, and systems designed to protect the most at-risk begin to strain under the weight of attrition and burnout.[24]

The same pattern appears in education. When teachers exit the profession due to safety concerns, students lose experienced educators, institutional knowledge disappears, and schools struggle to maintain instructional quality and stability. What looks like an individual career decision quickly becomes a systemic problem with long-term consequences for learning and community trust.[25]

In healthcare, particularly in emergency departments, the stakes are even more immediate. When healthcare workers leave because of repeated exposure to violence, threats, or emotional overload, communities lose critical care capacity. The COVID-19 pandemic made this reality impossible to ignore, revealing how fragile these systems become when skilled professionals are pushed beyond their limits.[26]

Retail and customer-facing industries are not immune. When workers quit due to abuse, intimidation, or unchecked hostility, businesses struggle to operate, services disappear from communities, and local economic opportunity erodes. These losses ripple outward, affecting not only workers and employers, but entire neighborhoods.[27]

Viewed collectively, this is not simply a workplace safety issue. It is a public health issue, an economic issue, and ultimately a question of what kind of society we are willing to tolerate. How we prepare professionals to manage crisis shapes not only individual outcomes, but the resilience and stability of the systems we all depend on.

Why Now? The Perfect Storm

Again, in an attempt to be descriptive rather than prescriptive, and to highlight observed patterns rather than assign blame, let's look at several factors that have converged to make this moment particularly critical:

Increased Mental Health Crises

America has a mental health crisis. More individuals are experiencing emotional dysregulation, substance use challenges, housing instability, and psychological distress. Public-facing professionals across all sectors encounter individuals in crisis more frequently.

The Substance Abuse and Mental Health Services Administration (SAMHSA) reports that in 2023, 58.7 million American adults experienced mental illness, representing 22.8 percent of the adult population.[28] These individuals don't only encounter mental health professionals. They interact with eligibility workers, retail staff, educators, security officers, and countless other public-facing workers who may have minimal preparation for responding effectively.

Emergency departments have reported substantial increases in visits for mental health and substance use concerns in recent years.[29] Many professionals in my training sessions consistently describe managing more patients in behavioral health crisis with fewer resources and less support than in previous years.

Erosion of Social Norms

Many social factors appear to have contributed to changes in behavioral norms in public spaces. The Federal Aviation Administration reported a high of 5,981 unruly passenger incidents in 2021, compared to historical averages of several hundred annually.[30] While this number has decreased since its 2021 peak, it remains substantially elevated compared to pre-pandemic levels.

Flight attendants, restaurant servers, retail workers, and other public-facing professionals describe hostile confrontations that feel qualitatively different from traditional customer complaints. Whether you attribute this to pandemic stress, political division, or other social factors, the result is the same: public-facing professionals experience more frequent and more intense hostile encounters.

Reduced Institutional Buffers

Many organizations have reduced staffing, eliminated experienced middle management, and pushed more responsibility onto frontline workers, often without the training or support needed. A retail sales associate is expected to handle situations that might once have been escalated to a supervisor. An emergency room nurse manages aggressive family members with minimal backup. A teacher addresses hostile parents with limited administrative support. They deserve better preparation.

Retail workers feel this acutely. In the Theatro survey, 63 percent said staffing shortages have made it harder to keep their stores safe, and 72 percent reported experiencing incidents in the past year where staff couldn't respond to a security or safety threat because the store was understaffed, with 22 percent saying this occurs frequently. When workers were asked what would help reduce stress during staffing shortages, 46 percent wanted improved in-store communication, 43 percent wanted enhanced security measures, and 40 percent called for better technology to streamline operations. Workers aren't just dealing with difficult encounters. They're dealing with them alone.[31]

Higher Stakes

In our hyperconnected world, workplace incidents don't stay contained. A hostile encounter captured on video can go viral within hours, bringing intense public scrutiny, media attention, and potential legal and reputational consequences. Organizations can no longer treat workplace violence as an unfortunate but isolated occurrence. Every incident is potentially a public crisis.[32]

Growing Recognition of the Problem

The positive aspect of all this: there's growing recognition that the status quo is unacceptable. Regulatory bodies are strengthening workplace violence prevention requirements.[33] Professional associations are calling for better training. Workers are demanding safer conditions. Labor unions are prioritizing workplace safety in contract negotiations. This moment of crisis is also an opportunity to fundamentally rethink how we prepare people for one of the most important aspects of their jobs.

The Training Gap: Why Traditional Approaches Fall Short

So, if the need is so obvious and the consequences so severe, why haven't organizations adequately addressed this gap? The answer is complex, but several factors contribute:

Misunderstanding What De-Escalation Is

Many organizations believe they're providing de-escalation training when they're actually teaching something else entirely. Common substitutes include:

Conflict resolution training: Useful for disputes between colleagues or parties who are both willing to problem-solve, but inadequate for encounters with individuals in emotional crisis who aren't capable of rational resolution in the moment.

Customer service training: Focuses on satisfaction and resolution, which can actually backfire when someone is emotionally dysregulated and doesn't want their "problem solved". Often, people want to be heard and validated.

Active shooter response: This is critical but often addresses only the most extreme end of the violence spectrum, providing no skills for the vast majority of encounters that haven't reached that level.

General communication skills: Helpful but not sufficient. Influencing a de-escalated outcome requires specific techniques for managing high-emotion encounters that differ significantly from everyday professional communication.[34]

Inadequate Delivery Methods

Even when organizations attempt to provide de-escalation training, they often rely on methods that don't build actual skill:

Streaming or pre-recorded video modules: Convenient and inexpensive, but insufficient on their own. Watching a demonstration may introduce basic concepts, but skill development requires practice. Just as CPR competence depends on hands-on training and feedback, de-escalation skills must be actively practiced to translate into real-world performance.

Conceptual instruction without application: Training that remains primarily conceptual may improve vocabulary and awareness but does not reliably produce behavioral change. Awareness, recognition and communication skills must be developed through applied learning that connects concepts to real-world decision-making.

"Check the box" compliance training: When training becomes primarily about meeting a regulatory requirement or protecting the organization from liability, it's designed to be completed, not to be effective.[35]

Retail workers confirm this gap in stark terms. In the Theatro survey, 40 percent of in-store workers reported receiving no training whatsoever in the past year on handling difficult situations such as theft or aggressive customers, and another 22 percent said the training they received was inadequate, a combined 62 percent who feel ill-equipped to deal with the encounters they face regularly. When asked what their stores need, 38 percent specifically requested additional training on handling difficult customer situations, and 36 percent wanted more frequent safety drills. Sixty-six percent of retail workers aren't confident that their employer has invested in the right technology for employees to request help during a safety crisis. Workers aren't asking for theory. They're asking for preparation that actually matches the situations they walk into every shift.[36]

Lack of Ongoing Practice

Even good initial training degrades over time without reinforcement. Organizations that provide solid de-escalation training during onboarding but never revisit it are setting their employees up for failure. Crisis communication skills are perishable. They require regular practice and refreshment.

Emergency response professionals understand this principle well. Firefighters don't receive fire suppression training once during the academy and never again. They drill regularly. EMTs and paramedics maintain certification through ongoing continuing education and skills practice. Yet many organizations treat de-escalation as a one-time training event rather than an ongoing skill development process.[37]

One-Size-Fits-All Approaches

Generic de-escalation training that doesn't account for the specific contexts, populations, and challenges of different professions or organizations often feels irrelevant to participants.

In my experience delivering From Crisis to Calm training across multiple sectors, I've learned that while the core principles and techniques are universal, the application must be contextualized. Healthcare workers need to understand de-escalation in the context of emergency departments and patient care. Social services workers need to understand it in the context of benefits eligibility and child welfare. Educators need to understand it in the context of parent conferences and student behavior management. Training that doesn't connect to participants' actual work feels theoretical and is less likely to be applied.

Insufficient Time Allocated

Perhaps most fundamentally, organizations often don't allocate sufficient time for meaningful skill development. A one-hour overview might raise awareness, but it won't build competence. Effective de-escalation training requires time for:

- Understanding the underlying principles
- Learning specific techniques
- Practicing those techniques in realistic scenarios
- Receiving feedback and coaching
- Reflecting on the application to participants' actual work contexts

That doesn't happen in an hour. It requires sustained, focused attention.[38]

What's Different About This Approach

This book, and the From Crisis to Calm program it's based on, represents a different approach to de-escalation training. It's shaped by established crisis negotiation principles and refined through a proprietary framework developed over years of real-world application, instruction, and evaluation across multiple professional sectors.

While this approach is informed by foundational crisis negotiation concepts originally developed within the FBI's Crisis Negotiation Unit, it is not a restatement of that model, nor is it limited to it.[39] Traditional crisis negotiation frameworks were designed for highly specific operational contexts: infrequent, high-risk incidents managed by specialized teams operating with time, structure, and defined authority. Most professionals don't work in those conditions.

From Crisis to Calm was developed in response to that gap. It translates and expands negotiation-based principles into a broader, more flexible framework suited to everyday, high-frequency encounters and situations where emotions escalate quickly, environments are uncontrolled, and decisions must be made in real time. Over nearly 30 years of experiencing difficult encounters and more than a decade of teaching thousands of professionals across dozens of sectors, I have observed consistent patterns in how crises unfold, how communication breaks down, and what reliably influences behavior before situations spiral into force, removal, or harm. This framework is the result of that observation, experience, and refinement.

It's Grounded in Evidence

From Crisis to Calm is grounded in evidence-based principles drawn from crisis negotiation research, neuroscience, behavioral psychology, and communication theory. These disciplines help explain how stress affects cognition, how emotions drive behavior, and how influence is established during moments of heightened arousal.[40]

Rather than relying on intuition or luck, this approach focuses on mechanisms that are observable, teachable, and repeatable. The goal is not to sound persuasive, but to understand what actually works when people are overwhelmed, defensive, or emotionally flooded. It applies those principles consistently across contexts.

It's Practical and Applicable

This approach is not theoretical and is deliberately practical. Every concept, technique, and framework presented is designed for use in the types of encounters participants actually face, not idealized scenarios or rare, extreme events.

Exercises and scenarios are drawn from personal experience and recurring real-world patterns observed across law enforcement, healthcare, education, social services, security, retail, and other public-facing professions. Participants don't just learn concepts; they apply them, practice decision-making, receive feedback, and engage in guided discussion. The emphasis is on leaving with usable skills, not just abstract understanding.

It Treats De-Escalation as an Outcome, Not a "Soft Skill"

Communication is often mislabeled as a "soft skill," implying that it is secondary to technical ability or tactical response. In high-stress, public-facing roles, this assumption is not just incorrect, it is dangerous.

Communication is a primary safety mechanism. It can influence perception, behavior, and decision-making before physical intervention becomes an issue. From Crisis to Calm treats de-escalation as an outcome that's shaped by choices, behaviors, and emotional regulation, not as a personality trait or a feel-good ideal. As such, it deserves the same seriousness, structure, and ongoing practice as any other safety-critical skill.[41]

It Teaches a Framework, Not a Script

Effective de-escalation can't be reduced to a script or a list of magic phrases. Human encounters are too complex and too varied. Instead, From Crisis to Calm offers a framework: a way of thinking about and responding to crisis encounters that can be adapted to so many different and unique situations. Participants learn principles and practice they can apply flexibly, not rigid procedures that fall apart when reality doesn't match the script.

It Emphasizes Professional Sincerity

At the heart of this approach is a concept I call Professional Sincerity: the ethical standard of influence, credibility, and respect that allows you to communicate authentically with people in crisis without requiring personal connection or agreement. It's the difference between manipulating someone's emotions and ethically influencing their behavior. It's the foundation that makes all the specific techniques work.

Professional Sincerity is about credibility, consistency, and respect. It enables authentic communication within clear professional boundaries, even when disagreement exists. This principle underpins the effectiveness of every technique taught in From Crisis to Calm and allows the framework to function across diverse roles, cultures, and power dynamics.

It Recognizes That Safety Includes Self-Care

De-escalation isn't just about managing others. It's also about managing yourself. The best communication techniques in the world won't help if you're emotionally dysregulated, exhausted from compassion fatigue, or so anxious about your own safety that you can't think clearly. From Crisis to Calm includes explicit attention to self-regulation, stress management, and the long-term sustainability of this work.[42]

What's Next

We've established that the need for effective de-escalation training is urgent, the consequences of inadequate preparation are severe, and that a better approach exists. But where did that better approach come from? The techniques in this book didn't emerge from a conference room or an academic theory. They were forged in tragedy, in moments when the old way of doing things got people killed.

In the next chapter, we'll trace the history and philosophy behind modern de-escalation, from the catastrophic failures of the early 1970s that forced law enforcement to rethink everything, to the development of crisis negotiation principles that have since saved thousands of lives. Understanding where these methods came from, and why they work, provides the foundation for everything that follows in this book.

Notes

1. Engel, Robin S., Corsaro, Nicholas, Isaza, Gabrielle T., and McManus, Hannah D. "Assessing the Impact of De-Escalation Training on Police Behavior: Reducing Police Use of Force in the Louisville, KY Metro Police Department." *Criminology & Public Policy* 21, no. 2 (2022): 199–233.
2. Occupational Safety and Health Administration, "Workplace Violence," U.S. Department of Labor, https://www.osha.gov/workplace-violence, accessed February 22, 2026.
3. OSHA guidance notes that workplace violence creates costs including medical expenses, legal fees, lost productivity, workers' compensation claims, and turnover expenses. See OSHA, "Workplace Violence," U.S. Department of Labor, https://www.osha.gov/workplace-violence (accessed February 22, 2026)
4. U.S. Bureau of Labor Statistics, "Nonfatal Occupational Injuries and Illnesses Requiring Days Away from Work," tables on "Intentional injury by another person," various years (2016–2022), https://www.bls.gov/iif/ (accessed February 22, 2026).

5. OSHA, *Guidelines for Preventing Workplace Violence for Healthcare and Social Service Workers*, OSHA 3148-06R 2016, https://www.osha.gov/sites/default/files/publications/osha3148.pdf (accessed February 22, 2026).

6. The Joint Commission, "Workplace Violence Prevention Standards," R3 Report, Issue 30 (June 18, 2021), https://www.jointcommission.org/standards/r3-report/r3-report-issue-30-workplace-violence-prevention-standards (accessed February 22, 2026). Note: The Joint Commission has marked this R3 Report as retired, though the standards it established remain in effect.

7. National Retail Federation, *2023 National Retail Security Survey*, https://nrf.com/research/national-retail-security-survey-2023 (accessed February 22, 2026).

8. Theatro (now a Motorola Solutions Company), *Retail Worker Safety Survey*. Full report available at https://www.theatro.com/resources/report/2024-retail-worker-safety-survey/ (accessed February 22, 2026).

9. U.S. Bureau of Labor Statistics, Job Openings and Labor Turnover Survey (JOLTS), "Retail Trade: Annual Total Separations Rate," 2023 data, https://www.bls.gov/jlt/ (accessed February 22, 2026); and various industry HR analyses summarizing frontline retail turnover above 60 percent.

10. Ringstad, Robin, "Conflict in the Workplace: Social Workers as Victims and Perpetrators," Social Work 50, no. 4 (2005): 305–313. For more recent research on workload, workplace safety, and violence in social service organizations, see also Aaron Turpin, Michael L. Shier, David Nicholas, and John R. Graham, "Workload and Workplace Safety in Social Service Organizations," Journal of Social Work 21, no. 3 (May 2021): 575–594, https://doi.org/10.1177/1468017320913541.

11. Child Welfare Information Gateway, "Worker Turnover," in *Child Welfare System Improvement* (Washington, DC: U.S. Department of Health and Human Services, Children's Bureau), https://www.childwelfare.gov (accessed February 22, 2026); see also Casey Family Programs, "How does turnover in the child welfare workforce impact children and families?" (strategy brief, updated January 2025), https://www.casey.org/turnover-costs-and-retention-strategies/ (accessed February 22, 2026).

12. U.S. Department of Education, National Center for Education Statistics, *Teachers Threatened With Injury or Physically Attacked by Students: Indicator A05* (Washington, DC: NCES, 2023), https://nces.ed.gov/programs/coe/indicator/a05/teacher-attacked-by-students (accessed February 22, 2026).

13. National Center for Education Statistics (NCES), *Indicators of School Crime and Safety: 2022*, NCES 2023-092 (Washington, DC: U.S. Department of Education, 2023), https://nces.ed.gov/programs/crimeindicators/ (accessed February 22, 2026). See also the updated edition: *Report on Indicators of School Crime and Safety: 2023*, NCES 2024-145, published jointly with the Bureau of Justice Statistics.

14. Linda Darling-Hammond et al., *Addressing California's Emerging Teacher Shortage: An Analysis of Sources and Solutions* (Palo Alto, CA: Learning Policy Institute, 2016), https://learningpolicyinstitute.org/product/addressing-californias-emerging-teacher-shortage (accessed February 22, 2026), and related teacher workforce studies on safety and working conditions as drivers of attrition.

15. U.S. Bureau of Labor Statistics, "Census of Fatal Occupational Injuries (CFOI), Fatal Occupational Injuries by Event or Exposure," tables on workplace homicides by circumstance, https://www.bls.gov/iif/fatal-injuries-tables.htm (accessed February 22, 2026).

16. U.S. Bureau of Labor Statistics, Occupational Employment and Wage Statistics, "Security Guards" (SOC 33-9032), reporting approximately 1.3 million security guards employed in 2024, https://www.bls.gov/ooh/protective-service/security-guards.htm (accessed February 22, 2026). For sworn law enforcement officers, see U.S. Bureau of Justice Statistics, "Law Enforcement Officers Employed," https://bjs.ojp.gov (accessed February 22, 2026). For the comparative scale of private security versus sworn law enforcement, see also ASIS International industry workforce analyses.

17. California Bureau of Security and Investigative Services, "Security Guard Registration Fact Sheet," https://www.bsis.ca.gov/forms_pubs/guard_fact.shtml; New York State Department of State, Division of Licensing Services, "Security Guard Training in New York State," https://www.dos.ny.gov/licensing/securityguard/sgtraining.html; Florida Department of Agriculture and Consumer Services, Division of Licensing, "Class D Security Officer License Requirements," https://www.fdacs.gov/Business-Services/Private-Security-Licenses/Class-D-Security-Officer-License-Requirements; Texas Department of Public Safety, "Private Security Training and Continuing Education," https://www.dps.texas.gov/section/private-security/training-and-continuing-education; all accessed February 22, 2026.

18. California Bureau of Security and Investigative Services, New York State Department of State Division of Licensing Services, Florida Department of Agriculture and Consumer Services Division of Licensing, and Texas Department of Public Safety, state regulatory agency continuing education requirements for security officers, accessed February 22, 2026.

19. Emily D. Buehler, PhD, State and Local Law Enforcement Training Academies and Recruits, 2022 — Statistical Tables, Bureau of Justice Statistics Statistical Tables, NCJ Number 309348 (Washington, DC: U.S. Department of Justice, November 2024), https://bjs.ojp.gov/library/publications/state-and-local-law-enforcement-training-academies-and-recruits-2022 (accessed March 11, 2026)

20. Federal Bureau of Investigation, "Hate Crime Statistics," https://www.fbi.gov/how-we-can-help-you/more-fbi-services-and-information/ucr/hate-crime (accessed February 22, 2026); and DHS–FBI joint bulletins on threats to faith-based communities.

21. National Alliance on Mental Illness (NAMI), "Crisis Intervention Team (CIT) Programs," accessed March 12, 2026, https://www.nami.org/advocacy/crisis-intervention/crisis-intervention-team-cit-programs/.

22. Learning Policy Institute, "Teacher Turnover: Why It Matters and What We Can Do About It," research brief (September 2017), by Carver-Thomas and Darling-Hammond, summarizing financial and educational impacts of teacher attrition, https://learningpolicyinstitute.org/product/teacher-turnover-brief (accessed March 11, 2026).

23. National Association of Social Workers, "Health Care Workforce Shortages and Solutions," written testimony submitted to the U.S. Senate Committee on Health, Education, Labor, and Pensions on March 20, 2023, https://www.socialworkers.org/Advocacy/Policy-Issues/Health-Care-Workforce (accessed February 22, 2026). For child welfare workforce turnover costs, see Casey Family Programs, "How does turnover in the child welfare workforce impact children and families?"(strategy brief,

updated January 2025), https://www.casey.org/turnover-costs-and-retention-strategies/ (accessed February 22, 2026).

24. Quality Improvement Center for Workforce Development (QIC-WD), "Worker Turnover Is a Persistent Child Welfare Challenge—So Is Measuring It," QIC-Take (University of Nebraska–Lincoln, 2022), https://qic-wd.org/qic-take/worker-turnover-persistent-child-welfare-challenge (accessed February 22, 2026). QIC-WD is a service of the Children's Bureau, Administration for Children and Families.

25. Darling-Hammond et al., *Addressing California's Emerging Teacher Shortage*.

26. National Academies of Sciences, Engineering, and Medicine, *The Future of Nursing 2020–2030: Charting a Path to Achieve Health Equity* (Washington, DC: National Academies Press, 2021), https://nap.nationalacademies.org/catalog/25982 (accessed February 22, 2026).

27. National Retail Federation, *2023 National Retail Security Survey*. See note 7.

28. Substance Abuse and Mental Health Services Administration, *Key Substance Use and Mental Health Indicators in the United States: Results from the 2023 National Survey on Drug Use and Health* (HHS Publication No. PEP24-07-021, NSDUH Series H-59), reporting that 22.8 percent of adults aged 18 or older (58.7 million people) had any mental illness in 2023, https://www.samhsa.gov/data/report/2023-nsduh-annual-national-report (accessed February 22, 2026).

29. Centers for Disease Control and Prevention, "Emergency Department Visits for Mental Health Conditions and Substance Use Disorders," analyses of National Hospital Ambulatory Medical Care Survey (NHAMCS) data, most recent data from 2022, https://www.cdc.gov/nchs/nhamcs/about/index.html (accessed February 22, 2026).

30. Federal Aviation Administration, "Unruly Passengers," https://www.faa.gov/unruly (accessed February 22, 2026). The FAA reported 5,981 unruly passenger incidents in 2021, the peak year. While incidents have declined substantially since then (2,102 reported in 2024), levels remain elevated compared to pre-pandemic averages of several hundred annually.

31. Theatro, *Retail Worker Safety Survey*; see note 8 for full citation.

32. Contemporary crisis communication and organizational behavior literature extensively documents workplace incidents that gained widespread public attention through video and social media, demonstrating the reputational and operational risks of poorly managed public-facing encounters. See, for example, analyses in W. Timothy Coombs, *Ongoing Crisis Communication: Planning, Managing, and Responding*, 5th ed. (Thousand Oaks, CA: SAGE Publications, 2019), Chapter 8.

33. See, for example, OSHA's evolving workplace violence prevention guidance and state-level healthcare workplace violence prevention laws, including California SB 553 (effective July 1, 2024), which requires nearly all California employers to implement written workplace violence prevention plans, provide training, and maintain incident logs; and New York Senate Bill S5294-B, signed into law December 12, 2025, requiring general hospitals and nursing homes to establish workplace violence prevention programs (effective September 2026).

34. For distinctions between conflict resolution, customer service, and crisis communication, see Michael J. McMains and Wayman C. Mullins, *Crisis Negotiations: Managing Critical Incidents and Hostage Situations in Law Enforcement and Corrections*, 5th ed. (New York: Routledge, 2013).

35. Adult learning theory emphasizes experiential practice; see Malcolm S. Knowles, Elwood F. Holton III, and Richard A. Swanson, *The Adult Learner: The Definitive Classic in Adult Education and Human Resource Development*, 8th ed. (New York: Routledge, 2015).

36. Theatro, *Retail Worker Safety Survey*; see note 8 for full citation.

37. Knowles, Holton, and Swanson, *The Adult Learner*; also standard continuing education requirements for EMTs, paramedics, and firefighters via state EMS offices and NFPA standards.

38. Knowles, Holton, and Swanson, *The Adult Learner*.

39. McMains and Mullins, *Crisis Negotiations*; also Gary Noesner, *Stalling for Time: My Life as an FBI Hostage Negotiator* (New York: Random House, 2010).

40. For crisis negotiation research and the development of influence-based approaches to behavioral change, see Gregory M. Vecchi, Vincent B. Van Hasselt, and Stephen J. Romano, "Crisis (Hostage) Negotiation: Current Strategies and Issues in High-Risk Conflict Resolution," *Aggression and Violent Behavior* 10, no. 5 (2005): 533–551. For the neuroscience of stress and cognitive impairment, see Amy F. T. Arnsten, "Stress Signalling Pathways That Impair Prefrontal Cortex Structure and Function," *Nature Reviews Neuroscience* 10, no. 6 (2009): 410–422. For behavioral psychology and the foundations of empathic communication, see Carl R. Rogers, *On Becoming a Person: A Therapist's View of Psychotherapy* (Boston: Houghton Mifflin, 1961). For communication theory and emotional contagion in crisis contexts, see Stephen W. Porges, *The Polyvagal Theory: Neurophysiological Foundations of Emotions, Attachment, Communication, and Self-regulation* (New York: W. W. Norton, 2011).

41. International Association of Chiefs of Police (IACP), *National Consensus Policy and Discussion Paper on Use of Force* (January 2017, updated July 2020) which recognizes de-escalation and crisis communication as core components of officer safety and effective policing, https://www.theiacp.org/resources/policy-center-resource/use-of-force (accessed February 22, 2026).

42. For compassion fatigue and self-care in helping professions, see Charles R. Figley, ed., *Compassion Fatigue: Coping with Secondary Traumatic Stress Disorder in Those Who Treat the Traumatized* (New York: Brunner/Mazel, 1995); for more recent synthesis, see Françoise Mathieu, *The Compassion Fatigue Workbook: Creative Tools for Transforming Compassion Fatigue and Vicarious Traumatization* (New York: Routledge, 2012), and B. Hudnall Stamm, "The Concise ProQOL Manual", 2nd ed. (2010), https://proqol.org (accessed February 22, 2026).

CHAPTER 2:

THE HISTORY AND PHILOSOPHY OF DE-ESCALATION

In Chapter 1, we established that the need for effective de-escalation is urgent and widespread: from retail floors and classrooms to emergency departments and social services offices. We've seen the human, financial, and organizational costs of getting it wrong, and we've made the case that a better approach exists. But that raises a fundamental question: *Why* does that work? Why does patience outperform pressure? Why does slowing down produce better outcomes than speeding up?

The answers didn't come from a textbook. They were forged in tragedy. In the late 1960s and early 1970s, the world witnessed several traumatic and violent incidents where fast, aggressive intervention resulted in catastrophic loss of life. Each tragedy became a lesson and each failure forced a reckoning. And slowly, painfully, law enforcement and crisis response professionals began to realize that the tools they'd relied on for generations (speed, force, and tactical dominance) were making certain situations worse instead of better.

Understanding this history matters for everyone in this field, not just law enforcement. The principles that emerged from these events (principles built on patience, communication, and human connection) are the same principles that work when a nurse faces a combative patient, when a social worker sits across from a desperate client, or when a teacher manages a student in crisis. Before we build the specific frameworks and skills you'll use in your daily work, you need to understand where they came from and why they work. Because when you know the "why," the "how" makes a lot more sense.

When Force Failed: The Crises of the Early 1970s

The traditional law enforcement model had been built on swift, decisive action. When criminals took hostages or barricaded themselves, the instinct was to move quickly, overwhelm the threat, and end the situation before it could escalate further. This approach worked well in many contexts, stopping active crimes, apprehending fleeing suspects, halting ongoing violence. But when applied to emotionally driven standoffs, barricaded subjects, and hostage situations, speed became the enemy of safety. The faster responders moved, the more desperate subjects became. The more cornered people felt, the more likely they were to hurt others or themselves.

Throughout the late 1960s and early 1970s, a series of high-profile incidents exposed the deadly consequences of this force-first mentality. Police departments, military units, and international agencies were confronting situations where people in crisis (whether criminals, terrorists, or individuals experiencing mental health emergencies) were holding others' lives in their hands. And in incident after incident, the outcome was the same: bloodshed, trauma, and the haunting question of whether there might have been another way.

Attica: The Cost of Rushing In

One of the most devastating turning points came in September 1971 at the Attica Correctional Facility in upstate New York. What began as a prisoner uprising quickly spiraled into one of the deadliest prison riots in American history. More than 1,200 inmates seized control of a large portion of the facility, taking 42 staff members hostage. The standoff lasted four days. Negotiations were attempted, and journalists, lawyers, and civil rights activists were brought in to mediate. Inmates presented demands for better living conditions, medical care, and amnesty. For a brief moment, it seemed possible that dialogue might resolve the crisis.

But patience ran thin. Political pressure mounted. On September 13, 1971, New York State Police launched a full assault on the prison yard. Troopers fired more than 2,000 rounds of ammunition in less than ten minutes. When the shooting stopped, 39 people were dead, 29 inmates and 10 hostages. Nearly all were killed by police gunfire, not by the inmates. The hostages had been killed by the very force sent to rescue them.[1]

The Attica assault became a symbol of what happens when urgency overrides strategy, when force replaces communication, and when the pressure to act fast eclipses the discipline to act right. Investigations revealed that negotiations had been undermined by a lack of structure, training, and commitment to the process. There was no coherent plan for managing the standoff, no clear strategy for using time as a tool, and no framework for building trust with the inmates. The result was a tragedy that could have been prevented.

The lesson from Attica was painfully clear: rushing in without influence, without understanding, and without a commitment to communication can cost lives, even when the intention is to save them.

Munich: When Speed Becomes Chaos

Just one year later, the world watched in horror as another crisis unfolded on live television. During the 1972 Summer Olympics in Munich, West Germany, eight members of Black September infiltrated the Olympic Village and took eleven Israeli athletes and coaches hostage. They demanded the release of prisoners held in Israel and safe passage out of Germany. The standoff lasted nearly 24 hours.

German authorities attempted negotiation, but the efforts were disorganized and half-hearted. There was no unified command, no clear negotiation strategy, and no plan for managing the crisis beyond hoping for a peaceful surrender or finding an opportunity to use force. As the deadline approached and the terrorists prepared to leave with the hostages, German police decided to mount a rescue operation at the airport. The plan was hastily conceived, poorly coordinated, and catastrophically executed. Snipers were positioned without adequate training or equipment. No assault team was in place. Communication between units was minimal. When the shooting started, chaos erupted. In the firefight that followed, all eleven Israeli hostages were killed, some shot by the terrorists, some caught in the crossfire, and some killed when a terrorist threw a grenade into the helicopter where they were bound and helpless. Five of the eight terrorists and one German police officer also died.[2]

Munich became an international case study in how not to handle a hostage crisis. The failure wasn't just tactical. It was philosophical. Authorities treated the situation as a military problem that required a military solution, rather than recognizing it as a human problem that required patience, communication, and careful planning. The urgency to resolve the crisis quickly overrode the discipline needed to resolve it safely.

The Pattern Emerges

By the early 1970s, a troubling pattern had emerged. Domestically, American cities were experiencing a wave of armed bank robberies and hostage situations. In many of these incidents, police officers, trained to respond quickly and decisively, were making situations worse by moving too fast. Suspects who might have surrendered peacefully became desperate when they felt cornered. Hostages who might have survived were killed in the chaos of rushed tactical interventions.

In New York City, this problem reached a breaking point. Between 1971 and 1973, the NYPD responded to multiple bank robberies where suspects took hostages and barricaded themselves inside. In early cases, officers instinctively used dynamic entry tactics, the kind built for catching criminals before they could act. But in emotionally charged hostage situations, those tactics backfired. Suspects became more violent the moment officers rushed them. Hostages died. Officers died. Innocent bystanders were caught in the crossfire.

A well-known incident occurred on August 22, 1972. John Wojtowicz and Salvatore Naturile attempted to rob a Chase Manhattan Bank branch in Brooklyn. When police arrived quickly, the two men took bank employees hostage and barricaded themselves inside. What followed was a 14-hour standoff that drew massive media attention and became the subject of the 1975 film *Dog Day Afternoon*.[3]

Another incident in particular became the catalyst for change. On January 19, 1973, four armed men attempted to rob John and Al's Sporting Goods store in Brooklyn in order to steal weapons. When police arrived, a shootout erupted. Officer Stephen Gilroy was killed, two other officers were wounded, and one of the perpetrators was shot. The gunmen retreated into the store with twelve hostages, and what followed was the longest standoff in NYPD history, lasting 47 hours. The department's established protocol called for issuing an ultimatum and then responding with overwhelming tactical force. Hundreds of officers flooded the area, but there was no trained negotiation capability, no psychological expertise on scene, and no doctrine for managing a prolonged hostage situation.

Into this volatile situation came Dr. Harvey Schlossberg, an NYPD officer who held a doctorate in psychology. Schlossberg convinced his superiors to try something unprecedented: rather than storming the building, he advocated for patience, dialogue, and psychological engagement with the hostage-takers. He opened lines of communication, worked to understand the men's motivations, and kept talking. Over the course of the 47-hour standoff, three hostages were released through negotiation, and the remaining nine escaped safely via a concealed rooftop staircase. All four perpetrators ultimately surrendered without further bloodshed. The incident demonstrated something that had never been proven on this scale: that communication, patience, and a willingness to understand the people on the other side of the door could resolve even the most dangerous situations.[4]

The Birth of a New Philosophy: "Talk to Me"

In the wake of these incidents, the NYPD made a decision that would revolutionize crisis response worldwide. In late 1973, they created the world's first dedicated hostage negotiation team. This wasn't just a tactical adjustment. It was a philosophical transformation. The department recognized that relying solely on force in emotionally driven incidents too often led to unnecessary deaths. Someone had to design a different path.

The architects of this new approach were Harvey Schlossberg, the NYPD psychologist who had been instrumental in resolving the Brooklyn event, and Lieutenant Frank Bolz, a seasoned officer who understood both the streets and the limits of traditional tactics. Together, they built a program that selected officers not because they were the biggest, the strongest, or the most aggressive, but because they could communicate. They could remain calm under pressure. They could influence behavior with words instead of weapons.[5]

Schlossberg and Bolz trained these officers to do something counterintuitive: slow the moment down. Instead of rushing in, they would create time. Instead of forcing a conclusion, they would guide the situation toward a peaceful resolution. They taught negotiators to build rapport, to learn what the subject wanted, to understand the emotions driving the crisis, and to use that understanding to steer the person toward surrender.

From the very beginning, that new approach had a simple and powerful motto: "Talk to me." It wasn't just a slogan. It was a declaration of purpose. It said that communication has value. It said that every human being, no matter how desperate or dangerous the situation may seem, still has a voice that can be reached. It reminded negotiators that their job wasn't to overpower someone but to understand them. To learn what they feared, what they needed, and what would help them feel safe enough to stand down.

"Talk to me" changed the culture of crisis response. It shifted the priority from ending the situation quickly to ending it safely. It recognized that when a person feels heard, their sense of threat begins to fade. And once that threat fades, thinking returns, and cooperation becomes possible. That simple invitation, *talk to me*, opened the door to rapport, influence, and resolution. It took the most volatile moments imaginable and turned them into opportunities for human connection instead of violent confrontation.

"Talk to me" is exactly what we want them doing. If they're talking, chances are they are not hurting you, someone else, or themselves.

Dynamic Inactivity: The Power of Doing Less

What made the NYPD model so revolutionary was that it flipped the traditional response on its head. Instead of rushing in, instead of forcing a fast conclusion, negotiators embraced what they called **dynamic inactivity**: the strategic choice to slow everything down.[6] It sounds contradictory: how can inactivity be dynamic? But that's precisely the point. Dynamic inactivity isn't passivity. It's not waiting and hoping something changes. It's active patience. It's deliberate restraint. It's doing less physically so you can do more verbally. It's taking control of the clock and refusing to let emotion or urgency dictate the pace of the encounter.

In traditional law enforcement thinking, action meant movement: advancing, breaching, overwhelming. But in crisis negotiation, action meant communication. The negotiator was actively listening, actively building rapport, actively managing the subject's emotional state. They were working, strategizing, and influencing, but they were doing it through words instead of force.

This shift required profound discipline. It's human nature to want to resolve a crisis as quickly as possible. When lives are at stake, every minute feels like an eternity. The pressure from commanders, politicians, media, and even fellow officers can be overwhelming. But the NYPD team learned that the best outcomes came when they resisted that pressure and gave the process time to work. Time for emotions to settle. Time for the subject to exhaust their adrenaline. Time for rational thinking to return. Time for rapport to take root.

Dynamic inactivity became the foundation of what we now call de-escalation. It taught responders that in certain situations, the most powerful thing you can do is not act. At least not in the traditional sense. Instead, you create space. You control the environment. And you use that space to communicate, connect, and influence.

The Three Keys: Contain, Isolate, Negotiate

From this philosophy came three foundational principles that became known as the **"Three Keys"**: **Contain**, **Isolate**, and **Negotiate**.[7]

Containment means keeping the situation from spreading or escalating. Negotiators and tactical teams would secure the area, limit movement, and create boundaries so no one else could be pulled into the crisis. Containment prevented the problem from getting bigger. It protected bystanders, prevented the subject from accessing additional hostages or weapons, and created a controlled environment where negotiation could occur safely.

Isolation meant removing the individual from external influences: crowds, noise, friends who might escalate the situation, or environmental triggers that intensified fear or anger. By reducing stimulation and limiting distractions, negotiators helped the person feel less overwhelmed and more capable of listening. Isolation wasn't about cutting the person off from humanity. It was about creating a calm, focused space where communication could happen without interference.

Negotiation was the heart of the process. This is where negotiators took the time they'd earned through containment and isolation and turned it into communication. The goal was to understand the motive (why the person felt trapped or desperate) and to understand the personality (how they saw themselves and the world). Were they scared? Were they angry? Hopeless? Were they trying to make a point, or were they trying to survive something inside their own head? By slowing down the incident and showing the individual that someone was there to listen, negotiators began influencing behavior in the safest possible direction. The person was no longer reacting to a rapidly closing threat. They were responding to a steady, calm human being who was offering them a path out.

The Three Keys proved something profound: if we create space, communication can take root, and cooperation can grow. And when cooperation grows, violence shrinks.

Evolution and Expansion: The Three C's

Over time, as tactics and training continued to evolve, the NYPD model was refined and adapted for broader applications. The original framework of Contain, Isolate, and Negotiate evolved into what many agencies now teach as the **Three C's**: **Contain**, **Control**, and **Communicate**.[8] The goal remained the same (create safety, create space, and create opportunity for influence), but the language reflected the wider environments where these principles were being applied.

Containment is still the first priority. Whether it's a barricaded subject, a person in mental health crisis, or an escalating confrontation in a hospital emergency room, we need to ensure the situation cannot spread or get worse. We protect bystanders, limit the person's movement if necessary, and stabilize the physical environment.

Control doesn't mean domination. It doesn't mean using force. It means taking control of the tempo, the tone, and the tactical posture. We manage the scene, coordinate roles, eliminate confusion, and ensure there is only one calm voice leading the moment. Control is about shaping the environment so communication can succeed. It also means staying in control of yourself, your emotions, your body language, and your reactions.

Communicate is the anchor of all of it. Not every situation involves formal negotiation. Not every person is barricaded. Not every encounter involves demands. But every situation requires communication. Communication is how we build rapport. Communication is how we influence behavior and how we take someone from chaos back to reasoning, from fear back to safety, from crisis to calm. Without communication, there is no connection. Without connection, there is no cooperation. And without cooperation, de-escalation fails before it even has a chance.

The Fourth C: Connection

I like to teach a fourth "C" that truly makes the difference: **Connection**. It's not enough to talk at someone or to deliver commands or instructions. Communication becomes meaningful only when the person feels a connection to the one speaking.

Connection is where trust begins and where influence takes hold. It's where a frightened, angry, overwhelmed individual realizes that the person in front of them is not a threat, but a lifeline. When connection forms, defenses lower. People stop fighting against us and start working with us. Their emotions begin to settle because someone finally sees them as more than a problem. They see them as a person.

Connection is born through empathy. It's built through patience. It strengthens every time we show respect, validate feelings, and treat the individual the same way we would want someone to treat our own family. Without connection, communication becomes noise. With connection, communication becomes the bridge that leads a person safely out of crisis.

Contain. Control. Communicate. Connect.

That's how we bring someone back from the edge. Not by force, but by humanity.

Defining De-Escalation

We've talked about it, where it comes from, why we use it, but how is "de-escalation" defined? Well, first of all, as I mentioned earlier and it bears repeating: de-escalation is not a single specific tactic or skill that we'll talk about in this book and in my FC2C classes. It's a lot of verbal and non-verbal skills put together to achieve an *outcome*. A de-escalated outcome.

The Merriam-Webster Dictionary defines it as "to decrease in extent, volume, or scope."[9]

That's fine... but it's not enough for me. That's why, when I was in the New York State Police and I was tasked with developing a de-escalation training program, I wanted a more detailed, concise definition of de-escalation, especially since I was approaching it as an outcome.

I ended up using the Ontario Police College definition of de-escalation, which states, "The use of verbal and non-verbal strategies, intended to prevent escalation or reduce the intensity of a situation without the application of force, and, if force is necessary, reducing the amount of force, if reasonably safe to do so."[10] I particularly like this definition, because I think it states exactly what I wanted to do as a police officer: try to bring things down without using force. If I had to use objectively reasonable force, I wanted to use the least amount of it that was safe. Safety is paramount. This definition preserves that.

I also like this definition as applied to any other profession, industry or service. Sometimes in professions other than enforcement or protection, the best way to achieve a de-escalated outcome may be to remove yourself from the situation or encounter. Keeping that in mind, we can apply this definition to any other industry or field by simply deleting some of the words and keeping this as our definition: "The use of verbal and non-verbal strategies, intended to prevent escalation or reduce the intensity of a situation." Preventing escalation or reducing the intensity of a situation helps us get to our goal of safer encounters. Our goal of a de-escalated outcome.

From Law Enforcement to Everywhere

The principles born in those early NYPD hostage negotiations didn't stay confined to law enforcement. Over the decades, crisis negotiation techniques spread to federal agencies, military special operations, correctional facilities, and eventually to civilian sectors. Mental health professionals recognized that the same communication strategies that worked with barricaded criminals also worked with individuals in psychiatric crisis. Hospital staff found that de-escalation techniques reduced violence in emergency departments. Social service workers discovered that patience and empathy, the core tools of crisis negotiation, helped them manage emotionally charged encounters with clients who felt desperate and unheard.

By the 1990s and 2000s, de-escalation training was being adapted for teachers, retail workers, customer service representatives, and anyone whose job required them to interact with people under stress. The language changed. Terms like "hostage negotiation" gave way to "crisis negotiation" or "verbal de-escalation" and "crisis intervention." But the foundational principles remained the same. Slow down. Create space. Communicate with empathy. Build connection. Influence behavior through understanding rather than force.

What began as a response to tragedy in the 1970s became a universal framework for managing human conflict. The lessons learned from Attica, Munich, and those early New York City bank robberies are now taught in hospitals, schools, social service agencies, and places of worship. The motto "Talk to me" echoes in every interaction where someone chooses patience over pressure, connection over control, and understanding over force.

Where Traditional Training Falls Short

The history of crisis negotiation gave us powerful principles, but somewhere along the way, much of de-escalation training lost its connection to those roots. By the time these concepts reached civilian professions (healthcare, social services, education, retail), they had been watered down, genericized, and stripped of the very elements that made them effective in the first place.

Walk into most de-escalation training sessions today and you'll find a familiar pattern: a PowerPoint presentation with bullet points telling you to "remain calm," "use active listening," "don't take it personally," and "give them space." The instructor, often someone who has never worked in your field, clicks through slides and maybe plays a video of a scripted scenario with actors that bears no resemblance to the real situations you face. Then you're sent back to work with a certificate, expected to apply these abstract concepts when an actual crisis erupts in front of you.

The problem isn't that the advice is wrong. It's that it's incomplete, impractical, and disconnected from the realities of your work. Traditional training treats de-escalation as a checklist of steps to follow rather than a set of principles to internalize. It focuses on what to say instead of how to think. It assumes that everyone you encounter fits neatly into textbook categories and will respond predictably to textbook techniques. And most importantly, it fails to prepare you for the emotional weight of these encounters, the fear, the frustration, the self-doubt, and the split-second decisions you'll have to make when someone's behavior is spiraling and you're the only one standing between them and a worst-case outcome.

These aren't isolated failures. They're systemic problems with how de-escalation is taught. To sum it up, traditional training makes several critical mistakes. First, it treats de-escalation as a universal skill that works the same way in every context, ignoring the enormous differences between calming a psychiatric patient, managing a frustrated customer, and responding to a student in crisis. Second, it focuses on techniques rather than understanding, teaching people what to do without helping them understand why those techniques work or how to adapt them when circumstances change. Third, it underestimates the emotional toll these encounters take on professionals, offering no framework for managing your own stress, fear, and frustration while simultaneously trying to de-escalate someone else. And fourth, it fails to address the organizational and systemic pressures that make de-escalation so difficult, the understaffing, the time constraints, the conflicting priorities, and the lack of support when things go wrong.

What Makes *From Crisis to Calm* Different

From Crisis to Calm is built on a different foundation. Instead of starting with generic communication tips, it starts where crisis negotiation started, with the recognition that people in crisis are not problems to be managed with scripts. They're human beings whose capacity to cope has collapsed, and our job is to help them find their way back. This isn't just a philosophical difference. It's a practical one that changes everything about how we approach these encounters.

FC2C is grounded in the same principles that transformed hostage negotiation from a deadly gamble into a science: slow down, create space, build connection, and influence behavior through understanding rather than force. But it doesn't stop there. It translates those principles into frameworks and language that make sense for the specific work you do. If you're a healthcare worker, you learn how to apply crisis negotiation techniques in a hospital setting where time is limited, emotions run high, and patient safety is paramount. If you're in social services, you learn how to build rapport with clients who feel powerless and abandoned by systems that were supposed to help them. If you work in education, security, or any other public-facing role, you learn how to adapt these tools to your environment, your constraints, and the unique pressures you face.

The core of FC2C is Professional Sincerity: the principle that effective de-escalation isn't about performing empathy or following a script. It's about showing up as a genuine human being who sees the person in front of you as worthy of dignity and respect. Professional Sincerity recognizes that people in crisis can detect inauthenticity instantly, and that the moment they sense you're manipulating them or going through the motions, trust collapses and cooperation becomes impossible. This is why FC2C doesn't teach you what to say. It teaches you how to think, how to regulate your own emotional state, and how to build the kind of authentic connection that allows influence to take root. We'll explore Professional Sincerity in the next chapter and return to it in depth later in the book.

Why This History Matters

You might be wondering why we're spending so much time on history and events that happened fifty years ago in contexts that may be very different from your own. Here's why it matters: the principles that saved lives in hostage situations are the same principles that can help keep you safe in your encounters.

Whether you're a social worker sitting across from a client whose benefits have been cut, a security officer approaching someone who's acting erratically, a teacher managing a student in crisis, or a nurse facing a family member's frustration in an emergency room, you are in a version of the same situation those early NYPD negotiators faced. Someone's emotions have overwhelmed their ability to think clearly. They feel cornered, desperate, unheard, or misunderstood. And how you respond in that moment will determine whether the situation de-escalates or spirals into something worse.

The history of de-escalation teaches us that we don't always need to be bigger, louder, or more forceful to be effective. We need to be calmer, more patient, and more connected. The tools that worked in the most extreme circumstances imaginable, like armed standoffs, hostage crises, life-and-death negotiations, may work in your everyday encounters too. Because at the end of the day, every crisis is still a human being struggling to cope.

Now that you understand where these principles came from and why they work, it's time to see how From Crisis to Calm organizes them into a framework you can actually use. In the next chapter, we'll lay out the three interconnected components that guide everything else in this program: the Five Pillars of FC2C, Professional Sincerity, and the G.U.I.D.E. framework. These are the tools that translate fifty-plus years of crisis negotiation wisdom into something you can apply in your next difficult encounter.

Notes

1. New York State Special Commission on Attica, *Attica: The Official Report of the New York State Special Commission on Attica* (New York: Bantam Books, 1972).
2. Simon Reeve, *One Day in September: The Full Story of the 1972 Munich Olympics Massacre and the Israeli Revenge Operation "Wrath of God"* (New York: Arcade Publishing, 2006).
3. P.F. Kluge and Thomas Moore, "The Boys in the Bank," *Life*, September 22, 1972. See also Randy Borum and Thomas Strentz, "Borderline Personality: Negotiation Strategies," *FBI Law Enforcement Bulletin* 61, no. 8 (1992): 6–10.
4. Harvey Schlossberg and Lucy Freeman, *Psychologist with a Gun* (New York: Coward, McCann & Geoghegan, 1974). See also Stefan Forbes, dir., *Hold Your Fire* (IFC Films, 2021), documentary; Frank Bolz and Edward Hershey, *Hostage Cop* (New York: Rawson Associates, 1980).
5. Thomas Strentz, *Psychological Aspects of Crisis Negotiation*, 3rd ed. (Boca Raton: CRC Press, 2017).
6. Frank Bolz and Edward Hershey, *Hostage Cop* (New York: Rawson Associates, 1980).

7. Gary Noesner, *Stalling for Time: My Life as an FBI Hostage Negotiator* (New York: Random House, 2010).

8. The evolution from Contain, Isolate, and Negotiate to Contain, Control, and Communicate reflects adaptations made across multiple agencies over several decades. For a comprehensive overview of these frameworks, see Michael J. McMains and Wayman C. Mullins, *Crisis Negotiations: Managing Critical Incidents and Hostage Situations in Law Enforcement and Corrections*, 5th ed. (New York: Routledge, 2014).

9. Merriam-Webster, s.v. "de-escalate," accessed February 22, 2026, https://www.merriam-webster.com/dictionary/de-escalate.

10. Ontario Police College, as cited in Toronto Police Service, *Chapter 15: Incident Response (Use of Force/De-Escalation) & Equipment*, Toronto Police Service Procedures (Toronto: Toronto Police Service, 2024). See also Ontario Police College, *Public-Police Interactions Training Aid Framework Document* (Aylmer, ON: Ontario Police College, 2023).

CHAPTER 3:

THE FROM CRISIS TO CALM FOUNDATION

In the last chapter, we traced the history that shaped modern de-escalation, from the tragedies at Attica and Munich to the Brooklyn standoffs that gave birth to the NYPD's first hostage negotiation team, and eventually to the spread of those principles across healthcare, social services, education, and every other field where people face crisis. What emerged from that history was a set of core principles: slow down, create space, build connection, and influence behavior through understanding rather than force. Those principles work. But without a structure to live in, they stay theoretical. With one, they become something you can actually apply under pressure.

This chapter lays out that structure, the standards that everything else in this book is built upon. Three interconnected components work together to translate those historically grounded principles into something that works: the From Crisis to Calm Five Pillars as your guiding framework, Professional Sincerity as your ethical core, and the G.U.I.D.E. framework as your process for navigating from crisis to calm. None of these are rigid sequences. They are interrelated components designed to support sound judgment under stress.

We're going to cover all three here, so you have the full map before we go further. The Five Pillars get real depth in this chapter because they're operating in the background of every skill you'll learn, from reading situations to setting boundaries to communicating under pressure. Professional Sincerity and G.U.I.D.E. get a look here so you understand how they connect to the Five Pillars, then get their full depth in later chapters when you're learning the specific communication techniques that bring them to life.

The Five Pillars: Standards That Guide Every Encounter

When you're in the middle of a difficult encounter, when someone's escalating and you need to know what to do, you need standards that guide your decisions and actions moment to moment. Not a script, not a formula, but a set of reliable touchstones that apply across different situations and different people.

That's what the Five Pillars provide. They're standards that apply simultaneously throughout an encounter. Think of them as five conditions that, when present, create the environment for de-escalation. When one or more are missing, escalation becomes more likely. When all five are present, you're creating the strongest possible foundation for moving from crisis to calm.

The Five Pillars are: Regulation, Boundaries, Validation, Collaboration, and Options.

Regulation: Managing Your Own State First

The first pillar is the one that professionals most often overlook because it seems obvious: before you can help someone else regulate their emotions, you need to regulate your own.

This isn't about suppressing your emotions or pretending you don't feel stressed. It's about managing your physiological and emotional state well enough that you can think clearly, communicate effectively, and serve as an anchor rather than adding your own reactivity to the situation.

In a difficult encounter, it's easy to unconsciously mirror someone's emotional intensity; raising your voice to match theirs, tensing your body to match their agitation. When you do this, you're failing at regulation. You've allowed their dysregulation to trigger your own, and now you're both escalated.

Regulation means you maintain enough control over your own nervous system that you can be the stable point in the encounter. You don't want to be robotic or emotionless. That comes across as cold and dismissive. You need to be grounded, present, and able to think while under stress.

When you take a breath and stay in control, your breathing stays relatively slow and deep rather than becoming rapid and shallow. Your voice stays stable rather than getting louder or higher pitched. Your body language stays open and oriented rather than becoming closed and defensive. These aren't just self-management tools. They may influence the other person's nervous system too.

Regulation also works in the mind. When you're regulated, you can actually think. Consequences get considered before you act or speak. Multiple response options open up rather than reflexively defaulting to the first thing that comes to mind. Training kicks in and appropriate techniques get applied rather than just reacting. Safety considerations get assessed while you're simultaneously managing the communication, and how your responses are landing becomes something you can monitor and adjust in real time. None of that is possible when your brain is stuck in fight-or-flight mode.

Here's what makes this hard: nobody gets to practice regulation when things are calm and easy. The skill only gets tested when the pressure is real, when someone is in your face and every instinct is telling you to fight back, shut down, or walk away. That's why regulation improves with repetition, not with willpower. The more you work with your own stress signals through techniques like controlled breathing, through developing awareness of your physical cues, through practicing in lower-stakes situations, the faster you recognize them when the pressure is on, and the sooner you can manage them before they manage you. The more accessible that regulation becomes in practice, the more reliably it shows up when you need it most.

This doesn't eliminate that stress response. You still need it. What regulation does is give you the ability to notice your stress response and manage it well enough that it doesn't control your behavior. You feel your heart rate increase, and you deliberately slow your breathing. You notice your jaw clenching, and you consciously relax it. You feel the impulse to snap back or shut down, and you pause long enough to choose a different response.

And here's what's remarkable: when you regulate yourself effectively, you often help regulate the other person. When you stay grounded, you pull others toward calm. Your slow breathing, steady voice, and present demeanor signal safety to the other person's nervous system, which can help them begin to down-regulate even before any specific de-escalation techniques are applied.

Regulation is the first pillar because without it, the other four become nearly impossible to implement effectively.

Boundaries: Maintaining Safety and Dignity

The second pillar is boundaries, the limits on acceptable behavior, the lines that protect both your safety and the other person's dignity. They're not punishment or threats. They're clear statements about what behavior is acceptable in this professional interaction and what happens if those limits are exceeded. This is where "I" statements become effective. They have several characteristics:

They're behavior-focused, not person-focused. "The volume needs to come down" rather than "You're being too loud." "That language isn't acceptable here" rather than "You need to watch your mouth." The boundary addresses the behavior without attacking the person's character.

They're stated clearly and directly. Vague boundaries or implied limits don't work because people in crisis aren't picking up on subtle cues. "I need you to step back" is clear. "You're kind of in my space" is not.

They explain the reason without justifying at length. "I can't hear you clearly when we're both talking at once" gives context. "Our hospital policy section 3.4.2 requires..." is usually too much detail in the moment.

Boundaries preserve dignity for all parties involved. Even when setting firm limits, boundaries can be stated in ways that maintain respect. "I'm going to stop you there" is more respectful than "Shut up and let me talk." Allowing someone to keep their dignity is extremely important. Chances are you or someone you work with may encounter the same person again. You may not remember them, but they will remember you and how they felt they were treated.

Boundaries offer choice about compliance. "I need the volume to come down. Can you do that, or do we need to take a break and try this again later?" works far better than "Lower your voice or I'm ending this conversation."

Once you've stated a boundary, you don't defend it or explain it repeatedly. You enforce it. Boundaries aren't apologies or negotiations. "I'm sorry, but I need you to..." weakens the boundary. Either you need it, or you don't. If you need it, state it directly.

They're not threats disguised as choices. "You can calm down or I can call security" presented in an aggressive tone isn't a real choice. It's a threat. "I want to help you, and that works best when we can keep this conversation respectful" followed by "If that's not possible, I'll need to get my supervisor involved" is a real boundary with real consequences.

The boundaries pillar is what prevents the other pillars from being exploited. You can validate someone's emotions while setting boundaries on their behavior. You can offer options while maintaining firm limits on what's non-negotiable. You can invite collaboration while being clear about what you will and won't accept.

"We can work this out. But the swearing needs to stop so that can happen. Can you do that?" Validation plus boundary. The emotion is acknowledged. The behavior is limited.

Here's the sophisticated part about boundaries: they're acts of respect. When you allow someone to continue behavior that's inappropriate, yelling, threatening, being abusive, you're not being kind. You're allowing them to damage the interaction and often to damage themselves. Setting a clear boundary gives them the opportunity to self-correct before consequences become more serious.

And boundaries protect you. Your safety comes first and your dignity matters. None of this ever requires you to accept abuse, tolerate threats, or remain in situations where you're unsafe. Boundaries are how you maintain those protections while still engaging professionally.

Validation: Acknowledging What's Real

The third pillar is validation, and it's the one that causes the most initial resistance among professionals learning this approach. It sounds like, "Why should I validate someone who's being unreasonable?" "If I validate their emotions, won't that reinforce their bad behavior?" "Doesn't validation mean I'm agreeing with them?"

Nope, no, negative.

Validation means acknowledging what's real about someone's experience without necessarily agreeing with their conclusions, their behavior, or their demands. It means recognizing that from their perspective, their emotions make sense, even if you would respond differently in the same situation.

Let's be clear about what we're validating: emotions, not actions. "It looks like you're really frustrated" validates the feeling of frustration. It doesn't validate yelling, threatening, or being abusive. The emotion, or how someone feels about something, is always acceptable. The behavior might not be. Validation addresses the emotion.

To understand why, it helps to know a little about how the brain processes threats. Two regions do most of the heavy lifting here. The amygdala is the brain's alarm system, a small structure deep in the temporal lobe that detects danger and triggers the fight-or-flight response. It operates fast, automatically, and without much nuance. The prefrontal cortex, sitting right behind your forehead, is the brain's executive. It handles reasoning, judgment, impulse control, and decision-making. Under normal conditions, these two regions work together. The amygdala flags a potential threat, and the prefrontal cortex evaluates whether that threat is real and decides on an appropriate response.

The problem is that this partnership breaks down under extreme stress or emotional overload.

Here's why validation matters neurologically: when someone's amygdala has hijacked their prefrontal cortex, when they're in emotional crisis, they're stuck in that state partly because their brain hasn't received the signal that it's safe to down-regulate.[1] Validation provides that signal.

When you say, "This must be really hard for you," the person's brain registers: Someone sees me. Someone understands that something is wrong. I'm not fighting alone here. That recognition, even from someone who can't give them what they want, often begins to reduce the emotional intensity.

Contrast that with invalidation. When you say, "There's no reason to be so upset" or "Calm down" or "You're overreacting," the person's brain registers: This person doesn't see my distress. They're dismissing my experience. I need to escalate more to make them understand how serious this is. And the intensity increases.

Validation doesn't require you to solve the person's problem. It doesn't require you to give them what they want. It doesn't require you to agree that they're right. It only requires you to acknowledge that they're experiencing something difficult from their perspective.

"I can hear how important this is to you." "This situation would frustrate anyone." "This caught you by surprise, didn't it?" "That sounds incredibly stressful."

Notice that none of these statements agree with any particular factual claim or promise any particular outcome. They simply acknowledge the emotional reality the person is experiencing.

Here's the sophisticated part of validation: you can validate contradictory emotions simultaneously, and you can validate emotions while maintaining firm boundaries.

"That's a lot to deal with all at once, and it makes sense that you'd feel overwhelmed. Let's look at what options are available."

"It sounds like you feel dismissed, and nobody should have to feel that way. Let's walk through what happens next, so you know exactly where things stand."

"Anyone in your position would feel blindsided by this. And I need us to stay in this conversation calmly so we can actually work through it together."

Validation plus boundary. Acknowledgment plus limit. This isn't contradiction; it's strategic communication.

The pillar of validation is foundational because people cannot move past emotional crisis until they feel heard. You might have the perfect solution to their problem, but if they don't feel heard first, they won't be in a state where they can receive that solution. Validation creates the conditions for rational engagement.

A Golden Rule: The Power of Two Minutes

Before we move into the next pillar, collaboration, I need to share what might be the single most powerful de-escalation tool at your disposal. It costs nothing. It requires no special training. And it often works across almost every setting and situation.

Give people validation by giving them time to vent.

Not forever. Not until they're done. But for thirty seconds. For one minute. And if the situation allows, for the gold standard: two minutes. Think of it as "Two Minutes to Calm" rather than Iron Maiden's "Two Minutes to Midnight."

For those unfamiliar, Iron Maiden's 1984 song referenced the Doomsday Clock, the symbolic countdown to nuclear catastrophe during the Cold War. That clock was ticking toward midnight, toward disaster. But in our work, two minutes represents something different: the window of opportunity before an encounter reaches its crisis point. It's the time we have to move the clock backward, away from midnight, toward safety. Those two minutes aren't counting down to explosion, they're the investment that prevents one.

Here's what most people experience when they try to get help, report a problem, or resolve an issue: they get cut off. They're told to go somewhere else. Stand in a different line. Call back later to a different number. See someone else. Fill out a form. Come back another day. It happens so consistently, so universally, that people expect it. They're used to it.

What they're not used to is someone giving them time. Time to explain what's bothering them. Time to talk about their issue or their problem or whatever brought them to you. Time to be heard without being interrupted, redirected, or shut down.

And here's the remarkable part: even when you can't solve their problem, even when what they're saying won't change the outcome, even when the documents they want to show you or the explanation they want to give won't make a difference to their case, giving them that time still matters enormously.

A participant in one of my classes shared this with me. She worked in a benefits office, and a person came to her window extremely upset and irate. They demanded to show her documentation they believed was crucial to their case. She looked at the papers. They were completely irrelevant. The documents did absolutely nothing to help their situation. Policy-wise, these papers changed nothing.

But here's what she did: she listened. She let this person explain everything they thought was important about those documents. She didn't interrupt. She didn't immediately shut them down with "this doesn't matter." She gave them time to explain what they believed these papers proved, why they thought this documentation was significant, what they wanted her to understand about their situation.

The transformation was remarkable. The person's agitation decreased visibly. Their voice lowered. Their body language shifted from confrontational to conversational. And here's what she told me: "No one before had ever let this person just vent about what they thought was important. Just giving them that time, even though those documents changed nothing about the decision, went such a long way toward calming them down."

This is the power of venting. This worked for me time after time during my law enforcement career. When people are emotionally activated, they need to discharge that emotional energy. They need to express what's frustrating them, frightening them, angering them. Trying to shut that down prematurely, trying to solve the problem or move forward before they've had a chance to vent, often makes things worse. They escalate further because they don't feel heard.

But when you give them time, that thirty seconds, one minute, two minutes, something shifts. The pressure releases and the emotional intensity decreases. They move from a state where rational conversation is nearly impossible to a state where they can actually hear you and work with you.

Now, this doesn't mean letting someone rant at you indefinitely and it certainly doesn't mean accepting abuse. It doesn't mean allowing someone to become more escalated without intervention. The key is this: when it's safe to do so, give them time. Two minutes is the gold standard. But even thirty seconds of uninterrupted time to express what's upsetting them can make an enormous difference.

This ties directly back to the Five Pillars. You're regulating yourself enough to remain calm while they vent. You're validating their need to express themselves. You're creating a collaborative dynamic rather than an adversarial one. You're restoring some sense of agency so they get to speak; they get to be heard. And you're maintaining appropriate boundaries. You're giving time, not surrendering control.

So, before you rush to solve the problem, before you explain the policy, before you redirect someone to another department or another day, give them two minutes. Let them talk. Let them vent and feel heard. You'll be amazed at how often those two minutes transform an escalating encounter into one you can actually resolve.

Collaboration: Creating Partnership Instead of Conflict

The fourth pillar is collaboration, and it fundamentally shifts how encounters feel.

In many professional interactions, especially those involving compliance, boundaries, or limited resources, the default dynamic becomes adversarial. You have something the person wants (approval, service, access) or you're enforcing something they don't want (rules, consequences, limits). This creates a natural us-versus-them dynamic where the person feels like you're the obstacle to what they need.

Collaboration reframes that dynamic. Instead of you standing between them and their goal, you position yourself alongside them, looking at the problem together. You're not adversaries. You're partners trying to navigate a difficult situation with constraints that neither of you controls.

This isn't about pretending you don't have authority or that constraints don't exist. It's about how you present the reality of the situation.

Adversarial framing: "You can't do that. It's against policy."

Collaborative framing: "Let's figure out what we can do within these constraints."

Adversarial framing: "That's not my department. You'll have to go somewhere else."

Collaborative framing: "Let's get you to the right place. Here's who can assist with that."

Adversarial framing: "You should have brought the right documents. Now you'll have to come back."

Collaborative framing: "Let's look at what you have and figure out what's still needed so your next visit can be successful."

Notice the shift in pronouns. "You can't" versus "Let's figure out." "You'll have to" versus "Let me help you." "You should have" versus "Let's look at." Small language changes that signal partnership rather than opposition.

The collaboration pillar is especially powerful when combined with validation. First you validate the emotion, then you invite collaboration on the solution.

"This is a frustrating situation. Let's figure out together what our options are from here." That combination, acknowledgment plus partnership, transforms encounters from confrontational to cooperative far more often than you might expect.

Options: Restoring Agency

The fifth pillar is options, and it addresses one of the core drivers of escalation: feeling trapped.

When people feel like they have no choices, no control, no way forward except through a wall they can't get through, their stress response intensifies. They might escalate their emotional intensity trying to force the situation to change or they might shut down in helpless resignation. Either of these makes it harder to achieve a resolution.

Options restore agency. Agency is the feeling that you have some control over what happens to you. When people in crisis lose that feeling, and every choice seems made for them, desperation sets in. Options give that sense of control back. Even small choices, even limited options, shift someone from feeling completely powerless to feeling like they have some influence over what happens next.

Here's what's important: the options don't have to be ideal. They don't have to solve the entire problem. They just have to be real choices that the person can actually make.

"The application can't be processed today without that document. But here's what we can do right now: let's go over exactly what's needed and get an appointment set up for later this week so there's no waiting in line again. Would Thursday afternoon or Friday morning work better?"

Notice what just happened. The main thing the person wanted, application processed today, isn't possible. That's a real constraint. But instead of ending with "you'll have to come back," which leaves them feeling powerless, the response included collaboration and provided real options: specific information about what's needed, an appointment instead of waiting in line, and choice about when to return.

Those are small options. But they're real, and they shift the person from feeling completely stuck to feeling like they have some path forward and some choice in how that path unfolds.

The pillar of options is especially powerful in situations where you're enforcing boundaries or delivering unwelcome news.

"If you don't have an ID we can't just let you in, but the person you're here to see can be called down to verify your identity. Would that work?"

"We can't accept this return without a receipt. How about store credit at the current price, or we can check if your purchase is in our system under your phone number. Which would you prefer?"

Boundary plus options. Limit plus choice. This isn't about undermining your authority or pretending constraints don't exist. It's about presenting the full picture: here's what's not possible, and here's what is possible. That second part, what is possible, is what people need to hear to move forward.

Sometimes the only option you can offer is choice about process rather than outcome.

"We need to collect some information from you. Would you rather do that here at the counter, or would you prefer to sit down over there where it's more private?" The outcome (information collection) isn't optional. But the process (where and how) offers real choice, and that choice reduces resistance to the unavoidable outcome.

The options pillar also applies to how you present consequences. Threat-based framing sounds something like, "If you don't calm down, I'm going to call security and have you removed." This presents one path: continued escalation leads to removal.

Option-based framing invites a resolution and can incorporate a boundary. "I want to help you, and I can do that best when we can talk at this volume. Can we bring it down together?" Now we have two paths: we can lower intensity together and move forward, or the intensity continues and we reach limits. It invites the person to choose cooperation rather than forcing it.

Here's the sophisticated truth about options: you're always making choices about what to offer and what to withhold, and you almost always have more flexibility than you might initially think. Part of developing skill in de-escalation is developing creativity in finding real options even in highly constrained situations. It comes with practice.

Professional Sincerity: The Ethical Core

You were introduced to Professional Sincerity in Chapter 1 as the ethical core of FC2C, the principle that effective de-escalation is about showing up as a genuine human being who sees the person in front of them as worthy of dignity and respect. Now that you've seen the Five Pillars in action, there's one idea about Professional Sincerity that needs to be understood, because every pillar depends on it: You can treat people with dignity and respect without liking them.

We'll explore Professional Sincerity in depth, its five principles, how it differs from customer service friendliness or therapeutic rapport, and exactly how it operates in practice, when we get to the communication chapters later in this book. For now, hold onto the core idea: you can be authentic, ethical, and effective without faking a connection you don't feel. That's what makes everything else in this program work.

The G.U.I.D.E. Framework: Your Process for Moving from Crisis to Calm

Professional Sincerity tells you how to show up. The Five Pillars tell you what standards to apply. But when you're in the middle of an encounter and you need to know what to do next, you need a process, a framework that guides you from initial contact through to resolution.

That's what G.U.I.D.E. provides. It's a framework of five elements that give you a structure for managing these difficult encounters, not as a rigid sequence, but a way to think through what's happening that helps you make better decisions in real time. G.U.I.D.E. stands for:

- **G**round Yourself
- **U**nderstand Emotion
- **I**dentify Shared Goal
- **D**irect the Interaction
- **E**nsure Safety and Support

Each element serves a specific purpose. Grounding yourself means checking your own emotional state and assessing the environment before you engage. It connects directly to the pillar of Regulation. Understanding emotion means identifying what's actually driving the person's behavior beneath the surface. Identifying a shared goal reframes the encounter from adversarial to collaborative. Directing the interaction means actively guiding the conversation toward resolution rather than letting it spiral. And ensuring safety and support means maintaining awareness of risk throughout while ending encounters in ways that preserve dignity.

One critical thing about G.U.I.D.E.: it flows and doesn't always go in strict order. In a real encounter, you might ground yourself, start to understand the emotion, realize you need to re-ground because your own stress is rising, redirect the interaction, circle back to understanding a new emotion that's surfaced, and ensure safety throughout. The letters give you a framework, not a rigid checklist. You return to whichever element the moment requires. We'll go fully into G.U.I.D.E. in later chapters.

For now, you have the map, and you may have noticed that the Five Pillars, Professional Sincerity, and G.U.I.D.E. share overlapping concepts. That's intentional. These three components aren't separate systems running in parallel. They're different lenses on the same core principles, designed to reinforce one another. The Five Pillars define the standards you maintain throughout an encounter. Professional Sincerity defines the ethical foundation that makes those standards credible. G.U.I.D.E. gives you a process for putting them into action. Where they overlap is where the framework is strongest, because the skills that matter most in a crisis aren't isolated techniques. They're principles that show up again and again, in different forms, at different moments, until they become second nature.

What's Next

Before you can communicate effectively with someone in crisis, you need to see what's actually happening. You need to read the room, read the person, read the behavioral cues that tell you whether you're dealing with someone who's venting frustration or someone who's preparing to hurt you. Those situations require very different responses, and misreading one as the other can be catastrophic.

That's where we turn next: to the critical skill of situational awareness, truly seeing what's happening around you, reading behavior accurately, and knowing what you're actually dealing with before you respond.

Notes

1. On the amygdala's role in emotional crisis and the neurological basis of validation, see Daniel Goleman, *Emotional Intelligence: Why It Can Matter More Than IQ* (New York: Bantam Books, 1995); Amy F. T. Arnsten, "Stress Signalling Pathways That Impair Prefrontal Cortex Structure and Function," *Nature Reviews Neuroscience* 10, no. 6 (2009): 410–422.

CHAPTER 4:

SITUATIONAL AWARENESS - SEEING WHAT'S ACTUALLY THERE

People are unpredictable. Because of that, we never want to get complacent. We never want to assume just because we've had a similar situation before that worked out okay or an encounter with a particular person turned out fine, that every encounter or person will follow the same path.

Every encounter has three contributing factors that shape the outcome: you, the other person, and the circumstances that brought you together in that moment. These three forces are constantly interacting with each other. If any one of them shifts, even slightly, the entire tone and direction of the situation can change. A small change in how we interpret someone's behavior, a misunderstanding in how they interpret ours, or a sudden shift in the environment can quickly turn a manageable moment into one that feels unpredictable and unsafe.

A person who seemed calm a second ago may suddenly feel threatened because of something we didn't see coming. We might misread their stress as hostility and react defensively. The setting might introduce a distraction or pressure that neither of us planned for. Any movement in any one of these factors ripples through the entire encounter, sometimes in ways that help, but often in ways that make things harder.

Most of us have reacted quickly and later realized that we misunderstood what was really going on. We treated one visible moment like it was the entire story, only to discover afterward that there were important pieces we didn't know, pieces that would have changed the way we responded. That's where the real danger lies. When we respond to assumptions instead of reality, we can escalate a situation that didn't need to escalate at all. Frustration, confusion, and fear become anger, resistance, and a fight-or-flight response. And assumptions turn misunderstandings into conflicts.

But here's the good news. We don't have to fix everything that led someone to this moment. In fact, often we can't fix the crisis that they are in. We don't have control over the stress or struggles they walked in with. What we do control is how we show up, our own piece of the equation. When we slow our assumptions, remain curious, and give ourselves room to recognize that we might be missing something important, we keep the door open to better outcomes. We keep their options open too. And suddenly, even small adjustments in our behavior can help guide the encounter toward a safer, more cooperative direction.

This has to be done with safety in mind and that starts with being and staying situationally aware.

"You see, but you do not observe."

We open this section with a quote from *Sherlock Holmes*: "You see, but you do not observe."[1]

The great, fictional detective Holmes is calling out a flaw in how most people move through the world. We see everything in front of us, shapes, colors, people, motion, but we rarely observe the meaning behind what we're seeing. Our brains are designed for efficiency, not accuracy, so most of what enters our eyes gets filtered, ignored, or oversimplified. We focus only on what we expect to matter.

To Holmes, "seeing" is the passive act of taking in visual information. "Observing" is the active process of paying attention to detail, noticing patterns, and recognizing what doesn't fit.

Most people look at a room and think they've gathered all the information. In reality, they often only take in enough to function, not enough to understand. Holmes knew that the real clues, the real risks, the real opportunities are almost always in what others overlook.

Observation means:

- Curiosity over assumption, asking, "what does that mean?"
- Details over generalities, noticing a specific change, not just the general scene
- Context over snapshots, understanding not only what it means, but why it might matter

This distinction is the heart of situational awareness.

Two people could stand side-by-side watching the same individual in crisis. One might only see anger. The other sees fear, shame, or panic because they're truly observing, connecting behavior to emotion, to context, and to risk.

Situational awareness is being aware of your surroundings and identifying potential threats and dangerous situations. It's the ongoing comparison of observed behavior and the environment to what is expected in that context. It's not about assuming everyone is dangerous or approaching every interaction with suspicion. It's about noticing when things don't fit, when behavior doesn't match the environment, when reactions don't align with circumstances, when someone's demeanor shifts from their baseline pattern.

And importantly, it isn't about being paranoid or scanning for danger every second. Hypervigilance actually creates blind spots. When we treat every person like a potential threat, we burn out, we lose the ability to think clearly, and we damage trust. True situational awareness is balanced; it's about observing what matters and noticing change, because change is usually what signals risk. Looking specifically for a threat everywhere, every minute is also bad for your mental health.

Think about walking through a parking lot at night. Most people are moving with purpose, heading to their cars, walking steadily, keys in hand, focused on their destination. That's the expected pattern. If you see someone moving differently, pacing between cars, looking around repeatedly, changing direction without apparent purpose, your brain registers that something doesn't fit. That noticing is situational awareness.

Of course, that same pattern of behavior, the pacing, the repeated glancing around, the backtracking, might simply be someone who parked on level 3 and is now hopelessly wandering level 4. Context matters. Situational awareness isn't about assuming the worst; it's about noticing what doesn't fit and then gathering more information before you decide what it means.

The same principle applies in professional encounters. In a hospital waiting room, most people are sitting, maybe looking at their phones, maybe reading, waiting with the patience or impatience typical of waiting rooms. If someone is pacing rapidly, muttering to themselves, repeatedly approaching the desk and backing away, checking the exits, that behavior doesn't match the context. It warrants attention.

In a retail environment, typical customer behavior includes browsing, comparing products, asking questions, moving through the store with normal shopping patterns. If someone enters, makes no eye contact, moves directly to high-value items, appears to be scanning for cameras or security personnel, keeps hands in pockets near those items, that doesn't fit normal shopping behavior.

Situational awareness is that comparison process: What would I normally expect to see here? What am I actually seeing? Do they match?

When they don't match, that discrepancy deserves attention. It doesn't automatically mean danger, there could be perfectly innocent explanations. But it means you should pay closer attention, adjust your positioning, maybe engage the person to understand what's happening.

The Five Levels of Awareness

Awareness isn't binary. You're not either completely aware or completely oblivious. It exists on a spectrum, and understanding that spectrum helps you recognize where you currently are and where you need to be for different situations.

In From Crisis to Calm, we talk about five distinct levels of awareness and relate them in a manner most can understand: to driving. These aren't arbitrary categories, they describe real states that you move through multiple times every day, often without conscious recognition. Learning to identify these levels in yourself helps you stay in the right state for the situation you're in.

Tuned Out

This is when someone is mentally checked out. On the road, it's the driver who is daydreaming or glued to their phone (dangerous in more than one way), barely aware they're even driving. Maybe you're driving to work and all of a sudden you realize you're there. You don't remember going over the bridge, stopping at the stop sign, what song was on the heavy metal satellite radio station. In a workplace or during an encounter, it's the employee who is so distracted or stressed that they miss the obvious cues right in front of them. They are present in body but not in mind, and in that state, they won't notice rising risk until it's too late.

We've all been here. You're thinking about what happened yesterday, worrying about what needs to happen tomorrow, replaying a conversation in your head. Meanwhile, the person in front of you is showing signs of escalation, and you don't notice because you're not actually present in the moment.

Tuned Out is dangerous not because you're doing anything wrong, but because you're simply not processing what's happening around you. You can't respond to what you haven't noticed.

Relaxed Awareness

This is the ideal baseline for most moments in everyday life. On the road, you're paying attention, scanning mirrors, noting traffic patterns. But you can still have a conversation, drink a cup of coffee. Nothing seems threatening, but you are ready to respond if something changes. Interpersonally, it means recognizing behaviors, reading the environment, and being aware of exits, hazards, and emotional energy in the room. You're calm, alert, and capable.

This is where professionals should spend most of their time during encounters. You're engaged, you're noticing, but you're not tense or hypervigilant. You can have a normal conversation while still registering body language, tone shifts, and environmental changes.

Relaxed Awareness doesn't drain you. It's sustainable. It's the state that allows you to notice the early indicators that something might be shifting, giving you time to adjust before a situation escalates.

Focused Awareness

In driving, this is when traffic gets heavier or something starts to concern you, maybe a car is drifting within its lane or weather starts changing. You are paying deliberate attention to a specific element. In an encounter, this is when you narrow your focus on behavior or risk indicators: shifts in body language, access to weapons, rising agitation. You're still in control, still thinking, but your attention is now actively directed.

Something has triggered this shift. Maybe the person's tone changed. Maybe they moved closer than appropriate. Or their hands went to their waistband. Whatever it was, your brain has flagged it as worth watching more carefully.

Focused Awareness is not panic. It's targeted attention. You're still capable of conversation, still able to use your communication skills, but now you're also monitoring specific behaviors or environmental factors that could become relevant to safety.

High Alert

This is the "brake pedal slammed" moment. When you perceive an immediate danger, when a collision seems possible, or a hazard jumps right in front of you. Physically, stress responses spike and reaction time speeds up. In a crisis interaction, this may mean a person suddenly becomes aggressive, a weapon appears, or someone else's panic spreads. High Alert isn't a place to stay; it's a place to act quickly and get to safety.

Your body responds before your conscious mind fully processes what's happening. Your heart rate increases, your muscles tense, and your focus narrows dramatically. This is your survival system taking over.

High Alert is appropriate when there's an immediate, observable threat. But it's also exhausting and unsustainable. The goal is to recognize threats early enough, through Relaxed and Focused Awareness, that you rarely need to reach this level.

Comatose

We talk about this one because sometimes, when people perceive intense threat or shock, they shut down entirely. They freeze. It's not cowardice, it's biology. The brain becomes overwhelmed and disconnects from decision-making. On the road, this is the driver who doesn't react at all when danger strikes. In a real-world interaction, this could be panic, confusion, or total shutdown. Recognizing this response matters, because people in Comatose mode need leadership, direction, and calm reassurance to move toward safer behavior.

You've probably seen this in others, the person who goes completely still when confronted with a threat, who stops responding to questions, whose eyes go distant. Their brain has essentially hit the circuit breaker. They're not making decisions because they can't.

Understanding that Comatose is a biological response, not a choice, changes how you interact with someone in this state. They don't need more information or louder instructions. They need calm, clear, simple direction that helps their brain re-engage.

Situational awareness gives us the earliest warning signs that a situation is changing. And when we see the change early, our options remain open. We can communicate better and influence behavior sooner. We can keep ourselves and others safer.

Behavioral Symptom Analysis: Reading the Change

Behavioral Symptom Analysis (BSA for short) allows us to stay situationally aware. It begins with establishing a reliable baseline: how the person naturally behaves when they are calm, unguarded, and answering questions that are easy for them to answer truthfully. We create that baseline during the early, low-pressure phase of a conversation, using simple, non-threatening questions or comments that invite comfort rather than defensiveness. We also note the environment and the baseline there as well, which helps us consider everything in context.

This is entirely about behavior, and nothing else. Not how the person looks, talks, where they're from, age, sex, religion, or anything of the sort. Behavior is what shows us intent, not any of those other things.

BSA gives us a way to recognize those early indicators that someone is heading toward risk. When we spot those changes early, we can intervene sooner, connect more effectively, and prevent harm before things spiral into a real crisis. To help us do that consistently, we use a simple, three-part threat assessment model. The truth is, we already do this in everyday life without thinking about it. What we're doing now is making the process intentional, so our reactions become safer and more effective, especially in stressful environments.

Identify

The first part is Identify. We do this in Relaxed Awareness. You, as an observer, should observe the person's typical patterns: how they sit, how they use their hands, their facial expressions, breathing rhythm, tone of voice, and how quickly they respond. These behaviors form a "normal" range unique to that person, not compared to the observer's expectations or assumptions. Once we have that baseline, we look for changes from it.

Assess

From there, next is Assess. We're entering Focused Awareness. Here, we ask ourselves whether what we're seeing is merely unusual or whether it is starting to move toward unsafe. The circumstances matter here. This means noticing the person and their behavior and asking yourself what stands out as different from the norm or different from what the environment would typically suggest. You might see signs like agitation, pacing, fixation, withdrawal, raised voice, clenched fists, or heavy breathing.

Timing and consistency become important here. When someone is relatively calm or regulated, their behavior tends to follow a predictable rhythm, steady speech, relaxed posture, and responses that fit the situation. But when a person becomes agitated, anxious, or overwhelmed, we may see sudden shifts in tone, unexpected pauses, restless movement, or body language that doesn't quite match the words being spoken. That doesn't prove anything by itself. Behaviors are signals, not verdicts. But it tells us where to slow down, pay closer attention, or build more rapport before moving forward.

A loud voice during a sporting event is normal; the same loud voice in a quiet office may be cause for concern. We're looking at whether the behavior is escalating, whether the environment increases or reduces risk, and whether the individual seems able to regulate themselves. This step keeps us focused on behavioral facts rather than assumptions or fear. We are not labeling the person as a threat here. Again, we are simply paying attention to behavior, especially behavior that changes suddenly or seems out of place.

Manage

Finally, if we determine that there is indeed a threat, we Manage. Here we should be in High Alert and may have to take action. This is where we engage in a way that helps lower tension and keeps everyone safe. Our communication strategies come into play here, things like validation, boundaries, and offering options that guide behavior toward calmer ground. Sometimes that means talking and building rapport. Sometimes it means creating space or redirecting. Sometimes it means asking for help if the risk continues to rise or suddenly spikes. The earlier we intervene, the more influence we have and the safer the outcome tends to be for both us and the individual in distress.

Ultimately, Behavioral Symptom Analysis is a comparison process. We compare behavior:

- From before and after a sensitive topic is introduced
- Across different types of questions or requests
- Against information we already know to be true

When we talk about Behavioral Symptom Analysis, we're really talking about reading the moment. Individual actions, like what someone is physically doing right now, are critical indicators. Are they engaged with the surrounding environment or fixated elsewhere? Do they react appropriately to external stimuli, such as the presence of a uniform, a specific topic or statement, or a sudden change in crowd behavior? Or do they fail to react at all when everyone else does? The absence of a reaction when one should be present can be just as telling as an overreaction.

Our job is to identify potential hostility early enough to change the outcome. Ideally, we'd like to catch violent behavior during planning, while intent is forming. But we know that isn't always possible. Sometimes identification happens just moments before the attack. And when that's the case, recognizing the behavior of an imminent attacker, and having an understanding of how they (and we all) make decisions may very well be the last line of defense.

The OODA Loop: How Decisions Happen

Everyone you deal with is running a mental cycle that helps them make sense of what is happening and decide what to do next. We call that cycle the OODA Loop: Observe, Orient, Decide, Act. It is not just a "tactical" thing or a "police" thing. It is a human thing. Your brain is doing this in traffic, in the grocery store, at a concert, even while you're reading this sentence.

The OODA Loop was developed by Col. John Boyd, USAF (Ret.), a fighter pilot instructor and student of tactical operations who noticed that in many engagements, one side presented the other with a series of unexpected and threatening situations with which they had not been able to keep pace. The slower side was constantly defeated. What Col. Boyd observed was the fact that conflicts are time competitive.[2]

The OODA Loop works like this: something happens, you take it in, you process what it means based on everything you know, you decide what to do, and you do it. Then the cycle starts again with the next piece of information. It runs continuously, often so fast you don't realize it's happening, and it's running in the person across from you at the same time.

Let's break down each stage and use an example throughout each of people gathered to watch the motorcade of an important dignitary:

Observe

Observe is the raw input stage. It's everything coming in through your senses: what you see, hear, smell, feel, and sometimes what you already know about the environment. In a crowd watching a motorcade, most people are observing the motorcade itself, the noise, the crowd energy, the flashing lights, the cameras. But different people can be observing the same scene while focusing on very different elements.

Orient

Orient is where the brain says, "What does this mean for me?" This is where past experiences, training, beliefs, fears, and goals all start shaping the picture. Two people can observe the same thing and orient to it completely differently. A supporter sees the dignitary and thinks, "This is exciting, I'm lucky to be here." A trained agent sees the same scene and thinks, "Where are my angles, where are the gaps, who doesn't fit?" Someone with hostile intent may be orienting in a very different way: "This is my chance. This is the moment I've been planning for." The same environment, completely different meaning.

Decide

Decide is where options are weighed, even if only for a split second. The brain picks a course of action based on that orientation. The average person decides to wave, cheer, take a photo. The agent decides to scan faces, watch hands, track movement. Someone planning an attack decides, "When the target gets close enough and the timing lines up, I am going to act."

Act

Act is the visible part, the behavior everyone else can see. Most people act by clapping, shouting, holding up signs. The agents act by positioning themselves, moving with the protectee, watching the crowd. The person with hostile intent acts by drawing a weapon, moving toward the target, or executing whatever plan they've been running through their Orient and Decide stages. An action will always have an effect on the environment and start the loop all over again.

Here is why this matters to us in Behavioral Symptom Analysis: if you can interfere with that loop, you can sometimes change what happens next. When you step in and speak to someone, you are not just "being friendly" or "doing customer service." You are stepping into their OODA Loop and forcing their brain to start the cycle over.

If an agent, or even another person in that crowd, had noticed someone's detached, mismatched behavior and walked up and said, "Hey, how's it going? You here by yourself today?" or "Do you know what time it is?", that simple interaction may have forced their brain to re-run the loop. Now they have to observe you, orient to why they're getting attention, decide what to do about this new problem, and act in response to you, not just their original target. That shift may not guarantee anything, but it could delay them, rattle them, expose them, or change the timing just enough that the opportunity disappears.

The bigger lesson for your work is this: everyone you deal with is running an OODA Loop, all day long. The person in crisis, the angry customer, the confused client, the co-worker who is about to say something they shouldn't, all of them are observing, orienting, deciding, and acting. When you learn to read behavior, and when you choose the right moment and the right words to engage, you are not just "talking." You are intentionally stepping into that loop to influence how the rest of it plays out.

Recognizing Hostile Intent

Now that we've spent time looking at behavior, the environment, and how we observe and process information, we can put all of that together into something that matters tremendously in real life: hostile intent. When we talk about intent, we're really describing someone's internal plan or desire to take action. Hostile intent means the person is not just upset. They are preparing or positioning themselves to do something harmful, whether that danger is physical, criminal, or otherwise aimed at causing damage.

Because we can't scan someone's thoughts directly, intent is always inferred. We learn to read it from the outside based on indicators that tell us what direction things may be headed. Sometimes those indicators show up as suspicious behavior, someone acting in a way that stands out from their environment or from what would normally be expected, through their clothing, their pacing, or their unusual focus on objects or people. Small details matter, and the worst thing we can do is dismiss what appears slightly "off" simply because it isn't dramatic yet.

Hostile intent can also show itself as overt hostility, and recognizing that shift can give us just enough time to act safely.

Another common sign is deception. A person's story may start smooth but then becomes fragmented, inconsistent, or full of gaps. Their body language may contradict what they are saying. The truth doesn't need rehearsal. Deception requires energy, and the cracks reveal where the energy is going. We're not going to talk much about deception. That is enough for a whole separate class and book in itself!

We want people to understand that hostile intent rarely reveals itself all at once. It comes in clues, patterns, and behaviors that don't quite fit the scene. The more someone practices identifying those patterns, the more they consciously and subconsciously scan for anomalies, the greater their safety, and the greater the chance they can protect others around them.

These are the clues people give us through their behavior, body language, tone, and positioning that something might be heading in a bad direction. To identify hostile intent, we watch for change from the baseline behavior. Change in tone, posture, emotional state and so on. When someone shifts from anxious to aggressive, or from cooperative to guarded, that change matters. The goal is not to assume someone is dangerous, the goal is to notice when something might be heading in the wrong direction, and stay ahead of it.

When we're assessing behavior in real time, our attention is never on just one thing. We watch several lanes at once, noticing how the person speaks, how they move, and how their emotional state shifts. Tone changes can tell us a lot, a sudden edge in the voice, an unexpected spike in anger, or a narrowed focus that locks onto us or someone else. At the same time, body language gives its own set of clues through blading of the body, fists tightening, eyes scanning for exits or opportunities. Positioning matters too, especially when someone starts closing distance, drifting into a flanking angle, or directing their attention toward a specific person or object. Then there are emotional transitions that don't make sense in the moment, it could be anger, dropping into a cold, flat affect or an instant flip from calm to explosive behavior.

A Word of Caution

It's important to note that you are not diagnosing, labeling, or accusing anyone based on a single action. What you are doing is noticing change, comparing what you're seeing now to what you saw just moments ago. And woven through all of this is our professional standard: context before conclusion. We must understand where we are, what is happening around us, and why the person might be reacting this way before we decide whether the behavior is actually threatening. Observation gives us the information. Context gives it meaning.

Before we start listing indicators, I want to make one thing clear: no single indicator means someone is about to become violent. Human behavior has context. A clenched fist might mean someone is angry, or it might mean they're cold. Someone pacing could be working themselves up, or just anxious or impatient.

So, we don't judge behavior in isolation. We look for clusters of behaviors that, taken together, make sense for the situation we're in. The goal isn't to label or assume. It's to notice changes, shifts in body language, tone, or proximity, and ask, "Does this make sense here?"

For example, if someone's been calm and suddenly starts avoiding eye contact, backing away, and their tone changes, that's information. Not proof of intent, but a pattern to pay attention to. The more changes you see happening at once, the more important it becomes to slow things down, adjust your distance, and keep your tone steady. You're shifting into Focused Awareness.

Cultural and individual differences matter too. What looks like aggression in one culture might be normal expressiveness in another. Even within the same culture, people have different baselines, some are naturally loud, animated, or physically expressive. Others are more reserved. That's why context and baseline behavior are key. We notice changes from that person's normal, not just from what we think is normal.

So, when we talk about indicators of hostile intent, think of it as a constellation, several points of light forming a picture. One star alone doesn't tell us much. But together, they form a pattern we can recognize early and act on before things escalate.

That's how we can stay ahead of danger: by increasing our awareness and reading behavior, not judging it.

Contextualizing Indicators: Behavior Doesn't Happen in a Vacuum

Contextualizing indicators of hostile intent ensures a more accurate and fair assessment of behaviors. Someone pacing at a bus stop is different from someone pacing while staring at staff. Someone sweating in July is different from someone sweating in a cold room. Someone angry because they're in crisis is different from someone angry because you told them "no." By considering environmental, situational, personal, and cultural factors, professionals can reduce the risk of misjudgments, avoid unnecessary escalation, and foster safer, more respectful interactions.

This matters because in the real world, the people you encounter aren't textbook case studies with clean behavioral profiles. They bring their entire history into that moment, their medical conditions, their disabilities, their trauma, their neurology, their culture, their communication abilities. And all of those factors can produce behaviors that look like hostility but aren't. If we don't account for that, we risk creating the very aggression we hoped to prevent.

Let's walk through some of the most common situations where behavior can be misleading, and how professionals can tell the difference between distress and danger.

When Behavior Mimics Aggression: Neurodiversity and Disability

One of the most challenging realities in behavioral threat assessment is that the same outward behavior can come from entirely different internal places. Pacing, clenched fists, poor eye contact, rocking back and forth, repeating phrases, or appearing "over-alert" can absolutely be indicators of rising aggression, but they can just as easily be self-regulation strategies for people experiencing anxiety, responses related to autism spectrum disorder, sensory overload, or disability-related stress. The person in the waiting room who is pacing may be trying not to panic. The driver of the car stopped for speeding who is staring may be trying to process language. The social services client avoiding eye contact may be overwhelmed, not disrespectful.

Our responsibility is to recognize the difference between distress and danger. The safest approach is to remain curious long enough to figure out whether the behavior is part of a survival strategy that protects us or a coping strategy that protects them.

Consider a hospital emergency department. A family member is pacing, fists tight, chest rising quickly, all classic escalation cues. But when a nurse establishes calm contact, they share that movement helps them keep control during autistic shutdown. The appearance was tense and intimidating, but the intent was self-soothing, not aggression.

This is why context and clusters matter. Remember, our own OODA Loop is spinning all the time too. One cue alone is not enough to justify a defensive response, but noticing patterns without assumptions protects everyone. What looks threatening could be someone trying to stay calm. Before we assume aggression, we should ask: Could this be discomfort? Fear? A disability-related behavior? People often look the most threatening when they're actually trying not to fall apart. If we treat that person as hostile, we may create the very aggression we hoped to prevent.

Communication Challenges: Vulnerability, Not Hostility

A person struggling to communicate, whether from a language barrier, a developmental disability, neurodiversity, or emotional overload, often acts in ways that can be misinterpreted as opposition. They may delay responding because their brain is working hard to process information. They may appear flat or expressionless because their nervous system is overwhelmed. They might laugh or smile during tense moments because anxiety is spilling outward in a socially mismatched way.

From the outside, these can look like defiance, deception, or disrespect. From the inside, they are often vulnerability, not hostility.

Picture a social services benefits office. A client avoids eye contact, freezes when asked simple questions, and repeats phrases instead of answering. Staff initially believe they are refusing to cooperate, but the behavior stems from struggling to translate stress into language. Their needs outweigh their communication abilities, and the breakdown becomes the spark for escalation.

When someone is losing their words, the worst thing we can do is treat them like they're refusing. If they can't communicate, they can't negotiate. Our tone, patience, and clarity become critical right here. Struggle with communication is not a sign of noncompliance.

Medical and Neurological Conditions: Involuntary Doesn't Mean Intentional

Not all physical cues are voluntary. Tremors, tics, jerking motions, rigid body posture, and clenched muscles can result from medical conditions like Parkinson's, Tourette's, epilepsy, chronic pain, anxiety disorders, or side effects of medication. These motions can mirror pre-assault indicators almost perfectly.

This means a person's body language can look dangerous even when their intentions are not.

Consider a transit scenario. A passenger on a bus platform repeatedly touches their waistband, shifts weight aggressively, and holds one arm tightly. Security identifies what appears to be a strong pre-attack cluster, until the individual explains that nerve pain and muscle spasms make them brace their waist constantly. The movement matched a weapon-access cue, but the intent did not.

Professionals must focus on patterns and escalation, not a single flicker of tension. Sometimes what we see has nothing to do with us at all. It might be an involuntary movement, a pain response, or a side effect of medication. The key is reading the whole person, not overreacting to a single cue. Not all rapid movements are intentional, or directed at you.

Intellectual Disabilities: Slower Processing Is Not Resistance

Some individuals take more time to understand direction, especially when the stakes are high or stress is elevated. Slow processing can look like refusing to listen. Performing a task incorrectly can appear manipulative. A blank stare can be interpreted as attitude. Lots of times, none of that is true.

When someone does not immediately follow instruction, we tend to repeat, faster, louder, more intensely. But for individuals with cognitive impairments or developmental disabilities, pressure lowers comprehension, and attempts to speed things up can inadvertently make the situation worse.

Think about a retail loss prevention scenario. A customer walks through the exit with a paid item still in the cart. When stopped for a receipt check, they freeze, unable to process multiple requests in a crowded environment. The pause looks like resistance, but is actually cognitive overload.

Here, professionalism means slowing ourselves down, not speeding the confrontation up. If they can't process your request, meaningful compliance becomes unlikely, delayed, or incomplete. Our patience protects the outcome. Slowing down buys cooperation.

Trauma and Mental Illness: When the Reaction Is to a Memory, Not to You

Trauma changes the brain. Hypervigilance, scanning, defensive posture, and rapid shifts in tone can all appear to be indicators of hostile intent, and they can be. But for someone with trauma history, the nervous system may trigger a fight-or-flight response even without real danger present. Uniforms, crowded rooms, loud voices, and authoritative commands can all activate survival memory.

The challenge becomes this: people who feel terrified can look terrifying.

A woman is waiting in a long line to enter a concert. The crowd is loud and packed tightly together, and security is conducting routine bag checks as people approach the entrance. As the line moves forward, her breathing becomes shallow and rapid. She keeps glancing over her shoulder and shifting away from anyone who comes too close. When a security officer asks to check her bag, she freezes and pulls the strap closer to her body, keeping it shielded from reach. Her voice becomes sharp, her responses are clipped, and she blurts out, "No one is touching my stuff!"

From the outside, the behavior checks boxes for pre-assault cues: increased tension, defensive posture, refusal to comply, and vigilant tracking of staff. The officer might interpret this as resistance, suspicion, or an attempt to conceal something dangerous, and without context, that's a reasonable concern.

But in this case, her behaviors stem from trauma associated with a past assault and violations of boundaries. The unexpected contact, loud environment, and perceived loss of control act as trauma triggers. Her brain isn't preparing to attack. It is preparing to survive. Fight-or-flight is activated without a conscious choice, and her protective behavior may escalate further if handled like a threat rather than a trauma response.

The security officer who recognizes this possibility doesn't take the reaction personally. They step back slightly to give space, lower their volume, and use calm reassurance: "Your bag stays with you, we'll go step-by-step at your pace. Tell me when you're ready." That small shift acknowledges fear rather than challenging dignity, and is often all it takes to lower the emotional temperature and regain cooperation.

Trauma isn't visible, but its impact is. Even in a calm setting, someone may be fighting a battle we can't see. A trauma-informed approach keeps us from becoming the trigger. Sometimes the reaction is to a memory, not to you.

Why This Matters: Observable Behavior, Not Assumptions

Any single behavior can be misleading on its own and we must base our decisions on observable behavior, not assumptions about who a person is. This approach builds trust, reduces bias, and enhances outcomes in high-stakes scenarios. The professional who takes a moment to consider context before reacting doesn't lose anything. They gain accuracy, credibility, and the ability to respond appropriately to what's actually happening rather than what they assumed was happening.

Context matters and so does recognizing what we bring to it. Every one of us carries biases, shaped by our experiences, our training, our environment, and sometimes by assumptions we don't even realize we're making. Our job is to observe behavior accurately, not to filter it through fear, stereotypes, or worst-case assumptions. When we let bias drive our assessment instead of behavior, we risk escalating encounters that never needed to escalate, and we risk missing the real threats because we were focused on the wrong person for the wrong reasons.

None of this means you ignore warning signs or that you give someone the benefit of the doubt when multiple indicators are clustering and the situation is clearly escalating. It means you stay curious long enough to tell the difference. It means you read the whole person, not just the one behavior that caught your eye. And it means you hold yourself to a standard that protects both your safety and their dignity, because in the end, that standard protects everyone.

Now we're going to move into the actual indicators that we've been mentioning throughout the block. These are patterns you can see, hear, and feel in real time. But the key is this: accuracy comes from seeing clusters of behaviors, not reacting to one isolated action. Anyone can clench their fists once or look away for a moment. It's when multiple cues start to show up together that our concern should rise and our focus should sharpen. One behavior might mean nothing, but when we see a cluster of warning signs, a pattern of escalation, and a shift in someone's focus (like fixating on staff or targets), that's when we need to pay attention.

This highlights that it's not about one-off behaviors; it's about trends and combinations that suggest intent.

The Seven Key Indicators of Hostile Intent

As we walk through these seven indicators, we are continuing everything we've already covered, staying aware of our biases, preserving legitimacy through fairness, and making safety decisions based on behavioral evidence. Clusters give us the context, the confidence, and the professionalism to respond appropriately. Now let's take a look at each of the seven indicators and how they show up before a situation turns dangerous.

1. Body Language Cues

One of the strongest early indicators of hostile intent is found in a person's body language. Our bodies react to stress and aggression before we ever say a word. When someone begins clenching their fists, tightening their jaw, puffing out their chest, or raising their shoulders, their body may be shifting into a state of readiness. These changes aren't random. They may be physical signs that adrenaline is rising, and the person may be preparing for a confrontation.

We also want to pay close attention to stance and positioning. When someone squares up directly toward us, moves into our personal space, or takes on an overly dominant posture, it is often a nonverbal way of testing our boundaries or signaling challenge. They might lean forward aggressively, angle their feet as if preparing to advance, or shift their weight like they're bracing for action. Their movements become tighter, sharper, and less casual.

But remember, context matters. A clenched fist by itself does not mean a fight is coming. People clench fists when they're cold, anxious, or even trying to control strong emotions. What raises concern is when multiple cues appear together, body tension, aggressive stance, escalating tone, and protesting behavior. When these indicators start clustering, it gives us a clearer signal that someone may be transitioning from anger to action.

Our job is to observe without assuming. We look at the body language, we compare it against what we're seeing and hearing, and we stay proactive and professional in our response.

Loss Prevention Example: Body Language Cues in Retail

A customer at a department store seems increasingly anxious as they move through the aisles. At one point, they stop near a high-value display, look around, and their shoulders rise and tense. Their jaw tightens and their movements change from casual browsing to more rigid, guarded gestures. When an associate walks nearby, the person squares their body, takes a wider stance, and shifts into a posture that looks ready, either to flee or to challenge the interaction. Their fists briefly clench, and their breathing becomes more pronounced.

None of these cues, by themselves, prove intent. Customers can be stressed or uncomfortable for many reasons, family finances, social anxiety, or maybe they simply want to be left alone. But when multiple cues cluster together, the rising tension, defensive posture, scanning behavior, these physical signs might be telling us the person is preparing to take action. The LP associate doesn't assume guilt based on how the person looks or who they are. They continue observing behaviors, maintain appropriate distance, and notify another team member to be aware and possibly help if the behavior escalates further.

In this way, behavior drives the decision, not bias or guesswork. By identifying physical signs early, the LP professional can take proactive safety steps without unfairly confronting someone who may simply be having a stressful moment.

2. Verbal Aggression

Another strong behavioral indicator of hostile intent is verbal aggression. When someone begins using hostile language, such as shouting, making threats, using profanity, or issuing personal insults, they are often signaling a desire to intimidate or provoke a reaction. They're trying to push your buttons. Their words become sharper, louder, and more targeted as emotion takes over. This shift in tone is usually not random; it's a sign that the conversation is moving from problem-solving to confrontation.

But verbal aggression isn't always loud. Sometimes it shows up as sarcasm, mocking comments, or belittling remarks designed to undermine our credibility or bait us into responding emotionally. The person may start questioning our authority, announcing what they "won't" do, or using language meant to embarrass us in front of others. These behaviors tell us the individual is becoming less concerned with resolution and more focused on conflict.

Bear in mind, the surrounding situation matters. People can curse when they drop their phone or raise their voice simply because they are overwhelmed or scared. But when verbal hostility combines with other indicators, such as closing distance, tracking movements, or escalating body tension, we should recognize the cluster for what it is: a potential shift toward aggressive action.

Don't let the language wind you up. Recognize that words often reveal what someone is preparing to do next. Verbal aggression is a warning sign. When you hear it, increase your awareness, manage your own self-control, and maintain communication that keeps the situation from tipping over the edge.

Social Services Example: Verbal Aggression

A client arrives at a public assistance office already stressed from transportation challenges, childcare issues, and fear that their benefits may be reduced. When they are told they are missing documentation needed to complete their case, frustration spills over. Their volume rises, profanity begins to appear in their sentences, and their complaints shift from the situation to personal attacks, implying the staff doesn't care, is "just trying to make people suffer," or is "too lazy" to help.

The yelling isn't just about anger; it's an attempt to regain control over a situation where the person feels powerless. As their verbal aggression escalates, they may talk over staff, demand immediate action, or attempt to draw others into the conflict by loudly proclaiming unfair treatment.

A trained staff member recognizes that this isn't simply disrespect. It is a behavioral indicator that emotions are approaching the point where impulsive actions become more likely. Instead of reacting defensively or matching tone, the staff member maintains calm, listens long enough for the person to feel heard, and uses empathy to redirect and clarify the path to a solution. At the same time, they increase situational awareness and stay alert for other indicators in the cluster, such as physical posturing, pacing, or boundary testing, that might signal a transition toward physical aggression.

By focusing on the behavior instead of the insult, the employee can remain professional, preserve safety, and maintain the legitimacy of the organization while working to de-escalate the situation.

3. Targeted Focus

When a person is shifting toward aggressive intent, their attention often becomes very specific and very sharp. They may fixate on a particular individual, a staff member, another customer, or someone they perceive as a threat, and that focus becomes noticeably intense. Their eyes track the target continuously, and they check frequently to make sure that person is still within reach or in sight. This isn't casual watching, it's intentional monitoring.

They may appear to stare right through you, sometimes referred to as a "thousand-yard stare", or they may focus on an object. Be aware that this could indicate a potential target of attack. For example, when I was a Trooper, if someone continually stared at my sidearm, I wanted to tactically reposition myself so that it was not accessible to them.

Targeted focus can also involve scanning behaviors. The person may dart their eyes repeatedly toward exits, security equipment, unattended belongings, or anything that could give them an advantage. They might quickly assess where staff members are positioned or look for blind spots in the environment. This kind of scanning may show planning, and planning tells us escalation may be moving from emotional outburst toward physical action.

As always, what surrounds the behavior matters. Someone might stare because they are confused or stressed, or they may scan a room because they feel unsafe themselves. It's when this behavior appears alongside other indicators, like clenched fists, aggressive stance, raised voice, that targeted focus becomes a real warning sign. They are no longer trying to solve the problem verbally, they may be preparing for what comes next.

By recognizing this cluster early, we can adjust our positioning, bring in support if needed, and start working to interrupt the momentum before the behavior breaks the boundary into aggression.

Healthcare Example: Targeted Focus

In a hospital emergency department, a patient's family member becomes increasingly distressed while waiting for an update. At first, they are pacing and expressing frustration to anyone nearby. But then their attention shifts and becomes locked onto a specific nurse, the one who last spoke to them. Their eyes stay fixed, following her movement through the unit even when she's interacting with other patients. Their body starts turning toward her with each pass, and their pacing becomes less random and more directed.

At the same time, they begin scanning the environment in a way that doesn't match casual observation. They glance repeatedly toward doorways, badge-controlled entrances, and supply cabinets. They check where security is standing and look for moments when the nurse is isolated. The behavior suggests they are not just upset. They may be calculating opportunities. This careful monitoring might reflect intent forming into possible action.

None of this means a confrontation is guaranteed. They may simply be overwhelmed and afraid for their loved one. But when targeted fixation and environmental scanning occur in a cluster with other cues like clenched jaw, raised voice, or boundary testing, it signals that the emotional tipping point may be approaching. Recognizing these signs early allows staff to reposition, call for support discreetly, and use communication to intervene before the behavior becomes physically aggressive.

4. Increased Physical Tension

As a person moves closer to aggressive behavior, we often see a clear shift in their physical tension. The body prepares for action before the mind fully commits to it. Rapid or shallow breathing is a major sign, it tells us adrenaline is rising and the nervous system is preparing for a fight-or-flight response. We may notice muscles tightening in the neck, shoulders, arms, or face.

Movements become quicker, sharper, and less relaxed than before. The person may begin pacing, not to "walk it off," but because their body is searching for an outlet for that building energy. These are all physiological signs that the body is preparing for action.

Another category of tension cues involves the hands. Fidgeting can shift into balling the hands into fists, gripping items tightly, or flexing fingers repeatedly as if preparing to grab or strike. Gestures may become more exaggerated and forceful. Even someone who hasn't raised their voice may be showing aggression through increased physical readiness. These cues tell us the person is no longer just emotionally upset, their body could be gearing up for a possible confrontation.

Of course, tension alone doesn't confirm hostile intent. A person may be nervous, cold, or simply under stress. What matters is the cluster, tension combined with targeted focus, boundary testing, or verbal aggression. The more these indicators stack together, the clearer the picture becomes. Our role is to recognize the shift early and respond with calm professionalism, adjusting our distance, stance, and communication so we stay safe while still working to keep the situation constructive.

City Clerk Example: Increased Physical Tension

A resident arrives at a municipal service counter frustrated about a permit delay that is holding up a home project. The initial conversation is tense but manageable. As the clerk explains the required steps, the resident's breathing quickens and their posture becomes more rigid. Their shoulders tighten while their jaw flexes repeatedly. They grip the edge of the counter with whitening knuckles and begin tapping their foot rapidly, signaling that patience is giving way to agitation.

As the interaction continues, the resident begins pacing in short bursts, stepping away and then returning with increased tension in each movement. Their hands become more active, opening and closing into fists, jabbing the air when making a point, or sweeping their arm in wide, forceful gestures. These cues represent more than irritation; they might show their body preparing for confrontation or to push past boundaries.

The clerk who recognizes these signs doesn't ignore them or hope they go away. They maintain a calm, respectful tone while discreetly creating space, angling their body slightly, ensuring that exits remain accessible, or involving a coworker to increase presence. They remain attentive to whether these tension cues appear alongside other indicators like verbal escalation or targeted focus. By responding early and professionally, the clerk protects both their safety and the reputation of the agency, while still working to resolve the resident's concerns.

5. Escalating Resistance

Another key behavioral indicator of hostile intent is escalating resistance. This shows up when a person begins refusing to follow simple, reasonable instructions, not because they misunderstand, but because they are pushing against boundaries. They may ignore requests, interrupt repeatedly, or reject options that would help resolve the situation. The more they resist direction, the more their behavior shifts from emotional frustration into a control struggle.

Escalating resistance often includes subtle but meaningful changes. A person may refuse to step back from a restricted area, attempt to move past a staff member, or talk over every effort to assist them. They might repeatedly say comments like, "You can't tell me what to do." Each refusal becomes a test, a way of seeing how much control they can exert over the situation or over you.

On its own, resistance can simply mean someone is upset, overwhelmed, or confused. But when resistance appears in combination with other indicators, like clenched fists, raised voice, targeted staring, or pacing, it tells us the person may be transitioning from verbal or emotional conflict toward physical escalation. The boundaries they ignore now may be the same boundaries they attempt to physically breach next.

We have to notice the shift and stay calm, keep expectations clear, and enforce boundaries professionally, using the skills we've already discussed to slow the escalation and maintain safety.

Loss Prevention Example: Escalating Resistance

A customer is stopped just past the point of sale because the associate noticed a high-value item at the bottom of their cart that was never scanned. At first, the customer denies it, expressing annoyance. When the associate politely asks them to return to the register to resolve it, the customer immediately pushes back, "No, I paid for everything," and attempts to keep moving toward the exit. The associate repeats the request and tries to clarify what was observed, but the customer interrupts aggressively, cutting off every word with escalating defiance.

Their refusal isn't just verbal. They angle their body toward the exit, pull the cart closer, and take quick steps forward each time the associate pauses. Each boundary set, "Please stop for a moment" or "Let's go back to the register", is ignored or met with a louder "No!" or "I'm not doing that." These are deliberate tests of whether the rule will hold or whether they can push past it.

When escalating resistance appears alongside other indicators we've discussed, elevated tension, clenched fists on the cart handle, scanning for security, raised voice, it signals a high likelihood that the person may attempt to run, push through staff, or create a distraction for escape. The LP professional recognizes the shift and adjusts strategy, increasing distance, bringing in support, maintaining clear verbal direction, and letting communication stay factual and professional rather than argumentative.

The goal is safety first, observe behavior, enforce boundaries appropriately, and avoid being physically trapped or engaged while still working to keep the situation from tipping into aggression.

6. Pre-Attack Posture

As a person moves closer to physical aggression, their body often gives us clear signals that they are preparing to act. One of the most important is pre-attack posture, the way they position themselves in anticipation of launching forward or defending against intervention. We may see a shift of weight onto the back foot so they can drive forward with power. They might square their shoulders and torso directly toward us, eliminating a neutral stance and replacing it with a fighting position. Their steps may become more deliberate and angled as if they're lining up their approach.

But the biggest and most reliable indicator is what a person does with their hands, because the hands are what hurt us. The hands control weapons, strike targets, and grab objects. If someone begins adjusting, patting, or repeatedly touching an area on their waistband, pocket, or jacket, especially where a weapon could be concealed, that's usually not by accident. It's likely an instinctive check to ensure access to the weapon and that it's still positioned where they expect it to be. This is especially common with someone not authorized or permitted to carry a weapon or not used to carrying one. They're constantly seeking reassurance that it's there. The person may keep one hand hidden, turn their body to shield a draw motion, or reposition clothing to gain quicker access.

These cues are early warning signs that the person is preparing to shift from words to action. They may not have thrown a punch yet, but their body may be preparing for the moment when they do. That's why it is critical to watch the hands more than the face. The face can lie, and so can words, but the hands rarely do. They reveal what the body plans to do next.

Of course, adjusting clothing alone does not confirm intent, people fix their shirts or adjust their waistband all the time. But when those movements appear in a cluster with other hostile indicators, such as clenched fists, verbal aggression, narrowing distance, or scanning for advantages, we must respond as if a transition to physical violence is imminent. Reading these cues early allows us to increase distance, improve our angle, call for support, and prioritize safety before that intent turns into action.

Social Services Example: Pre-Attack Posture

A client meets with a caseworker after learning that their visitation is being adjusted. At first, their frustration is verbal. They're raising their voice, interrupting, and insisting the system is unfair. But as the conversation continues, their body begins to tell a different story. The client squares their stance toward the caseworker's desk, stops shifting their feet randomly, and plants themselves firmly as if rooting into position. Their shoulders rise and tense, and they lean slightly forward, closing space instead of maintaining it.

Most critically, their hands become the loudest communicator. They repeatedly tug at the front of their hoodie and keep one hand near their waistband, patting or adjusting it every few seconds, behavior that suggests they are checking something concealed or ensuring quick access to an object they may be carrying. Their breathing increases, fingers flex and curl tightly, and their eyes shift rapidly between the caseworker, the doorway, and the area where security typically stands.

The caseworker recognizes this cluster of cues as a pre-attack posture. Instead of confronting the person or challenging their behavior directly, the worker keeps their voice steady, sets a respectful boundary, and creates time: "We'll figure this out together, but I need you to take a step back so we can talk safely." They also discreetly reposition, angle their body for an exit path, and signal for assistance if available. These moves protect their safety while still giving the individual a chance to calm and regain control.

In this example, the staff member doesn't wait for the situation to become physical before taking action. They saw the transition, from anger expressed through words to aggression preparing to come through the hands, and responded early enough to shape the outcome.

7. Facial Expressions

Up to this point, we haven't talked directly about facial expressions, but now is the right time. Facial expressions can be a significant indicator of hostile intent and understanding them means understanding something deeper. When we read someone's face, we're not just reading muscle movements. We're reading emotion. Emotions are the engine that drives facial expression. They leak out whether someone wants them to or not. And in the environments you work in, emotions show up fast. Sometimes faster than words, faster than rational thinking, and almost always faster than a threat can turn into action.

Facial expressions matter because they tell the story before the person does. A glare, a clenched jaw, that brief flicker of panic, these signals reveal what's happening inside someone long before they choose a behavior. And within our From Crisis to Calm framework, emotions are not just background noise. They're woven into every step we take: recognizing what the other person is experiencing, making them feel understood, setting boundaries that reduce uncertainty, and guiding them toward safer behavior. Each of those steps is influenced by how well we acknowledge and respond to the emotion we see.

So when we look at facial expressions, we're not staring for clues like detectives in a crime show. We're tuning into the humanity in front of us. We're asking: What is this person feeling? What just changed? And what does that mean for what might happen next?

Understanding Emotion

Emotion is one of the most universal human experiences we have, and also one of the most unpredictable. It comes, it goes, and sometimes it hits like a freight train. Some of us feel emotions intensely; others keep things more contained. But no one gets through a single day without emotion playing a role in how they act, speak, and respond to other people. We're all emotional people, some of us just more so than others.

Emotions don't always show up fully formed. Often, they're triggered, sometimes by obvious things, and sometimes by something that wouldn't bother anyone else in the room. We share a lot of emotional triggers as human beings: fear, embarrassment, frustration, disrespect, uncertainty. But how much we feel it and how quickly that feeling floods in, varies wildly from person to person based on their past experiences, their current stress level, trauma history, mental health, physical condition, or what kind of day they've already had before they walked through your door.

To understand emotion as an indicator of behavior, it helps to see that not every moment of someone's life is emotional, but emotional moments happen routinely, and they influence everything that comes next.

Let's talk about a universal trigger: a real threat. Imagine a social worker conducting a routine home visit. She's been to this address before, nothing unusual. She steps through the front door into the living room, and a large dog she's never seen before lunges off the couch straight at her, snarling, teeth bared, closing the distance before she can even step back. For a split second, her face tells the whole story: fear, shock, survival instinct. Luckily, the dog's owner was able to stop the dog and gated him in the kitchen for the duration of the visit, so there were no more problems.

But here's the key question: Did she pause to think about how to look afraid? Did she analyze the scene, weigh possibilities, and choose an emotional response? Of course not. The emotion hit faster than conscious thought. The body reacted before the brain could organize a plan. The face revealed everything inside, whether she wanted it to or not.

That's because emotions are sudden, automatic, and deeply tied to our survival. Dr. Paul Ekman explains it like this:

"Emotions are a process, a particular kind of automatic appraisal influenced by our evolutionary and personal past, in which we sense that something important to our welfare is occurring, and a set of psychological changes and emotional behaviors begins to deal with the situation. This is a simple idea, but a central one, emotions evolved to prepare us to deal quickly with the most vital events in our lives."[3]

In other words: emotions are fast, they're powerful, and they're designed to protect us. They show up on our face before our words have time to catch up.

And when we're working to achieve a de-escalated outcome, we must learn to see those emotional signals early, respond to them instead of reacting to them, and guide the interaction before emotion turns into action.

The Role of Emotion and Facial Expressions

Dr. Paul Ekman, one of the leading researchers in human emotion, spent more than forty years studying the human face and what he discovered fundamentally changed how we understand emotional communication.

Back in the 1960s, Dr. Ekman set out to answer a question that had been debated for generations: Are emotional expressions learned from culture, or are they universal to all humans?

Ekman took that question as far away from outside influence as he could. In 1967, he traveled to Papua New Guinea to study the Fore people, a tribe of indigenous people who had been isolated from Western contact. Ekman showed members of the tribe pictures of Western faces expressing different emotions: happiness, sadness, anger, fear, disgust, and surprise. Even though the Fore people had never seen Westerners before, never watched television, never been exposed to Western cultural norms, they identified the emotions correctly. The expressions meant the same thing to them as they did to people halfway around the world.

Then Ekman reversed the experiment. He told the tribespeople emotionally charged stories and asked them to show what their face would look like in those situations. He recorded this and when Western observers watched those recordings, they identified the emotions accurately. The conclusion was clear: certain facial expressions are not learned. They are hardwired into us as human beings.[4]

This showed that there are seven universal facial expressions. Universal, as in we all have them. Unlike other avenues of communication, such as gestures and language, we all share these emotions and their corresponding facial expressions: anger, fear, disgust, surprise, sadness, happiness, and contempt. We may call them different things, in fact it's helpful to do so when we label emotions. You can use the Emotional Labeling handout in the Appendix to help you do just that.

Ekman didn't just stop after discovering universal facial expressions. He spent decades studying how emotions show up on the face, even when someone is trying hard to hide them. All of that work came together in one of his most influential books: *Emotions Revealed*.[5]

In this book, Ekman breaks down how emotions work inside us, the triggers, the rapid automatic reactions, the changes in our breathing, heart rate, posture, and especially the way our face broadcasts those changes to the world. What makes the book powerful is that it isn't written only for scientists. It's written for professionals who deal with people in high-stakes situations: law enforcement, healthcare, negotiators, educators, anyone who could change a moment for the better by noticing what others miss.

Ekman teaches us how to:

- Spot early emotional shifts before behavior changes
- Recognize when someone is trying to hide what they feel
- Distinguish between genuine and forced expressions
- Identify what triggers someone's emotional response
- Respond in a way that matches the reality of the emotion

What matters most for our work is understanding that emotions leak. Even when someone is trying to control what they show, their face will reveal fragments of what they're actually feeling. Those fragments, micro-expressions that flash across the face in a fraction of a second, can tell us when someone is more distressed than they're letting on, when fear is present beneath anger, when contempt is being masked by a smile.

Ekman's research reminds us that before we react to what we think we're seeing, we need to look more carefully at what's actually there. A person's face may show what they want us to see, but it also shows what emotion forces to the surface despite their efforts to conceal it.. But Dr. Ekman also discovered that people hide emotion in two ways: they mask genuine emotion with a false expression, or they leak true emotion through micro-expressions that appear and disappear in less than half a second.

Ekman discovered micro-expressions by accident. He was reviewing a filmed interview of a psychiatric patient who had requested to be discharged home for the weekend. But when Ekman slowed the video down, he caught something: a flash of anguish and despair that appeared on her face for a split second before she resumed her calm demeanor. The expression was so brief that it had been invisible at normal speed. That patient later admitted she had been planning to take her own life if she was released.[6]

Ekman realized that those micro-moments were the emotional truth, and had been hidden beneath the surface of what the person chose to present.

For professionals working with people in crisis or uncertainty, the lesson is clear: in addition to the hands, watch the face. Not just for what it's saying, but for what it's trying not to say.

Happiness shows in a genuine smile that reaches the eyes, what Ekman calls the "Duchenne smile." Sadness draws the inner corners of the eyebrows upward and pulls the corners of the mouth down. Fear shows in widened eyes and a dropped jaw. Anger tightens the lips and furrows the brow. Surprise raises the eyebrows, widens the eyes, and drops the jaw open. Contempt appears as a one-sided lip curl. Disgust wrinkles the nose.[7]

These aren't opinions. They're biological markers that appear across cultures and contexts. When you learn to recognize them, you gain insight into what someone is actually experiencing, not just what they're *telling* you they're experiencing.

Recognizing these micro expressions isn't just a skill for investigators or crisis negotiators. It's a skill for anyone who works with people in crisis or conflict. These quick flashes of emotion give us a rare look at what a person is really experiencing beneath the surface. And in many of the environments where you may work, such as hospitals, social service agencies, schools, retail settings, human resources, security positions, public counters, call centers, people don't always tell us directly how they feel. Sometimes they can't. Sometimes they won't.

But micro expressions help us detect that moment when a situation is shifting. We might see a brief flicker of fear when someone says they're "fine." We might catch a flash of anger when someone claims they're "just frustrated." Or we may notice a split-second of contempt, that early warning sign that respect is fading and resistance may be on the way.

For law enforcement officers, these cues can offer an early signal of deception or potential aggression, critical when time is short and choices are limited. But the same is true for a nurse standing between a stressed patient and a waiting room full of families, for a social worker entering a home where emotions are already high, for a retail employee who sees that first spark of hostility before a customer explodes.

The ability to recognize these tiny emotional leaks gives us something incredibly valuable: time. Time to slow the encounter down. Time to acknowledge the emotion. Time to validate, reassure, offer options, or set boundaries before the situation accelerates.

In every profession represented here, early recognition of emotion can be the difference between cooperation and conflict, between a conversation that moves forward and a situation that becomes unsafe. Micro expressions pull the curtain back just long enough for us to respond with purpose, before the person's behavior makes that response much harder.

When you consider the seven universal emotions and their accompanying facial expressions in difficult situations, the ability to recognize human expression and emotions can often assist in determining someone's state of mind and potential hostile intent.

And when you combine that facial awareness with the other skills we've discussed. Behavioral Symptom Analysis, understanding the OODA Loop, recognizing hostile intent, you begin to develop a comprehensive picture of the person in front of you and the direction the encounter might be heading.

The Situational Awareness Exercise

In From Crisis to Calm training, we run an exercise that brings all of these concepts together in a practical, memorable way. It's simple in design but powerful in what it reveals about how awareness actually works under realistic conditions.

Here's how it works. Participants partner up in groups of two or three. They're going to have a completely normal conversation for two or three minutes, nothing intense, nothing structured. Talk about where you're from, what you do for fun, your favorite movie or food, just regular, everyday conversation.

But here's the twist. Everyone receives a sheet of paper with a few physical actions listed on it. During the conversation, they casually perform those actions. No exaggeration, no cartoon-level acting, just subtle, natural movements while they talk. And the people they're speaking with are doing the exact same thing with their own list, which may or may not be the same.

Participants have two responsibilities during this drill. First, they need to hold a real conversation, stay engaged, and be present with what the other person is saying. Second, while doing that, they quietly observe any behavior that feels out of place, unusual, or inconsistent with normal conversation.

After a few minutes, we bring everyone back together and ask: what did you notice?

Almost universally, people realize they missed a whole bunch of behaviors happening right in front of them. The reason so many of us miss things is simple: our brains can only handle so much at once. When we're speaking, trying to find the right words, and worrying about how we look or sound, our ability to notice the small but important details drops fast.

We check a few specifics. Who noticed any fist-clenching? What about pacing or shifting weight? Did anyone pick up on scanning eyes, darting side-to-side or locking onto one spot? Did anyone see pocket-checking or sudden touches to the waistband?

And here's a big one: did you feel the discomfort in your body before you could explain why? That feeling is important. Sometimes your survival system senses a threat before your rational mind has processed what's happening. Tension, unease, that little "something isn't right" sensation, those cues are worth paying attention to. Listen to your gut instincts. Just follow them with observation instead of assumption.

The exercise demonstrates something critical: situational awareness is a skill. It requires practice. It requires deliberate attention. And most importantly, it requires operating from Relaxed or Focused Awareness rather than being Tuned Out. You can't read behavior if you're not present to see it. And you can't respond to escalation you didn't notice beginning.

Now that we have the tools to see the five levels of awareness, Behavioral Symptom Analysis, the OODA Loop, the seven indicators of hostile intent, and the ability to read facial expressions and emotions, it's time to put them to work. In the next chapter, we'll walk through real encounters that show what escalation looks like as it unfolds. We'll apply everything we've built so far to recognize the patterns, the decision points, and the moments where the right response changes everything.

Notes

1. Arthur Conan Doyle, "A Scandal in Bohemia," in *The Adventures of Sherlock Holmes* (London: George Newnes, 1892).
2. Ken J. Good, "Got a Second? Boyd's OODA Cycle in the Close Quarter Battle Environment," Progressive Combat Solutions, accessed February 22, 2026, https://www.progressivecombat.com/pdfs/OODA.pdf.
3. Paul Ekman, *Emotions Revealed: Recognizing Faces and Feelings to Improve Communication and Emotional Life*, 2nd ed. (New York: Owl Books/Henry Holt, 2007). See also Paul Ekman Group, "Universal Emotions," https://www.paulekman.com/universal-emotions/ (accessed February 22, 2026).
4. Paul Ekman and Wallace V. Friesen, "Constants Across Cultures in the Face and Emotion," *Journal of Personality and Social Psychology* 17, no. 2 (1971): 124–129. This landmark study documented recognition of basic emotions in facial expressions among the Fore people of Papua New Guinea, who had minimal exposure to Western media.
5. Paul Ekman, *Emotions Revealed: Recognizing Faces and Feelings to Improve Communication and Emotional Life*, 2nd ed. (New York: Owl Books/Henry Holt, 2007). Ekman's foundational research on universal facial expressions of emotion spans decades and is synthesized in this volume.
6. On micro-expressions and their timing (typically lasting 1/25th to 1/5th of a second), see Ekman, *Emotions Revealed*, 2nd ed., chapters 1–2.
7. For the facial expression markers of each universal emotion, see Ekman, *Emotions Revealed*, 2nd ed.

CHAPTER 5:

RECOGNIZING ESCALATION IN REAL TIME

In Chapter 4, we built the observation skills that let you see what's actually happening around you. Now, let's talk about recognizing escalation in real time. We've developed tools for situational awareness, the five levels of awareness, Behavioral Symptom Analysis, the OODA Loop, and the seven indicators of hostile intent. We learned to observe rather than just look, to read behavioral cues, to assess environments, to notice the details that tell us what's actually happening in an encounter.

Now it's time to put all of that into practice. Because the real test of these skills isn't in a classroom exercise, it's in the messy, unpredictable, emotionally charged encounters that professionals face every day. The bank lobby where a frustrated son is trying to help his elderly mother. The retail floor where an upset customer is squaring off with an employee. The front porch where a domestic disturbance is unfolding with compounding risk factors. Let's see what these encounters look like when we apply everything we've built so far.

Bad Policy: Can't Change it, Validate it

A man walks into a bank branch with a straightforward goal to make a cash payment on his mother's credit card. He has the cash in hand, so it should be simple. But when he reaches the teller window and explains what he needs, he's told the bank doesn't accept cash payments for credit card accounts.

His confusion is immediate. "That doesn't make any sense. My mother is 78 years old. She lives 138 miles away! She asked me to pay this for her. I have the cash right here. Why won't you just take it?"

The teller, following procedure, reiterates the policy, telling him that this is standard banking practice, clearly outlined in the bank's guidelines. Cash payments for credit card bills aren't accepted.

But watch what happens. The man's confusion shifts to frustration. His voice rises. "So you're telling me you won't take my money? That's the stupidest thing I've ever heard!" His hands gesture toward the cash, toward the teller, up in the air in exasperation. "What kind of bank won't take cash?"

Other customers are watching now. The man's face flushes. His movements become more animated, more agitated. The teller glances toward the branch manager's office.

Let me ask you to pause here and assess what you're seeing. At the beginning of this interaction, would you view this man as an immediate threat? Think about the specific behaviors visible in this moment: his tone, his body language, his physical actions. He's clearly frustrated. His voice is raised. His movements are animated. His focus is intense. But is there an indication that he intends harm?

This gives us a helpful example of a person who is clearly frustrated but not presenting an immediate threat. He's showing signs of agitation, raised voice, animated movements, and intense focus on the issue, but at this point, he's venting. There's no indication that he intends harm. That doesn't mean we assume safety. As I've said, people are unpredictable, and situations can shift quickly. But we're not yet at a point where we need to shift into a high-alert posture.

Think about what emotions are driving his behavior right now. What do you actually see beneath the raised voice and agitated movements? Frustration, certainly. But look deeper. Helplessness, perhaps? He came here to accomplish something for his mother, and he's being blocked at every turn. Embarrassment, possibly, as other customers watch this interaction unfold. These emotions matter enormously because they tell us what this person actually needs in this moment.

The teller continues defending the policy, explaining why it exists, justifying the bank's position. And you can see how quickly that causes him to get louder, more insistent. She's doing what many professionals do instinctively when challenged: she's explaining, she's justifying, she's trying to make him understand why the rule is the rule. This is what we call the explanation trap, and we're watching it unfold in real time.

Now, we could argue about whether the policy is frustrating or even ridiculous. But the teller can't change it. And when we argue with someone who is already upset, all we do is escalate. The teller begins to defend the policy, and the escalation accelerates. Instead of debating the rules, a far more effective approach would be to acknowledge his feelings. He is absolutely entitled to feel angry or disappointed. Emotions are always acceptable; actions are what must be managed. The teller missed out on Regulation.

This is where the third pillar, Validation, becomes essential. The teller doesn't need to agree that the policy is stupid. She doesn't need to promise that she can override it. She just needs to acknowledge that from his perspective, this is frustrating. "It sounds like this policy is really frustrating, and you have every right to feel that way," acknowledges emotion and builds a connection without promising anything she can't provide. It costs nothing, and it changes everything. Instead, she makes it about herself, doing everything we mentioned above, rather than making it about him.

Let's also consider the time investment here. How long does this whole encounter actually last? Maybe two minutes. Yet the teller spends that entire time trying to shut him down, trying to make him understand the policy, trying to defend the bank's position, instead of giving him thirty seconds to breathe and feel validated. When it's safe to do so, giving someone a little time and validation can change the entire trajectory. That one or two minutes can shift the outcome dramatically. She missed that opportunity here.

What ultimately happens in this encounter? He leaves. That's a successful de-escalated outcome. And in many encounters just like this one, the person vents their frustration, expresses their emotions, and the situation resolves naturally. Human beings have a core emotional need to feel heard. Think about when you've had a bad day: talking about it doesn't solve the problem, but it releases pressure. As emotions go down, rational thinking comes back up. In this interaction, that's exactly what happens. He vents, he feels heard enough, or at least says what he has to say to let out the pressure, and he leaves.

This is what the first element of G.U.I.D.E., Ground Yourself, enables you to recognize. When you've grounded yourself, when you're regulated enough to observe rather than just react, you can see that this man isn't a threat requiring immediate intervention. He's a person in emotional distress who needs acknowledgment. He needs to feel heard and validated. That recognition changes everything about how you respond.

Another critical point this encounter highlights is the presence of a built-in safety barrier. The bank counter gives the teller a physical advantage. If this man's behavior suddenly transitioned from frustration to an immediate threat, she has space to move, reposition, or remove herself entirely. This is situational awareness in action, recognizing what environmental features support safety even before an encounter begins. The counter isn't just furniture. It's a barrier that provides distance, time, and options if the situation changes.

Think about what the teller could have said differently to acknowledge his feelings without arguing the policy. What phrases come to mind? "You came here to help your mother, and this policy is getting in the way." "That would frustrate me too." "I hear you that this doesn't make sense from your perspective." Notice that none of those statements change the policy. None of them give him what he originally wanted. But they give him something he needs even more in that moment: acknowledgment that his frustration is valid.

Here's the biggest takeaway from this encounter: When it's safe, let them vent. Venting is one of the simplest, fastest ways to help someone regulate their own emotions. It requires patience, it requires presence, and you have to resist the urge to defend or argue. But it's often the first step toward getting back to calm and staying safe. This is the first pillar, Regulation, in action. When you stay regulated yourself, when you don't match their intensity, you create the space for their intensity to decrease naturally.

Consider your own threshold for response. At what point, if any, would you have shifted to a different strategy? What would be your threshold for a heightened safety response? These aren't theoretical questions. In every encounter, you're making real-time assessments about where someone sits on the dial from frustrated to threatening. This man remained frustrated throughout, but his behavior never transitioned toward threat. Recognizing that distinction, and responding appropriately to what you're actually seeing rather than what you fear might happen, is fundamental to effective de-escalation.

The Retail Encounter: Connection as a Safety Tool

In a large retail electronics department, a man is visibly upset. His voice is elevated, his gestures are animated, and his frustration is directed entirely at an employee standing in front of him. "You rammed the cart! You didn't say excuse me; you just rammed the cart! Listen, this is my wife, and you rammed her cart!" He's getting close to the employee's personal space. The environment is filled with valuable merchandise, other customers, and open aisles that can quickly become escape routes or danger zones if things turn physical. This situation represents a very common challenge in retail, customer service, and loss-prevention environments. If possible and in line with your responsibilities, the best thing to do here is to remove yourself from the situation.

But let's look at how the employee has positioned himself. He's standing very close to the agitated customer, with no barrier between them and no safe exit path available, so self-removal isn't really feasible right now. If this customer suddenly transitions from verbal anger to physical action, the employee is in a poor defensive posture. There's merchandise nearby that could be damaged or used as weapons. The employee has nothing to protect himself with. Even though this does not appear to be an immediate threat at this moment, we should always maintain awareness of how quickly frustration can shift into aggression. People are unpredictable.

This is what we mean when we talk about positioning as a de-escalation tool, not just a safety measure. A small change in positioning, so that even a partial barrier like a counter or display unit between them, would give the employee time and space to react safely if needed. Position isn't about expecting violence. It's about maintaining options. When you have distance and barriers, you have time to assess, time to respond, time to retreat if necessary. When you're standing within arm's reach with your back to merchandise and no clear exit path, you've eliminated your options for repositioning yourself before the conversation even starts.

Now let's look at what's actually being communicated. The employee is responding defensively, repeating that he's sorry and insisting he didn't ram the cart. He's talking about himself when the customer doesn't care about explanations or apologies right now. He cares about his wife and the perceived slight against her. Perceived is the key word here. It doesn't matter what the intention of an action or a statement is, it's how that action or statement is perceived by the other individual. That's what's driving everything. Someone hurt the person he loves, and nobody is acknowledging it.

This is where understanding the emotion beneath the behavior changes everything. This man isn't angry about a policy or frustrated about a transaction. He's protective. His wife was hurt, or at least startled, and his instinct is to stand between her and the person who caused it. Every defensive response from the employee, every "I didn't hit it," or "I said excuse me," misses the point entirely because none of it addresses what he actually needs to hear.

If the employee had stopped defending himself and said, "Is she okay? Is she hurt at all? Gosh, I thought I had more room," the entire dynamic could shift in a single sentence. That question does something powerful: it tells the customer that someone else sees what he sees. Someone else cares about his wife's wellbeing. He's no longer fighting alone against an employee who won't take responsibility. Now there's another person in the conversation who shares his concern.

That's the third pillar again, Validation, working alongside the fourth pillar, Collaboration. "Is she okay" validates the emotion driving his behavior, and it repositions the employee from adversary to ally. He's no longer the guy who rammed the cart and won't own up to it. He's someone who wants to make sure a woman is alright. From there, everything else becomes easier. "Let's make sure she's okay first, and then we can figure out what happened." Concern first. Details second. That sequence matters.

If his wife isn't injured and the immediate concern is addressed, the fifth pillar, Options, gives the customer a path forward. "Do you want to document what happened? Would you like to speak with a manager, or would you prefer me to get our incident report so we can put this on the record?" Those are real choices. They give the customer agency. He's not being dismissed or brushed off. He's being offered concrete next steps that acknowledge something happened and that it matters.

And if his volume stays elevated even after the concern has been addressed, the second pillar, Boundaries, gives the employee a way to set limits without dismissing the emotion. "You're looking out for your wife, and that makes complete sense. But the yelling needs to come down so we can actually take care of this. Can we do that?" Acknowledgment plus limit. The emotion is respected. The behavior is redirected.

But there's something else happening in this encounter: a missed opportunity that almost jumps off the screen when you know what to look for. The customer is wearing a Megadeth t-shirt. That's what we call a "hook." When someone displays an interest, a passion, a hobby through their clothing, jewelry, or tattoos, or anything else, they're offering us an instant connection point. We don't need to solve the problem with the first sentence we speak. Sometimes we address the person's emotional state first and find some non-threatening common ground.

A hook is anything about a person that tells you something about who they are, or what they're about, beyond the moment you're in. A t-shirt with a band logo, like we have here. A tattoo. A lanyard from a favorite sports team. A piece of jewelry that suggests a cultural background or personal story. A hat with a fishing brand. A phone case with a dog's picture on it. People wear their identities. They display and talk about what matters to them, often without thinking about it. And when you notice those things and acknowledge them, something shifts. You're no longer just the employee behind the counter, the officer at the door, or the case worker behind the desk. You're a person who saw them as a person. That moment of recognition, even a brief one, can interrupt an escalation pattern because it speaks to something deeper than the conflict. It says, "I see you. Not your problem. Not your behavior. You."

Hooks don't solve the problem. They don't replace validation, and they don't substitute for the work that still needs to happen. But they create a pause, a small opening where human connection gets in before defensiveness locks the door. And in that pause, the emotional temperature can drop just enough to give you access to the person underneath the anger. You don't have to share the interest. You don't have to be an expert. You just have to be observant enough to notice it and genuine enough to mention it. That's Professional Sincerity at work, which we'll get deeply into later.

You don't even have to know anything about it. You've never heard of the band on their shirt? "That's a cool shirt, what band is that?" works just as well. You have no idea what the tattoo means? "That's interesting, what's the story behind it?" is a genuine question that invites them to talk about something they care about. The hook works because you noticed and you asked, not because you already knew the answer.

If the employee had said, "Megadeth, cool shirt. Did you ever see them live?" the customer might have paused, even for one second, because someone saw him as a human being and not just a problem. That brief pause is often enough to shift emotional gears and give us access to rational thinking again. The employee doesn't have to be a Megadeth fan. He doesn't have to know anything about heavy metal to find that connection with the customer. But he can acknowledge what's visible and create a moment of human connection before diving into the issue at hand. This is one of the many ways to develop rapport, which we'll look at in depth later.

Think about where you see an opportunity for connection in situations you face. What could you notice and acknowledge that shows someone you see them as a person, not just as a transaction or a problem to be managed? This isn't manipulation. It's recognition of that fundamental human need to be seen, to be acknowledged, to matter as an individual.

Now let's look at the behavioral indicators this customer is displaying. He's upset, certainly. His language is loud. His gestures are expressive. His focus is intense. But behaviorally, he's not yet dangerous. He's not in a pre-attack stance. He's not hiding his hands. He's not looking for objects to grab. He's not scanning his surroundings for exits or witnesses. He remains a potential threat rather than an immediate one.

These distinctions matter enormously. Our goal is to keep him in the "potential" category rather than allowing escalation into the "immediate" category. We do that by giving him space, validating his concern for his mother, offering structured paths through Options, and when appropriate, redirecting him to a less public location where the audience can't feed the energy.

Consider how moving to a quieter or less public area might help de-escalate this situation. Right now, other customers are watching. That audience changes the dynamic. The customer feels like backing down means losing face in front of witnesses, and in front of his wife. The employee may feel pressure to "win" or maintain authority publicly. If they can move this conversation away from the audience, "Sir, let me take you and your wife over to customer service where we can sit down and take care of this properly," suddenly both parties have more flexibility. The customer can accept a resolution without feeling like he's surrendering publicly. The employee can offer options without feeling like he's setting a precedent that everyone watching will demand. Remember the importance of contain and control.

Ultimately, what we want is for the customer to feel heard and to accept a path forward that resolves the encounter safely. People rarely calm down because someone proved them wrong or insisted nothing happened. They calm down when they believe the person in front of them understands their frustration and is trying to help. That's why communication and connection come before solutions. By shifting the approach from defensive to collaborative, we stand a much better chance of guiding the customer toward cooperation rather than confrontation.

Think about what emotions appear to be driving this customer's behavior. How can acknowledging those emotions build influence? When someone feels understood, their defensive intensity often decreases. They don't need to keep escalating to make you hear them because you've already demonstrated that you hear them. That acknowledgment, that validation, creates the foundation for the second pillar, Boundaries, to work. Once someone feels heard, they're far more likely to accept limits on their behavior because the limits don't feel like dismissal.

At what point should security support be requested in a situation like this? What signals would indicate rising danger? These are the assessments you're making constantly in any elevated encounter. This customer is showing loud, emotionally driven speech with strong arm gestures but he's not grabbing things to throw or throwing punches. He's intensely focused on the employee as the person responsible, but there's no attempt to cut off exits or force the employee backward. Each one of these indicators can change rapidly, which is why we stay alert and ready to adapt. Right now, in this moment, this is an encounter that communication can still de-escalate.

Connection isn't a luxury in these situations. It's a safety tool. When someone feels understood, the risk of escalation decreases. This is why Professional Sincerity and the Five Pillars aren't abstract concepts. They're practical tools that directly impact safety outcomes in real encounters.

Poor Positioning

On a residential front porch at 9:47 PM, a police officer is responding to a domestic disturbance call. The officer is trying to understand what happened inside the house. The man who answered the door comes outside and is agitated, pacing in the small confined space of the porch, running his hands through his hair repeatedly, his voice tight with frustration and emotion.

“What's going on here tonight?” the officer asks, notebook out, pen ready. “What happened?”

“Erica!” The man's voice pitches higher, sharper. “That's what happened! Erica did this! She always does this!” He's pacing faster now, his gestures becoming more emphatic, more frantic.

The officer, doing exactly what officers are trained to do, tries to gather specific information about the incident. He needs facts, who, what, when, where. "Okay, so Erica did something. What did Erica do? Where's Erica now?"

The man's agitation spikes immediately, dramatically. "Erica! I told you; it's Erica! I try to do everything to make her happy! Why doesn't anyone listen? Erica is the problem!" His volume increases. His movements become more frantic. He's pacing the full length of the small porch now, his hands gesturing wildly, his breathing fast and shallow.

The officer continues trying to gather information: "I hear you that Erica is involved. But I need to know what specifically happened. Is Erica in the house? Did she hit you? Did you hit her? I need specifics here."

With each mention of Erica's name, the man's escalation climbs higher. His face reddens. His breathing becomes more rapid and shallow. His hands clench and unclench. The officer's attempts to gather information, perfectly reasonable, completely standard investigative protocol, are making the situation worse, not better.

This is what we call a "barb," the opposite of a hook. A barb is anything we say, intentionally or unintentionally, that drives the person deeper into their emotional reaction and pulls them further away from rational behavior. When that barb exposes a raw nerve or a sensitive issue, the escalation can become immediate. The barb is what we want to stay away from. The officer isn't doing anything wrong by standard protocol. He needs information about what happened. Erica is apparently central to what happened. So asking about Erica makes logical sense from an investigative standpoint. But logic and effective crisis communication don't always align.

Every time the officer says "Erica," he triggers an escalation response. The name itself has become the barb. The subject makes it extremely clear, through his increasingly agitated response every single time the name is mentioned, that he does not want that name brought up. Yet the officer keeps using it, keeps touching that trigger, and the man becomes visibly more agitated with each mention.

Once a barb is recognized, we should acknowledge it quickly and then remove it from the interaction entirely. Instead of repeating the name that's causing escalation, the officer could shift focus to the man's concerns without continuously poking the same emotional sore spot. A simple shift to "I want to make sure I'm understanding what happened here. Help me understand what's going on right now" would show understanding and keep the conversation focused on the present behavior rather than continually retriggering the escalation.

This is where the second element of G.U.I.D.E., Understand Emotion, requires us to look beneath the words to what's actually happening. The officer is trying to understand the facts. But what he needs to understand first is the emotional state. This man is highly elevated. His voice is raised, his gestures are animated, his responses are fast, and his emotional brain is clearly in control. The prefrontal cortex, the part of the brain responsible for providing coherent narrative information, has less access right now. Asking for detailed specifics when someone is this dysregulated rarely works.

But there's an even more critical safety issue unfolding in this encounter, and it has nothing to do with words, but with where this entire interaction is taking place. The officer is standing on an elevated porch, extremely close to the subject, with nothing separating them, his back to the railing, and no clear path to move away if the situation shifts.

Think about what could happen if this man's behavior suddenly transitioned. If he made physical contact with the officer, even accidentally, even without intent to injure, both could easily lose balance and go over the side. I've seen it happen in real life. That fall could cause serious harm, and the officer would have little ability to protect himself or regain control. This is poor positioning creating unnecessary risk.

Safe positioning isn't just a preference. It's a de-escalation tool. When you position yourself in a way that maintains options, you can focus on communication because you're not simultaneously as worried about your immediate physical safety. When you position yourself in a way that eliminates options, you're forcing yourself to think about exit strategies instead of de-escalation strategies.

There are also multiple risk factors present that complicate this situation. Let's throw these factors in: There's at least one dog nearby that we can see behind the screen door. There's also a person inside the home visible behind the subject, possibly Erica herself. Either of these additional elements could quickly enter the encounter, intentionally or not, and complicate the situation in ways that would be very difficult for the officer to manage once he's already in such a vulnerable position.

When dealing with one agitated individual, others around them can be triggered by loyalty, fear, or stress. The dog could become protective. The person inside could come outside. Suddenly the officer could be dealing with a much bigger conflict, and his positioning has left him with almost no good options for managing it safely. These are all things that good situational awareness picks up on.

The man's behavior in this encounter is highly elevated. While he may not yet be an immediate physical threat, he is very close to that line. His elevated emotional behavior includes loud voice and rapid pacing. There's zero reactionary distance between him and the officer and he's reacting strongly to a single repeated trigger. The officer is ignoring clear escalation cues.

Think about what environmental hazards increase the risk of physical harm in situations you encounter. How does positioning help or hurt safety? These aren't theoretical questions. In every encounter, the physical environment either supports de-escalation or undermines it. This encounter shows multiple ways that environment and positioning can create risk.

Consider why the repeated mention of Erica functions as a barb. What could have been said instead to validate emotion without triggering escalation? "We'll get to the bottom of what happened. Before we get into the details, let's just slow this down a bit. Can you take a breath with me?" That's the first element of G.U.I.D.E., Ground Yourself, extended to help the other person ground themselves too.

At what point should the officer have repositioned or disengaged from this particular physical setup? Ideally, upon approach or before the conversation even started. But certainly once it became clear that the man's agitation was increasing rather than decreasing, and that the current approach wasn't working. This is the fourth element of G.U.I.D.E., Direct the Interaction, which includes directing your own positioning and approach, not just the other person's behavior.

The fifth element of G.U.I.D.E., Ensure Safety and Support, means continuously assessing whether the current situation remains within safe parameters. It doesn't mean waiting until there's an immediate threat. Instead, recognize your positioning, your approach, or the environmental factors that have created risk, and make adjustments before those risks become actualized dangers.

Sometimes getting the information you need requires an indirect approach to the same destination. The officer needed to know what happened with Erica. But asking about her directly, repeatedly, while the subject was this elevated wasn't getting that information. It was just creating more agitation. Once the subject's breathing slowed, his pacing stopped, his volume lowered, then specific questions about what happened might be answerable. But not while he's this escalated.

This encounter illustrates why situational awareness matters on multiple levels. We need to be aware of emotional triggers like barbs that cause escalation. We need to be aware of environmental dangers like fall risks, confined spaces, and poor positioning. We need to be aware of additional people and animals who may enter the encounter. We need to be aware of how our own communication patterns are landing, whether they're helping or hurting. When we ignore these cues, we place ourselves into avoidable jeopardy, and the chance of a de-escalated outcome through communication drops significantly.

What These Encounters Teach Us

These three encounters, the bank customer, the retail confrontation, and the domestic disturbance call, illustrate different patterns of escalation and different critical decision points.

The bank customer needed space to vent and validation of his frustration, demonstrating the power of the third pillar, Validation, and the importance of the first element of G.U.I.D.E., Ground Yourself, which allows you to recognize venting for what it is rather than treating it as threat. His escalation was driven by feeling unheard and by the absurdity he perceived in the policy. The solution wasn't complicated: acknowledge his emotion through Professional Sincerity, give him a moment to express it, and maintain your own regulation so you don't add intensity to his intensity. After he vented, he left. Simple, effective, safe.

The retail encounter showed that hooks offer opportunities for human connection that change entire dynamics, and that the fourth pillar, Collaboration, transforms encounters from adversarial to cooperative. The employee's defensive explanation escalated rather than de-escalated because it positioned the employee as obstacle rather than partner. Better positioning would have maintained safety options. Recognition of the Megadeth t-shirt hook would have created human connection. Collaborative language may have created partnership. All three together (safety, connection, collaboration) create the conditions for successful de-escalation.

The domestic disturbance call showed that barbs cause escalation and must be avoided once identified, that positioning creates or eliminates options for safe response, and that environmental awareness isn't separate from communication. It's integrated with it. The officer's repeated use of Erica's name was a barb that kept triggering escalation. His poor positioning eliminated his options if the situation transitioned to physical. The additional risk factors, dog, bystander, elevated structure, compounded both issues. All three together created unnecessary danger that better situational awareness could have prevented.

Three encounters. Three different patterns. Three different appropriate responses. This is why formulaic approaches to de-escalation don't work. Scripts fail because every situation is different. But the framework of Professional Sincerity, the Five Pillars, and G.U.I.D.E. works across different situations because they're adaptable to context while remaining consistent in purpose.

These encounters all shared something in common: they were manageable. Communication had a chance. The bank customer was frustrated, not dangerous. The retail customer was upset, not violent. Even the domestic disturbance, with all its compounding risk factors, remained within the realm where better communication and positioning could have improved the outcome. The tools we've built, situational awareness, behavioral observation, foundational principles, and applied skills, are designed for exactly these situations, and they often work.

But not every encounter stays manageable. Sometimes, despite our best efforts, a situation transitions beyond the reach of communication. The person in front of us demonstrates means, opportunity, and intent. The behavioral cues shift from emotional distress to something more deliberate, more targeted, more dangerous. When that happens, our responsibility shifts too, from de-escalation to safety, from connection to distance, from calming the situation to getting out of it.

That's where we go next: to immediate threats and safety planning, the moment when everything we've learned about seeing and communicating meets the reality that sometimes, the safest response is action.

CHAPTER 6:

IMMEDIATE THREATS AND SAFETY PLANNING

In Chapter 5, we watched escalation unfold in real encounters. In each of those scenarios, communication still had a chance to work. The person across from us was elevated but reachable. The skills we built in Chapters 3 and 4, situational awareness, behavioral observation, the Five Pillars, G.U.I.D.E., were enough to guide those encounters toward safer outcomes.

But not every encounter stays in that range. Sometimes, despite everything we do, a situation crosses a line where communication alone can no longer keep us safe. When an immediate threat emerges, we no longer have the luxury of waiting to see how things unfold. Immediate threats justify immediate action, not based on assumptions or gut feelings, but on clearly articulable facts that any reasonable professional would recognize as dangerous.

Everything we've covered so far has been about seeing escalation early enough to intervene. Situational awareness, behavioral observation, the OODA Loop, the seven indicators of hostile intent, facial expressions, emotions, and reading context. The goal has been to catch behavior while it's still manageable, while communication still has a chance of working, while Professional Sincerity and G.U.I.D.E. can still help us create a safer outcome.

But this chapter is different. This chapter is about the moment when someone's actions have shifted into something that could cause injury right now. When our responsibility is no longer to de-escalate through words, but to protect ourselves and others through action.

This is when we move from influence to safety. From connection to distance. And in non-enforcement industries, from trying to calm the situation to getting out of it.

What Constitutes an Immediate Threat?

So what does an immediate threat look like in real encounters? A number of things.

It's when an individual is armed, and that weapon is accessible and relevant to the situation at hand. It's when an individual has made threats toward you or others, and the circumstances show they have the means and opportunity to carry them out right now. It's when an individual attempts to strike, grab, or harm someone, even if that attempt doesn't fully land, because the intent and capability have already been demonstrated.

An immediate threat is present when the behavior and the context combine to show that someone could take harmful action at any moment. It's not a vague possibility or a distant concern, it's a risk that is unfolding right in front of you. And the key here is that it is observable, describable, and explainable: what did you see, what did you hear, and why did those facts tell you the danger was real?

The answer is rooted in behavior, access, and intent, not assumptions or stereotypes. It's recognizing that the moment a person's actions shift into something that could cause injury right now, communication alone may not keep us safe. Our responsibility in those moments is to respond appropriately, using the level of intervention necessary to protect ourselves and others, while still being accountable for the decisions we make.

Means, Opportunity, Intent: The M.O.I. Framework

When we talk about an immediate threat, we're talking about a situation where harm could occur right now, not later. Three elements must be present at the same time for a threat to be considered immediate: means, opportunity, and intent. If any of those three are missing, the danger may be concerning, but it isn't yet immediate.

Let's break down each element and understand how they work together.

Means

Means refers to a person's capability to cause harm. Sometimes that involves a weapon, but not always. A person's size, strength, or access to objects that can be used as weapons can also establish means. The key point is that the person has the physical ability to hurt someone if they choose to.

Think back to Chapter 4, where we discussed the seven indicators of hostile intent. One of those indicators was Pre-Attack Posture, which included the person repeatedly touching or adjusting an area where a weapon could be concealed. That behavior signals access to means. When combined with the other elements (opportunity and intent), that access becomes immediately relevant to safety.

Means can also be environmental. In a hospital setting, medical equipment can become a weapon. In a retail environment, merchandise or tools can be grabbed and used. In a social services office, furniture can be picked up and thrown. The professional who has practiced Relaxed Awareness is already scanning for these possibilities before the crisis moment arrives.

Healthcare Example:

A patient in the emergency department has been waiting for hours, growing increasingly agitated. The nurse assigned to them has noticed the escalation: first verbal aggression, then increased physical tension, then targeted focus on specific staff members. The patient is a physically large individual who has been pacing, clenching fists, and making statements like "I'm done waiting" and "Someone's going to listen to me."

In this scenario, means exists. The patient's physical size and strength provide capability. The environment provides additional means: IV poles, medical equipment, chairs. The nurse who has been trained in BSA recognizes these factors early and begins adjusting positioning, maintaining distance, and preparing to call for support. They're not assuming violence will occur. They're recognizing that the capability exists and responding proactively.

Opportunity

Opportunity depends on time, distance, and circumstances, including the environment. If the person is close enough and nothing is physically stopping them from following through with the harmful action, then the opportunity exists. This is actually the factor we often have the most control over. By adjusting our positioning, increasing distance, or moving behind a barrier, we can sometimes remove the opportunity and reduce the immediate danger.

Think about the concept of Focused Awareness. When you narrow your attention to specific risk indicators, part of that focus should be on opportunity. How close is this person? What's between you and them? Where are your exits? Can they close the distance before you can react?

Distance equals safety. This is a principle that applies across every professional environment. The closer someone gets, the less reaction time you have. The more obstacles between you and a potential threat, the more options you maintain. This is where tactical positioning or repositioning becomes critical.

Social Services Example:

A caseworker is conducting a home visit to follow up on a benefits issue. The client has been cooperative during previous visits, but today something feels different. The caseworker notices the client is exhibiting several indicators: escalating resistance (refusing to sit down, ignoring requests to step back), verbal aggression (raised voice, profanity), and increased physical tension (rapid breathing, clenched fists).

The client is standing between the caseworker and the front door. That's the only exit from the small living room. Opportunity now exists. Even if the caseworker isn't certain about intent, and even if they're not sure if means involves a weapon, the simple fact that opportunity is present (close proximity with no clear exit path) creates an immediate concern.

The trained caseworker recognizes this and makes a tactical adjustment. They politely suggest moving the conversation to the kitchen table, which happens to provide a different angle toward the door. They're not being dramatic, not announcing their concern, but quietly repositioning to maintain options. They're removing opportunity while maintaining Professional Sincerity, still treating the client with respect while prioritizing their own safety.

Intent

Intent is shown through behavior, words, tone, or physical actions that reveal what the person is preparing to do. This must be based on what you can actually observe and articulate, not assume or stereotype. Examples might include someone making explicit threats, moving aggressively toward another person, or showing obvious signs of preparing to strike. It's happening right now. It's not a fear of something to possibly come later.

Remember our discussion of the OODA Loop. Intent is forming during the Orient and Decide phases, the person is processing the situation and making internal decisions about what action to take. Sometimes that intent leaks out through micro-expressions (as Dr. Ekman taught us), through changes in baseline behavior (BSA), or through the clustering of multiple hostile intent indicators.

Intent is never assumed based on how someone looks, what they're wearing, or demographic factors. It's inferred from observable behavior that shows preparation or movement toward causing harm.

Loss Prevention Example:

A customer has been observed exhibiting several concerning behaviors. It looks like they've been scanning for security cameras (targeted focus), moving between high-value items without browsing normally (behavior that doesn't match context), and repeatedly touching their waistband area (pre-attack posture indicator). When an associate approaches to offer assistance, the customer's facial expression shifts to what Ekman would identify as contempt: a one-sided lip curl that signals disdain or hostility. Their tone becomes sharp: "Back off. I don't need your help." One hand curls into a fist and starts to draw back...

The LP professional recognizes these behaviors as indicators of intent. Not definitive proof of criminal intent, but a pattern that warrants increased attention and positioning for safety. They're applying everything from Chapter 4: observation over assumption, context over snapshots, details over generalities. They maintain Professional Sincerity in their communication while simultaneously preparing for the possibility that this encounter could escalate.

When All Three Align

Importantly, this is not about fear of what might happen later. It's about what could happen in this moment. When an individual has the means to cause harm, the opportunity to act, and the intent to cause harm, the threat must be taken seriously and addressed without delay. That might mean disengaging, calling for security or support, or positioning yourself and others to stay safe until help arrives.

Recognizing these three elements and acting early is what keeps us ahead of harm instead of reacting after danger has already arrived.

Let's look at a scenario that pulls together everything from the previous chapters to show how M.O.I. works in real time.

Social Services Example: When All Three Converge

A caseworker arrives at a client's apartment for a scheduled benefits review. The visit was routine the last two times, but today the atmosphere is different. The client opens the door but doesn't step back to let the caseworker in. He's blocking the doorway, arms crossed, jaw tight. His baseline has changed.

The caseworker steps inside and immediately begins a quiet scan. The apartment layout is simple: a small living room, a kitchen off to the left, one hallway leading to the bedrooms. The front door is behind them. There's a sliding glass door to a balcony off the living room, but it leads nowhere useful. The hallway leads away from both exits. The caseworker chooses to stay in the living room, near the front door.

The client starts talking before the caseworker can sit down. His voice is elevated, his words pressured. "You people keep messing with my benefits. Every time I get something figured out, somebody changes the rules. I'm done playing games." His hands are clenched. He's pacing. His focus is locked entirely on the caseworker (Targeted Focus). His body language is shifting: weight forward, shoulders squared, the beginning of what we described as Pre-Attack Posture. The client is a large man, significantly bigger than the caseworker, and the room suddenly feels a lot smaller.

The caseworker is running their OODA Loop. Observe: elevated voice, clenched fists, pacing, squared posture, targeted focus on me, significant size disparity, and he's now positioned between me and the front door.

Orient: multiple indicators are clustering. This pattern matches what we learned about hostile intent. The client's baseline from previous visits was calm and cooperative. Today's behavior is a significant departure. Decide: I need to create distance and keep communication open while I figure out whether this encounter can be redirected.

Act. The caseworker takes a small step back, shifting their angle so the coffee table is between them and the client. They keep their voice calm, their posture open. "It sounds like something changed with your benefits, and that must be causing a lot of stress. Let's sit down at the table and go through it together so we can figure out exactly what happened."

The client doesn't sit. He takes a step closer. "No. I'm done sitting down and filling out forms. You're going to fix this right now, today, or we're going to have a problem." His voice has dropped in pitch. His pacing has stopped. He's now standing still, squared up, staring directly at the caseworker. That shift from agitated movement to controlled stillness is a very significant pre-attack indicator; combining increased physical tension and escalating resistance.

The caseworker recognizes what's happening. The client has the means: his physical size and strength alone establish capability. Intent is escalating: the verbal threat ("we're going to have a problem"), the posture, the stillness, the locked eye contact. And opportunity is there: they're in a small apartment, the client is between the caseworker and the most direct exit, and no one else is in the room.

This is the moment many agencies and organizations want this training for. Not every encounter can be saved through communication, and not every situation requires you to stay and try. The caseworker's agency has a clear policy: when your safety is compromised during a home visit, you leave. You don't escalate, you don't negotiate from a position of vulnerability, and you don't stay to prove a point. You get out, report it, and the visit gets rescheduled under safer conditions.

The caseworker keeps their voice steady. "We need to get this resolved, and it sounds like it needs to happen at a higher level. Here's what we'll do. The office is going to get a supervisor directly involved so this gets handled the right way. That's going to get you a faster answer than anything that can happen standing here right now."

That response does something important: it gives the client a reason to let the caseworker leave. It reframes the departure not as rejection or retreat, but as escalation on his behalf. The caseworker moves toward the door without rushing, maintains a calm tone, and exits the apartment.

Outside, they immediately drive to a safe location and text their supervisor the address and situation. They write down the key details while everything is fresh before making the full report.

The caseworker recognized that means, intent, and opportunity were all present or forming. They attempted redirection through communication, and when that didn't work, they made the professional decision to remove themselves from the situation. That's not failure. That's exactly what this training is for.

This is situational awareness, BSA, hostile intent recognition, and M.O.I. all working together. The caseworker never had to confront the client. They never had to match his intensity. They simply recognized the pattern early enough to get out before the encounter crossed a line that couldn't be walked back.

But what happens when disruption isn't possible? When all three elements are present and action is imminent? Up to this point, communication remains a powerful way to influence behavior and slow escalation. Beyond this point, however, the determining factors shift. Role, authority, and safety (not communication technique) define what comes next.

When Verbal De-Escalation Is No Longer Feasible

When faced with an immediate threat, the rules of communication change instantly. At that point, verbal de-escalation is no longer realistic or safe, because the person in front of you has already demonstrated the means, opportunity, and intent to cause harm. Once those three factors align, there isn't time to negotiate or attempt emotional calming strategies. Safety becomes the priority.

For civilians, the most appropriate and effective response in this moment is simple: remove yourself from the situation. Create distance, back away, and get to a safer space where help can be reached or where the threat can no longer reach you. Your responsibility is not to control the other person; it is to protect yourself.

When danger becomes immediate, staying in that proximity only increases the risk. Leaving may feel abrupt or uncomfortable, but it is the safest and most professional choice. Once separation is established and the immediate risk has passed, additional steps (contacting security, calling 911, notifying supervisors) can take place from a position of safety rather than vulnerability.

The goal is straightforward: do not stay in harm's reach when the threat is right in front of you. Safety first, everything else can happen afterward. This is also a point where Regulation becomes important in recognizing your limitations. In one of my classes, a caseworker told me about a home visit she went on. This visit had been rescheduled and taken on and off her calendar for weeks and she was determined to complete it this day. While at the client's residence, the client became very agitated and escalated to the point where he picked up a baton or club and started smashing things with it. Definitely a sign to leave! But the caseworker, determined to check this visit off of her to-do list, stayed and continued to try to talk to the individual, clearly in crisis. I'm happy to say she left without being harmed, but told me that she was reprimanded by her supervisor for continuing the visit.

Up to this point, we've focused on recognizing when a situation becomes an immediate threat and understanding the roles that define our response. Now we need to get practical. What do you actually do to keep yourself safe? What does preparation look like before the encounter, during it, and when everything falls apart? The rest of this chapter is about some specific tools, strategies, and habits that give you the best chance of staying safer in the worst case scenarios.

Personal Safety: Your Responsibility, Always

Every one of us has a role in our own safety, both at work and out in the world. No matter what policies exist, no matter what support is available, and no matter what someone's job title is, personal safety begins with the individual. You are the one in control of your awareness, your positioning, your decisions, and your willingness to take action when something doesn't feel right.

This isn't about becoming paranoid or assuming everyone we meet is dangerous. It's about acknowledging that our body gives us information, our instincts alert us to changes, and our choices can either increase or decrease our exposure to risk. When we take ownership of our safety, we move from being passive participants in an encounter to informed and prepared professionals who can influence outcomes.

Even in workplaces where other people are responsible for security (hospitals, government offices, retail environments, social service agencies), the truth remains the same: we are always the first line of our own defense. The choices we make in those first critical seconds of a situation often determine whether we stay safe long enough for additional help to arrive.

By understanding how to recognize risk early and by responding in ways that protect our space, our movement, and our options, we give ourselves a better chance to stay calm, stay aware, and stay safe. Personal safety enhancement is not about fear. It's about empowerment. It's recognizing that we have influence not just over others, but over our own environment and wellbeing. You are responsible for your safety!

Creating Your Personal Safety Plan

Most workplaces today have safety plans in place: written procedures, emergency protocols, security staff, panic buttons, evacuation routes, and response expectations. Those plans are critical, and they exist for a reason. But here's the thing: a workplace plan only protects you if you can access it in the moment. If you're in a hallway, a parking lot, a restroom, or off-site on a home visit, that formal plan may not be available to you when you need it most.

That's why every person (regardless of job title) needs their own personal safety plan everywhere they go. A safety plan isn't complicated; it's simply the choices you make ahead of time that give you a way out when the situation changes. It's knowing where the exits are before you need them. It's recognizing blind corners or confined spaces before someone corners you there. It's having a thought-out response to the question, "What would I do if things go sideways right now?"

We plan every day for things far less important than our own wellbeing: schedules, appointments, meal prep, errands and so on. Safety deserves that same level of preparation. It's not paranoia. It's professionalism and recognizing that control is easier to maintain when we think ahead, not when we're reacting under stress.

A personal safety plan might mean positioning yourself so you're never trapped between a person in crisis and a closed door. It might mean having a code word with a coworker that signals you need help without alarming the person you're dealing with. Outside of work, it might mean choosing where you park based on lighting and foot traffic, or where you sit in a restaurant based on what feels secure.

The goal isn't to live in fear. It's to live with awareness. A prepared mind stays calmer, thinks more clearly, and reacts faster than a surprised one. When you create your own safety plan, you give yourself permission to recognize when something doesn't feel right and to act before that feeling becomes a threat.

Personal safety planning is empowerment. It is acknowledging that you are worth protecting, then taking practical steps to make sure you can keep yourself safe and continue helping others.

Know Your Exits: Two, Not One

A major part of any personal safety plan (and one we often overlook) is understanding how to get out if we have to. Exits are not just architectural features; they are opportunities. They are the fastest way to turn a dangerous situation into a safe one. Whether we work behind a counter, visit people in their homes, interact with the public in a lobby, or move throughout a large facility, exits give us the ability to remove ourselves from danger the moment the situation demands it.

But here's the key: knowing only one exit isn't enough. If that path becomes blocked (by equipment, by a crowd, or by the individual who is escalating), we need another option. Two exits give us a choice. Three exits give us a plan. When we walk into a room, a hallway, an office, or a home visit environment, one of the first quiet assessments we should make is: *If I had to leave right now, where do I go?*

Once a crisis starts, tunnel vision narrows our focus dramatically. That's the worst time to be trying to figure out where the door is.

This applies everywhere:

At work, Before the public ever arrives, take a moment to learn where all the exits lead. Which ones open to secure areas? Which require a badge? What pathways become choke points during busy hours? Is there furniture or equipment that could block your escape route?

During home visits, Take a quick scan the moment you enter. Leave yourself a clear line back to the door. Don't allow the individual to position themselves between you and your exit. If possible, choose seating that keeps you closest to your way out while still remaining respectful and unobtrusive.

In the community, Parking lots, elevators, public events, awareness of your surroundings can give you crucial seconds if things shift. A simple decision like choosing a well-lit path or a seat near a service exit can change the outcome without anyone ever knowing you planned ahead.

Another smart part of personal safety planning involves varying the entrances and exits we use over time. Most of us are creatures of habit. We park in the same spot, take the same hallway, use the same door, and sit in the same chair. That consistency feels comfortable... until it works against us.

In a crisis, the body doesn't rely on creative thinking. It relies on muscle memory. Under stress, our brain shifts into survival mode, and it will automatically choose the path we use most often. If that path becomes blocked, unfamiliar, or suddenly unsafe, we can lose precious seconds trying to adjust.

By intentionally using different entrances and exits periodically when everything is calm, we create multiple mental maps of safety. We train ourselves to move without hesitation regardless of where we are in the building. Our body remembers the routes we've taken before, and that familiarity becomes a tool we can call on when our thinking gets narrow and fast.

This doesn't mean we change everything every day. It simply means we give ourselves more than one practiced option. Because the more options we have, the more control and regulation we maintain if something unpredictable happens. Preparedness is built in the calm moments so it's available in the chaotic ones.

ABC: A Framework for Active Threats

Pop culture can actually help us remember important safety principles, and one of the best examples is the movie *Die Hard*. Now, we're certainly not suggesting anyone become John McClane. No climbing through elevator shafts, no rooftop gunfights, and definitely no walking on shattered glass. But the reason that movie works so well as a teaching moment is because the basic survival model he uses is the same approach recommended today in active threat situations: **Run, Hide, Fight**, or as it's often referred to now as **Avoid, Barricade, Confront,** or **ABC.**

Using a pop culture reference here certainly does not make light of these kinds of situations. They are probably one of the worst things that someone can experience. Thankfully, even though we continue to read about these incidents and see them on the news, they are indeed very rare when you take into account population sizes and the number of buildings, schools, campuses, and so on there are.

But getting back to our *Die Hard* example, as soon as the threat begins, McClane doesn't freeze. He runs. He creates distance from danger because distance buys time and safety. When he can't run, he hides. He uses cover, concealment, and silence. He positions himself where the threat can't reach him, and he waits for the right moment to move. And only when there is absolutely no other choice, when his life and the lives of others hang in the balance, does he fight.

This is essentially the original Run, Hide, Fight model. From a late 1980's movie, before we considered this kind of response so often in civilian life.

The movie gives us a memorable framework: don't wait, don't negotiate with danger, and don't hope the situation improves on its own. Take action that keeps you alive long enough for help to intervene. Run if you can. Hide if you must. Fight only if there are no remaining options.

What makes McClane survive that situation isn't his toughness. It's his awareness, his mobility, and his willingness to make smart decisions under pressure. He keeps moving. He keeps adjusting. He keeps himself in a position where he has options.

That's exactly what I want for all of you. Not heroics or confrontation, but the mindset and awareness to protect yourself from harm. Because the safest win in any life or death situation is the one where you get out alive and go home at the end of the day.

Run is always the first choice. If there's a clear path to safety, take it. Don't wait to see if things get worse. Don't worry about looking dramatic or overreacting. Your life is more important than anyone's comfort level with your urgency. Get out and get out fast. Leave belongings behind, and when you exit, make sure that your hands are up, empty and you follow any commands from first responders.

Hide when running isn't possible. Find a room, lock or barricade the door, turn off the lights, silence your phone, and stay quiet. This isn't about permanent hiding. It's about making yourself unavailable as a target until help arrives or until you can safely run. Consider wedging something under a door that opens inward. For an outward swinging door, belts, pieces of clothing or other improvisions can be used to tie off the door to prevent it from opening.

Fight is the absolute last resort. Fight when the threat is directly upon you and there is no other option. Fight with everything you have. Improvised weapons, noise, aggression. Fight hard and fight dirty, because at that point, you're fighting for your life.

This framework applies to active threat situations where immediate danger to life has removed all other options. The key is making the decision quickly and committing to it fully.[1]

Cover vs. Concealment: Knowing the Difference

Another key piece of personal safety is understanding the difference between cover and concealment. In a dangerous situation, the protection you think you have may not actually protect you at all.

Concealment is anything that hides you from view. It keeps the person from seeing where you are, and that can absolutely be helpful. Concealment might give you a moment to breathe, to think, or to plan your next move. But concealment alone does not stop a bullet, a knife, or any physical force. Thin walls, furniture, curtains, even a closed door. Those may hide you, but they don't block harm. Concealment buys time, but not safety.

Cover, on the other hand, is something that stops the threat. It protects your body from bullets, strikes, and impact. Think about thick concrete walls, large pillars, heavy industrial equipment, or the engine block of a car. Cover keeps you physically shielded from harm. It is your best friend when danger is real and direct.

So when a situation shifts from "uncomfortable" to "unsafe," we want to prioritize cover over concealment whenever possible. If all you can find is concealment, take it. Disappearing from sight may still interrupt the attacker's focus. But if you have the option to move behind something that can actually stop the threat? That's where you want to be.

Understanding the difference in advance allows you to make faster, smarter decisions under stress. It's one more piece of your personal safety plan that can turn a moment of chaos into a moment of survival.

And this awareness isn't just for workplaces with security staff or controlled access. It's just as important when you're out in the community. This is especially true for those who conduct home visits or work in environments where surroundings can change from moment to moment.

When you're walking up to a residence, moving through a neighborhood, or even just approaching a building from the parking area, part of your personal safety plan is noticing what could serve as cover and what could serve as concealment if something suddenly breaks bad. A car's engine block might give you actual protection from harm, while a bush or fence might only hide you from view. Both have value, but for very different reasons.

This kind of awareness doesn't require fear or suspicion. It's a matter of quietly scanning your environment and giving yourself options before you need them. You might notice a fire hydrant or utility box that could shield you from impact, or a landscaping feature that could allow you to disappear from sight. You're simply taking mental note of what you could use if the situation changes quickly.

The goal is not to think constantly about danger. It's to give your brain a head start so it doesn't have to solve these problems in the middle of a crisis. Because when stress hits, the brain doesn't rise to the occasion. It falls to the level of its training and preparation. Knowing where your cover and concealment are ahead of time gives you a plan without anyone ever knowing you made one. Prepared doesn't mean paranoid. It means professional.

Barriers: Creating Friction Between You and Danger

Another element of personal safety planning involves recognizing barriers. This is something we mentioned in Chapter 5 in the bank encounter: objects in our environment that can slow down or block someone who is moving aggressively toward us. Barriers aren't necessarily cover or concealment; they are simply obstacles that create friction in the path of a person trying to close distance. And in a tense encounter, distance equals safety. In a worst-case scenario, it may be used as either, depending upon what it is made of.

In the workplace, we often have barriers right in front of us without realizing it. Chairs, tables, counters, desks, computer stations, file cabinets, even a heavy printer. Any of these can be used to interrupt someone's ability to rush or grab us. We don't need to move them dramatically or draw attention to them. Sometimes all it takes is a subtle step behind a chair or a shift so that a desk is between us and the individual. Just that simple repositioning can buy valuable seconds if the situation turns.

For those who conduct home visits, the barriers are the objects already in the living space: a dining room table between you and the person you're speaking with, a kitchen island that requires someone to walk around it to reach you, or even the simple structure of a stair railing. Furniture and fixtures can be allies as long as we position ourselves in a way that keeps those obstacles working for us and not against us.

This is where tactical repositioning matters. Our goal is to avoid becoming trapped, cornered, or pinned. We should always be aware of where our exit is and avoid letting someone cut off our path to it. That may mean taking a step to the side, changing angles in the room, or gently navigating a conversation to a more open area where we maintain mobility. These are small, intentional movements that maintain safety without escalating tension or signaling fear.

It is much easier to reposition early, while the conversation still feels manageable, than to try to force your way out once someone has closed distance or blocked your route. These quiet, professional adjustments help ensure that if something changes, you are not starting the moment already disadvantaged.

In short, barriers slow the threat down. Repositioning keeps you from being contained. And together, they allow you to maintain space, options, and control. Three things that are essential when safety is at risk.

Distance: The Most Underrated Safety Tool

Throughout this chapter, we've been circling around one fundamental principle: distance equals safety. The farther you are from a potential threat, the more time you have to react. The more space between you and an escalating person, the more options you maintain. Distance isn't just a physical measurement, it's a tactical advantage.

Think back to our discussion of M.O.I. Opportunity exists when someone is close enough to act on their intent with their means. One of the most effective ways to remove opportunity is simply to increase distance. Move back. Create space. Don't let someone close the gap.

This connects directly to what we discussed in Chapter 4 about the levels of awareness and the OODA Loop. When you're at Relaxed Awareness, you should be noticing distances naturally. How close are people? How quickly could they close remaining gaps? What positioning gives you the most reaction time? When you shift to Focused Awareness because you have recognized concerning indicators, distance becomes even more critical.

The challenge is that increasing distance can sometimes feel rude or defensive. We don't want to offend someone by stepping back, or we don't want to seem scared. But here's the reality: maintaining professional distance is not rude. It's appropriate boundary setting. And if someone takes offense at your need for space, that reaction itself can be telling.

Professional distance varies by context and culture, but as a general principle: if you can't react in time to protect yourself, you're too close.

Government Office Example:

Gil Emmett is a clerk at a municipal services counter. He's helping a resident who has become increasingly frustrated about a permit delay. The resident has been exhibiting several concerning behaviors: verbal aggression, escalating resistance to the process being explained, and increased physical tension. Initially, the interaction took place across the service counter. That counter was a natural barrier that maintained appropriate distance.

But now the resident has moved around the counter, eliminating that barrier, and is approaching Gil's workspace. The resident is still talking, still technically engaged in conversation, but their body language has shifted to Pre-Attack Posture: squared shoulders, weight shifting, fists up and at the ready.

Gil, a trained clerk, recognizes the loss of distance as a critical change. He doesn't freeze or confront. He simply takes two steps backward (creating space) while maintaining Professional Sincerity: "I want to help you get this resolved. Let's check with my supervisor on the best way to move this forward."

That backward movement accomplishes several things: it increases reaction time if the situation escalates, it signals a boundary without being confrontational, and it buys time for Gil to call for support if needed. He has removed opportunity by managing distance, even while still attempting to de-escalate through communication.

The GPS Analogy: When Your Safety System Fails

We rely on technology every single day. Most of us, myself included, can barely get across town anymore without pulling out our phones and tapping that little map app icon. We trust that tool to guide us turn by turn until we arrive exactly where we intended to go. It makes travel simple, predictable, and comfortable. We don't have to think too hard about the route, or memorize the turns, because the GPS handles it all for us.

But here's the catch: that confidence only exists when the technology is working the way we expect it to. When the signal is good, the battery isn't dying. When our hands are steady and we can think clearly enough to type where we need to go. We don't think about those conditions until suddenly they're not there.

Imagine you've driven somewhere unfamiliar. Maybe you didn't pay attention to how you got there, because why would you, right? Then something changes. Something feels wrong. You have to get out of there, now. And suddenly the GPS isn't cooperating. The service dropped or the screen freezes. The app crashes. Your heart rate spikes and your hands are shaking. Even the simplest task (typing in an address) becomes complicated. Now the tool you depended on is gone. So the question becomes: what do you do when your go-to system fails you?

This is where we shift from convenience to preparedness. From automatic to intentional. And in communication, safety, and crisis encounters (just like on that dark backroad), we need a plan for when the GPS stops guiding us.

So here's how we solve that problem before it ever becomes a problem. We build ourselves a backup map. Something simple, fast, and always available even when the tech isn't. Before you ever head out to a home visit, a client meeting, or a property check at a location you don't know well, take a moment while you're still calm and thinking clearly. Use your GPS to pull up the directions. Not just getting there, but getting back out. Then take a sticky note and write down the key turns or landmarks that will get you home or back to safety. Nothing fancy. Just "Right on Maiden Lane, left at the light, Route 9 to the interstate." The big moves that get you away from danger and headed in the right direction.

And then, stick that note right on your steering wheel or dashboard. Now if things go sideways (if someone becomes aggressive, if your safety instincts kick in, if you make the decision that it's time to leave), you don't have to think. You don't have to unlock your phone, fight with the GPS, or type with shaky hands. You simply get in, close the door, start the engine, glance at that sticky note, and go. You've already made the exit strategy easy.

Just like that, there goes the uncertainty out of a high-stress moment. You've given yourself a clear, fast path to safety. That little yellow square becomes the confidence you need when adrenaline tries to steal your brain's ability to problem-solve.

Accountability: Making Sure Someone Knows

There's another piece to staying safe in unfamiliar or unpredictable environments. This one has nothing to do with technology at all. It's about people. Specifically, the people who should know where you are and when to expect you back.

When you're heading out to a home visit, a field call, a client appointment (anywhere outside your controlled workspace), hopefully you're going with someone else. But we know that's not always the case. Personnel shortages, varying workloads, and sometimes even policy can dictate that you're going by yourself. Someone should know your destination, when you left, and when you plan to return. If something goes wrong and you don't check in, they can start looking for you a lot earlier instead of hours going by with no one realizing you needed help.

It doesn't have to be complicated. It can be as simple as using a whiteboard at the workplace with names, locations, and expected return times. It can be a quick text message to a supervisor before you walk in the door, and another when you're safely leaving. It can be a digital reminder, a shared calendar note, or even a phone alarm set to go off if you forget to check back in. All of these tools do one important job: they make sure someone knows you're out there and can raise the flag if something delays you.

Isolation increases risk. The longer a situation goes unnoticed, the more dangerous the outcome becomes. But when your coworkers, your supervisor, or anyone on your team has that simple piece of information (where you are and when you should be back), you have a built-in safety net. You're never just "out in the field." You are accounted for.

It's a small habit that pays off in huge ways. And just like that sticky note on the steering wheel, a tiny bit of planning on the front end can make all the difference when things don't go according to plan.

Connecting Everything: From Awareness to Action

In Chapter 3, we established that connection precedes influence through Professional Sincerity. We can't guide someone toward safer behavior if they don't see us as credible, sincere, and worth cooperating with.

In Chapter 4, we built the observational framework: the five levels of situational awareness, BSA, the OODA Loop, indicators of hostile intent, and the science of facial expressions and emotions. In Chapter 5, we watched those tools work in real encounters and saw how the Five Pillars shape communication when someone is escalating.

Across those chapters, we became observers, not just viewers. We learned to read behavior, understand emotion, and apply communication strategies that move encounters toward safer outcomes.

Now, in this chapter, we've learned what to do when seeing and communicating aren't enough. When the person in front of us has demonstrated means, opportunity, and intent and becomes an immediate threat. That's when communication yields to safety.

This is not a failure of de-escalation. This is recognizing reality and responding appropriately. The professional who has internalized all of these concepts (from connection to awareness to safety) operates with confidence. They know when to engage and when to disengage. They know how to read behavior early and position themselves for safety. They know that protecting themselves is not incompatible with treating others with dignity. It's a prerequisite for being able to continue helping others. Because you can't help anyone if you're hurt, you can't de-escalate effectively if you're trapped, and you can't use Professional Sincerity if you're in immediate danger.

The skills in this chapter aren't about being paranoid or assuming the worst. They're about being prepared for reality. They're about taking ownership of your safety so that you can continue doing the difficult, important work of helping people in crisis. And they're about going home at the end of the day, every day, so you can come back and do it again tomorrow.

In the next chapter, we're going to shift direction. We've spent six chapters building skills that help us do things right. Now we need to talk about the things we do wrong. The habits, the phrases, the instincts that feel natural but actually make escalation worse. Because sometimes the biggest threat to a safe outcome isn't the person in front of us. It's what we bring to the encounter ourselves.

Notes

1. Cybersecurity and Infrastructure Security Agency, "Active Shooter Pocket Card," U.S. Department of Homeland Security, accessed February 22, 2026, https://www.cisa.gov/resources-tools/resources/active-shooter-pocket-card.

CHAPTER 7:
HOW WE MAKE THINGS WORSE

There's a moment that happens early in nearly every From Crisis to Calm training session. We're doing the "Say It Better" exercise. This is where the class as a group works through phrases people use reflexively during difficult encounters, and that's when I usually start to see it: that look of recognition spreading across faces in the room. Someone shifts uncomfortably in their seat. Another person winces slightly. A few exchange knowing glances with colleagues and chuckle. They're realizing something uncomfortable: they've been making things worse.

Not intentionally and not maliciously. But consistently, reflexively, and with the best of intentions, they've been using responses that escalate rather than de-escalate the very encounters they're trying to resolve.

This realization isn't pleasant, but it's essential because you can't change patterns you don't recognize. And the truth is, most people have never been taught what actually works in high-emotion encounters. They're operating on instinct, mimicking what they've seen modeled, or falling back on approaches that work well in normal conversations but backfire spectacularly when someone is in crisis.

This chapter examines the most common ways well-intentioned professionals inadvertently escalate encounters, and more importantly, what to do instead. If you recognize yourself in these examples, good. These patterns are nearly universal among people who haven't received specific training in crisis communication and recognizing them is the first step toward changing them. Every mistake in this chapter maps directly back to the Five Pillars and Professional Sincerity we built in Chapter 3. When you see what goes wrong, you'll also see exactly which standard was missing.

Under stress, our brains want to defend, correct, argue, interrupt, or fix things fast. Those impulses come from a good place. We want to help, to get things resolved. But in a high-emotion moment, those instincts usually pour gasoline on the fire. We stop listening, start explaining, and match the other person's intensity instead of anchoring it. Sometimes, we rush to solve the problem before the person feels heard. We might get defensive when someone accuses us of something unfair. Every one of these reactions feels natural and justified in the moment, and every one of them makes the encounter worse.

When Good Intentions Make Things Worse

It's 2:30 on a Wednesday afternoon at County General's emergency department. Maria Coverdale has been a registration clerk here for six years, and she prides herself on staying calm under pressure. But right now, watching a man pace back and forth in front of her desk, she can feel her own heart rate climbing.

"Sir," she says, keeping her voice steady and professional, "you need to calm down. Getting upset isn't going to help your mother get seen any faster."

The man stops pacing. For a moment, Maria thinks it worked. Then he wheels toward her, and his voice (which had been merely loud) becomes something else entirely. "Don't tell me to calm down! My 84-year-old mother has been back there for two hours, and NO ONE will tell me what's happening! She could be dying and you're sitting here telling me to calm down?!"

Other people in the waiting room are watching now. Maria feels her face flush. She was just trying to help. Why did that make things worse?

Maria's instinct was to call out the behavior and correct it. It felt professional. It felt like taking control. But telling someone to calm down when their amygdala has hijacked their prefrontal cortex doesn't work for a simple neurological reason: the brain systems required to "calm down" on command are the exact systems that have been temporarily overridden by stress hormones.[1] Worse, it communicates three damaging messages at once: your emotional response is inappropriate, your concern isn't being taken seriously, and you're the out-of-control one who needs correcting. The man in that waiting room wasn't primarily upset about waiting. He was terrified for his mother. When Maria told him to calm down, he heard: "Your fear doesn't matter to me."

That scene plays out every day in retail stores, social services offices, school front desks, and hospital lobbies across the country. The words vary slightly, but the pattern is identical: a well-meaning professional tells an escalated person to calm down, and the situation gets worse. In terms of the Five Pillars from Chapter 3, this is a Validation failure. The person's emotional reality was dismissed instead of acknowledged, and without Validation, there is no path to Collaboration or options.

Patterns You Already Recognize

"Calm down" is just one of several patterns we've already seen in this book. If you've been paying attention, you'll recognize a few others.

The explanation trap is what happens when we try to logic someone out of an emotional state. In Chapter 5, we watched a bank teller explain a policy to a customer who was getting more frustrated by the second. The more she explained, the less he heard. She was giving the right answer at the wrong time, which made it the wrong answer. When someone is emotionally escalated, their capacity for rational processing is significantly impaired. The prefrontal cortex has less blood flow and less glucose available while the amygdala is hyperactive, scanning for threats,[2] and it's needed for rational thought. Detailed explanations don't land in that state. The person needs emotional validation before they can process logical content. Emotions down first, then rationality comes back up. When someone is still emotionally activated, they need Validation before they can engage in Collaboration or consider Options.

Matching energy is what happens when we unconsciously mirror the other person's intensity. We introduced this concept in Chapter 3, and it shows up constantly in practice: the louder they get, the louder we get. The more agitated they become, the more commanding we become. Instead of serving as an emotional anchor, we become a mirror, reflecting and amplifying the exact energy we're trying to reduce. This is what happens when Regulation fails. Regulation is the first Pillar for a reason: before you can help someone else manage their emotional state, you have to manage your own. Once Regulation is gone, every other Pillar collapses with it. The encounter becomes an escalation race, and nobody wins an escalation race.

These three patterns (telling someone to calm down, explaining when they need validation, and matching their intensity) account for a huge percentage of professional escalation. But they're also the ones you're most likely to catch now that you've spent six chapters building awareness. The subtler patterns are the ones that do damage without anyone noticing.

Minimizing and Dismissing

Sometimes escalation happens not through what we say but through what we dismiss or fail to acknowledge.

It's a Tuesday morning at a county mental health clinic. Intake coordinator Robert King is meeting with a new client, a woman in her late twenties who's describing symptoms of severe anxiety that have been affecting her ability to work and care for her children.

"I understand," Robert says, barely looking up from his computer screen as he types. "A lot of people feel anxious. Let's get scheduled for an assessment three weeks from now."

The woman's voice cracks slightly. "Three weeks? I can barely get through a day right now. My kids are scared because I keep having panic attacks. I lost my job last week because I couldn't make it in. I need help now, not in three weeks."

Robert, still typing, responds: "Everyone thinks their situation is urgent. We're very busy. Three weeks is actually pretty fast. Some people wait two months."

The woman stands up abruptly. "You know what? Never mind. This was a mistake." She walks out.

What just happened? Robert didn't raise his voice. He didn't tell her to calm down. He didn't launch into lengthy explanations. But he did something equally damaging: he minimized her experience. He communicated, through his words and his body language, that her crisis wasn't really a crisis. That her suffering fell within normal parameters and didn't warrant special concern. That compared to other people's problems, hers wasn't particularly significant. Maybe even more damaging, he said, "I understand," to a situation or experience that he can't possibly understand firsthand the way she does.

This is a subtle form of escalation because it doesn't always result in raised voices or obvious conflict. Sometimes it results in exactly what happened here: disconnection. The person stops trying to be heard because they've received the message that they won't be heard. They may physically or emotionally leave and they don't come back, or worse.

At the Anytown Police Department front desk, someone is trying to report ongoing harassment by a neighbor. The desk officer responds: "Unless he's made physical threats, there's really nothing we can do. People have disputes with their neighbors all the time." The person hears: "It's really not something you need to be afraid of. Deal with it yourself."

It happens across all settings and industries. The insurance agent says "That's just how insurance works." The retail associate says "This is the first complaint we've heard." In each case, the professional thinks they're providing perspective. What they're actually doing is invalidating the person's experience and dismissing their concern. And people whose concerns are dismissed don't become calmer. They often become more insistent, more emotional, and more desperate to make someone understand that their problem is real and significant. This is Validation at its most fundamental. When we minimize or dismiss, we communicate that the person's experience doesn't matter. And when someone believes their experience doesn't matter to the person in front of them, Professional Sincerity is dead on arrival. There is no credibility, no trust, and no path to cooperation.

Using "But" to Negate

This is one of the smallest but most destructive words in crisis communication: "but."

Emily Appice, a case manager at a child welfare agency, is meeting with a mother whose children were temporarily placed in foster care. The mother is in Emily's office, voice breaking, explaining how hard she's working to meet the court's requirements. She's attending parenting classes, she's going to therapy, she's maintaining stable housing, she's staying sober. All the things she's been told to do.

Emily nods along. "You're making the effort," she says. "But there have only been three months of sobriety, and the court requires six months before we can consider reunification."

The mother's expression shifts from hopeful to defeated in an instant. "So, nothing I'm doing matters? I'm doing everything you told me to do!"

What happened here? Emily actually started with validation. She acknowledged the mother's efforts. But then, literally, she used the word "but," which functionally erased everything she'd said before it. In human communication, whatever comes after "but" tends to be what people hear and remember. Everything before "but" gets discounted, dismissed, forgotten.

Think about how this construction works in various contexts:

"I love you, but..." "That was good work, but..." "I understand your concern, but..." "You're right, but..."

It signals, "disregard what I just said, because now I'm going to tell you what I really mean." It transforms validation into negation. The person doesn't hear "I can see the real efforts being made AND the court requires six months." They hear "Your efforts don't actually count."

This pattern appears constantly in high-stakes professional conversations.

At a housing authority office, a caseworker tells an applicant: "I understand the urgency, but there's a waiting list and this application is incomplete." The applicant hears: "Your urgency isn't my problem."

At a corporate HR investigation meeting, an employee relations specialist tells a complainant: "I believe something happened, but I can't substantiate the specific allegations made." The complainant hears: "I don't actually believe you."

The solution isn't to never present limitations or requirements. It's to use language that allows both things to be true simultaneously: validation AND boundaries, empathy AND constraints, understanding AND policies. The Five Pillars don't compete with each other. Validation and Boundaries can coexist in the same sentence. The word "but" forces them into opposition. The word "and" lets them stand together. Instead of "but," we can use "and" or simply pause between statements. We can also use collaborative language, such as "we" or "let's".

"The efforts being made here are real and they're clear." (Pause) "The court requires six months of sobriety before reunification can be considered" communicates the same information without negating the validation.

"This must be pretty urgent. Let's look at what we can do to move this complaint forward." creates collaboration instead of contradiction.

Being Right at the Wrong Time

Sometimes the problem isn't what we say but our need to say it in the first place.

Officer Alan Cooper has pulled over a driver for failing to signal a lane change. The driver, a woman in her forties, is already upset before Alan reaches the window.

"Do you have any idea how fast you were following me before pulling me over?" she says before Alan can introduce himself. "You were dangerously close! And I'm being pulled over for not signaling? That's ridiculous!"

Alan's jaw tightens. "Ma'am, I was maintaining a proper following distance. The lane change was made in violation of Vehicle and Traffic Law section 1163. License and registration, please."

The driver's voice rises. "I've been driving for twenty-five years without a ticket! This is BS!"

Alan's response: "If you have twenty-five years of driving, the law requiring turn signal use should be known. I'm going to need those documents now."

The encounter continues to escalate. Eventually, what might have been a warning becomes a ticket, a lecture, and a complaint filed against Alan for being "rude and dismissive."

What happened? Alan was factually correct about everything he said. The driver did violate the law. He was maintaining proper following distance. Turn signals are required. But Alan's need to be right (to correct the driver's mistaken perception, to defend himself against an unfair accusation), that need transformed a routine traffic stop into a confrontation.

This is one of the hardest patterns to recognize and change because it feels like we're just stating facts. We're not being mean or dismissive. We're simply correcting misinformation or defending ourselves against unfair criticism. But in crisis communication, being right often matters less than being effective.

The driver wasn't in a state where she could receive corrections or factual information. She was escalated, defensive, and looking for validation of her concern (even though that concern was misdirected). When Alan immediately corrected her and defended himself, he confirmed what she already *perceived*: that he wasn't interested in treating her fairly.

It doesn't matter what your intention is when you say something, what matters is how it is perceived. We see it, and continue to do it, in every professional setting where people interact under stress.

This pattern shows up everywhere: the customer service rep who cites a 94 percent satisfaction rating, the caseworker who says "we help thousands of people every month." They're stating facts. But those facts, delivered in that moment, serve only to invalidate the person's experience and escalate their emotional intensity. There's a time for facts and corrections, but it's not when someone is escalated. First comes validation and emotional labeling. Then, once the person is in a state where they can actually hear information, comes clarification and fact-sharing.

The Language of Accusation

Language patterns matter more than most professionals realize, and certain patterns consistently escalate encounters. One particularly problematic pattern involves phrasing that sounds accusatory, even when that's not the intent.

Consider these common phrases: "You need to calm down." "You're being unreasonable." "You have to fill out this form." "You should have brought that document." "You can't do that here."

Each of these sentences, regardless of their factual accuracy, can put the listener on the defensive because they sound like accusations or commands. They position the speaker as the one with power and judgment, and the listener as the one being corrected or controlled. That's the danger of "you" statements.

But here's where it gets more nuanced. Not all statements that include the word "you" are accusatory. There's a critical difference between "you" statements that focus attention on the person's needs, concerns, and experience versus "you" statements that judge, command, or criticize. They're very effective in From Crisis to Calm, as long as you use them correctly.

Watch how this distinction plays out in a probation office. Probation Officer Tom Rhoads is meeting with someone on his caseload who missed their last two appointments.

CRISIS VERSION: "You missed the last two check-ins. You know that's a violation of probation terms. You need to take this seriously. You're putting yourself at risk of going back to jail."

The person across from him, who missed appointments because they couldn't afford bus fare and didn't know how to explain that without sounding like they were making excuses, doesn't shut down. They fire back. "Oh, so now you're threatening me? That's all you people do. You don't give a damn about anything except locking people up. Go ahead, send me back. I don't even care anymore."

Now Tom has a full-blown escalation on his hands, and his own language lit the match.

CALM VERSION: "The last two appointments were missed, and that's concerning for what it could mean for your probation status. What's been happening?"

The person is still angry. "Man, I don't need a lecture. You have no idea what I've been dealing with."

But Tom stays with it. "It sounds like things have been rough. I'm asking so we can figure out what's getting in the way instead of just marking violations. What's going on?"

Notice that every "you" Tom uses in the CALM version is focused on understanding the person's perspective, inviting their input, and showing genuine interest in their situation. Even when the person pushes back, Tom doesn't match that energy with commands or accusations. He makes the person feel attended to rather than attacked. The attention is on them in a supportive way, not a critical way. It's a way to Say It Better.

Same information being addressed, but the second version invites explanation rather than sounding like an attack. The person feels like Tom is trying to understand rather than just enforce, and that shift creates enough space for the conversation to move forward instead of spiraling.

This pattern can happen in any encounter.

An administrator in a high school office tells a parent: "You need to sign this form and return it by Friday or your child can't participate in the field trip." The parent, who's working three jobs and barely keeping up with the paperwork demands of raising four kids, hears: "You're a bad parent who doesn't care about your child's experiences."

Compare that to: "This form needs a signature by Friday for the field trip. You're real busy, what's the best way to make sure that happens?"

Dr. Stanley tells a patient for the third visit now: "You have to lose weight and exercise more or the diabetes will get worse." The patient, who already feels ashamed of their weight and has tried unsuccessfully to change their habits for years, hears: "Failing at basic self-care is why being sick is happening, and it's all your fault."

Compare that to: "What have we tried before for managing weight? What have you done that felt doable versus what felt impossible?"

An overworked, underpaid caseworker in a social services office tells an applicant: "You didn't provide the right documentation. You'll have to come back with the correct forms." The applicant, who spent four hours in transit to get there and took unpaid leave from work, hears: "This is all your fault, and everyone's time was wasted."

Compare that to: "Looking at what you brought, we're still missing a couple of things. Let's be really specific about what's needed so when you come back, we can process this right away."

The information being conveyed might be accurate and necessary. But the way we frame that information (whether it sounds like an attack or an invitation to collaborate) determines whether people can actually hear and respond to what we're saying. This is the Collaboration and Options Pillars in action. When language sounds like a command, it removes choice. When it sounds like an invitation, it restores it. The same information, framed differently, can either fire someone up, shut someone down or open them up.

Say It Better: Translating Crisis Into Calm

Now that we've looked at common patterns that escalate encounters, let's talk about what to do instead. In From Crisis to Calm training, this is where we put into practice what I introduced at the start of this chapter: "Say It Better."

The concept is simple. I present phrases that we use reflexively in high-stress encounters: phrases that feel natural and appropriate in the moment but that actually escalate rather than de-escalate. Then we work together to translate those phrases into language that accomplishes the same goal while reducing emotional intensity rather than increasing it.

I'm going to present a series of common crisis phrases from various professional contexts. Before looking at the SAY IT BETTER version, take a moment to think about how it might be said differently. What would accomplish the same goal, setting a boundary, providing information, and redirecting behavior, while validating emotion and maintaining connection?

Let's start with some we've already discussed and add many more.

"You need to calm down."

How can it be said differently?

SAY IT BETTER: "This is clearly really important to you. Take a breath with me and let's figure this out together."

The improved version acknowledges the emotional intensity ("this is really important"), provides a specific action that's actually achievable ("take a breath with me"), and creates partnership ("let's figure this out together") instead of commanding behavioral change.

"There's nothing I can do."

What's a better way to communicate limitations?

SAY IT BETTER: "Here's what we can do..." followed by specific options, even if they're limited.

The shift from "nothing" to "here's what I can" changes the entire frame from powerlessness to agency. Even small options restore a sense of possibility. Changing "I" to "we" invites collaboration, not conflict.

These examples demonstrate communication principles, not scripts. Whether and how they're used depends on role, authority, and whether safety allows the conversation to continue.

"That's just our policy. I don't make the rules."

How would policy constraints be communicated without dismissing the person's concern?

SAY IT BETTER: "This must be frustrating. Let's take a look and see if we have any flexibility."

This version validates frustration, offers context, and leaves room for problem-solving rather than presenting the policy as an immovable wall.

"If you don't calm down, I'll have to call security / have you removed / end this conversation."

What's a way to set a necessary boundary without making a threat?

SAY IT BETTER: "If we keep talking over each other like this, it's going to be hard to sort this out. I want to help you, but I need us to bring the volume down so we can talk."

This states what's needed, expresses desire to help, and invites cooperation rather than threatening consequences.

"You should have..." (brought the right documents, read the instructions, called ahead, etc.)

How would what didn't happen be addressed without shaming?

SAY IT BETTER: "For next time, it helps to..." or "Moving forward, what we'll need is..."

This is future-focused rather than past-focused, providing guidance without blame.

"That's not my job / department / responsibility."

What's a way to redirect without dismissing?

SAY IT BETTER: "Let's connect you with the person who handles that. We want to make sure you get to the right place."

Instead of creating a dead end, this creates a bridge and demonstrates investment in helping them find the right resource. This is best accomplished after listening first.

"There's no need to be so upset / emotional / angry."

What's a way to respond to emotional intensity without telling someone their feelings are wrong?

SAY IT BETTER: "It looks like you're pretty angry about this. It makes complete sense to feel that way."

Validation of the emotion, not judgment of it.

"I've already explained this three times."

When information needs to be repeated, what's a better approach than expressing frustration?

SAY IT BETTER: "Let's go through this together so we can be sure we're on the same page."

This acknowledges that the previous explanation didn't land and commits to trying a different approach rather than blaming them for not understanding.

"You're the first person to complain about this."

What's a way to provide context without invalidating their experience?

SAY IT BETTER: "That sounds incredibly annoying. Tell me more about what happened."

Instead of suggesting their concern isn't valid because it's unusual, this simply invites more information so the specific situation can be addressed.

"That's impossible / We can't do that / No."

What's a way to communicate limitations while leaving room for alternatives?

SAY IT BETTER: "What other solutions can we work on together here?"

Again, the shift from what can't happen to what can happen changes the emotional tone of the entire interaction.

"You must be confused / mistaken / you're wrong."

When someone has incorrect information, how could it be corrected without being insulting?

SAY IT BETTER: "Let's make sure the right information gets to you" or "Sometimes this information is outdated. Here's what's current."

This provides correction without suggesting they're incompetent or wrong.

"I'm going to need you to..." (followed by a demand)

What's a way to make requests without sounding commanding?

SAY IT BETTER: "What would help is..." or "Let's do this..."

Framing used as a need or as an invitation to cooperate rather than as a command reduces resistance. This works to direct the interaction.

Industry-Specific Translation Practice

The following scenes show how ordinary interactions unfold when stress is already present. Each begins at the point where things start to go sideways, followed by an alternate response that slows the encounter without surrendering boundaries.

Healthcare – Prescription Delay

CRISIS VERSION:
The pharmacy counter is backed up, phones ringing behind the glass. The patient has been standing in the same spot for several minutes, checking the time, shifting their weight. When the technician finally looks up, the patient's frustration spills out, and they say, "Hello? I've been standing here forever! I got a notification my script was ready," with an edge to their voice. The tech, tired from a busy day says, "Sir, you need to calm down. We're slammed right now and doing the best we can. Your prescription will be ready when it's ready. If you keep yelling at me, I'm going to have to ask you to leave."

CALM VERSION:
The technician pauses, letting the moment breathe before responding, and taking a breath himself, lowers his voice. "That's frustrating. Being told it would be ready and finding out it's not. Let's check what's holding it up and get a realistic time. Will you be nearby, or should we call when it's done?"

Social Services – Documentation Requirements

CRISIS VERSION:
After a long bus ride and a security screening, an applicant sets a stack of documents on the desk. The worker flips through them quickly, then pushes the pile back across the desk.
"You should have read the letter more carefully. It clearly states what documents are required. There's nothing I can do without them. You'll have to come back another day."

CALM VERSION:
The worker slows down, spreads the papers out, and points to specific gaps.
"A couple of things might still be missing. Let's check and make sure we're clear about what's needed so we don't make extra work. There may also be a few things that we can start today."

Education – Behavioral Incident

CRISIS VERSION:
A parent sits rigid in the chair, arms crossed tight. The vice principal remains standing; folder tucked under one arm and says, "The rules are the same for everyone. Your daughter made a poor choice and now she's facing the consequences. That's how accountability works."

CALM VERSION:
The vice principal pulls out a chair and places the folder on the desk. "This is upsetting, especially when it involves your child. Let's walk through what happened and then hear your daughter's side. Our goal is helping her move forward."

Retail / Loss Prevention – Receipt Check at Exit

CRISIS VERSION:
A customer slows near the exit at the big box store, receipt still in hand, stiffens, glancing at other shoppers nearby. "I just paid for this. Why are you stopping me?" as the associate steps into their path. The associate crosses their arms slightly and barks, "I need to see your receipt. Everyone gets checked."

CALM VERSION:
The associate shifts a half-step to the side, keeping the exit visible. Voice steady. "That makes sense. It feels personal when it happens at the door." (Brief pause.) "If you want to clear it up right now, the receipt does that. If not, you're free to head out."

Security – Access Control

CRISIS VERSION:
The visitor steps closer to the desk, glancing toward the secured doors behind the officer. The officer

straightens and says, "You can't come in here without photo ID. Those are the rules. I don't make them, I just enforce them. You'll have to leave and come back when you have proper identification."

CALM VERSION:
The officer keeps their stance open and voice level. "We're supposed to see your photo ID to enter. Is there anything with a photo on it, even expired? Who did you say you're here to see? Let's see if the visit can be confirmed."

Corporate HR – Benefits Denial

CRISIS VERSION:
The employee leans forward, paperwork spread across their lap. The HR specialist scrolls through policy language. "Well, if the benefits booklet had been read, you would have known that procedure isn't covered under the plan. Everyone received the same information. I can't override policy just because coverage wasn't understood."

CALM VERSION:
The HR specialist turns the screen slightly away as the conversation slows. "We didn't expect this denial so that creates real stress. Let's look at what is covered and whether there's an appeal or another option."

Law Enforcement – Traffic Stop

CRISIS VERSION:
The driver grips the steering wheel, jaw set. The officer stands square to the window and says, "I pulled you over because you were speeding." When the driver starts to speak, the officer continues, "It's not up for debate. License and registration now, or I'll add failure to comply to the violations."

CALM VERSION:
The officer eases their stance. "Your speed was 52 in a 35. Can we take a look at your license and registration and we'll see where we go from there?"

Medical Clinic – Wait Time

CRISIS VERSION:
A patient checks the clock again, frustration clear. The medical assistant responds without looking up, "You're not the only patient here. Everyone has to wait. The doctor will see you when he gets to you. There's no need to get so worked up about it."

CALM VERSION:
The assistant turns fully toward the patient. "Looks like your wait's gone longer than planned. Let's check and get a real estimate."

Faith Community – Conflict Mediation

CRISIS VERSION:
Voices overlap in the small church office, tension thick. The pastor raises their voice to regain control.

"You both need to calm down and act like adults. This behavior is completely inappropriate in God's house. If you can't work this out maturely, you'll both need to find other places to worship."

CALM VERSION:
The pastor waits for the room to quiet. "This is something that really matters to both of you, so let's slow this down and hear what's most important for each of you."

Practicing Crisis Communication: The Collaborative Exercise

Seeing the difference between crisis language and calm language on the page is one thing. Being able to make that shift in the moment is another. In my training sessions, after we examine those contrasts, we move into practice. Not role-playing, participants often find role-playing uncomfortable and artificial, but collaborative problem-solving.

I present realistic scenarios from various professional contexts and invite participants to work together to figure out the calm response and then keep the conversation going. The goal isn't to find a perfect scripted answer, but to practice the thinking process: What's happening here? What does this person need? What would make this better versus worse?

Let me give a few examples of how this works.

Scenario: The Denied Service Request

Context: Customer service desk at a retail store. A customer is trying to return an item that's outside the return window and doesn't have a receipt.

What the customer says: "This is ridiculous! I spend thousands of dollars here every year and you're telling me you won't take back one defective item because I don't have a little piece of paper? That's the worst customer service I've ever experienced! I want to talk to your manager!"

What would make this worse? What would make this better?

Crisis responses that would escalate:

- "That's our policy and I can't override it."
- "You should have kept your receipt."
- "I don't make the rules."
- "Getting angry isn't going to change anything."

Calm responses that may be effective:

- "This must really get you, especially since you shop here regularly. Without a receipt we can't do a full refund, but let's see what options we do have."
- "It must feel like we're not taking care of you. That's not what we want. Let me get the manager involved. Not to pass you off, but because there's more flexibility at that level."

Scenario: The Missed Deadline

Context: County benefits office. An applicant missed a deadline and their case was closed. They need to reapply.

What the applicant says: "What do you mean I have to start over? I did everything you people told me to do! This isn't fair! I've been trying for three months to get help and now you're telling me I have to start from scratch because of some deadline I didn't even know about?"

What would make this worse? What would make this better?

Crisis responses that would escalate:

- "We sent you multiple notices. You should have read them."
- "The rules are the same for everyone."
- "If you had called us, we could have explained the deadline."
- "I don't make the rules, I just follow them."

Calm responses that may be effective:

- "You must be fed up! Three months of effort and now feeling like you're back at the beginning. Let's see what we can do to make the reapplication process as quick as possible, and make sure you have all the information you need this time."
- "The deadline issue can be incredibly overwhelming, especially if it wasn't clear that that date mattered so much. While we can't undo the closure, what we can do is walk you through the reapplication step by step right now, so we don't lose any more time."
- "This feels like starting over, but you've already gathered most of the documentation, so the second application should be much faster. And now you know the system, which helps. Let's get this done today."

Why This Matters

You might notice a pattern in the calm responses. They don't avoid the problem. They don't give people everything they want. They don't eliminate consequences or override policies. What they do is validate emotion, demonstrate understanding, and find ways to move forward that preserve the person's dignity and restore some sense of agency.

The crisis responses we've examined throughout this chapter all have something in common: they put people on the defensive, dismiss their concerns, or make them feel unheard. The calm responses acknowledge what's real about the person's experience, even when limits exist on what can be done about the problem.

This isn't about being nice or soft. It's about being effective. When someone feels heard, understood, and treated with respect, they're far more likely to accept limitations, follow directions, and work with you to find solutions. When they feel dismissed, controlled, or disrespected, they're far more likely to escalate, resist, and make the situation harder for everyone.

Moving Forward

We've covered a lot in this chapter. We've looked at how we make things worse through our language, our tone, our timing, and our focus. We've seen how each pattern maps to a specific Pillar failure: telling someone to calm down violates Validation, matching their energy violates Regulation, rushing to explain skips Collaboration, removing choices violates Options, and doing all of it with the wrong tone violates Professional Sincerity at its core. We've practiced translating crisis language into calm language. And we've worked through collaborative exercises that mirror real-world encounters.

But knowing what not to do and having some better phrases available still isn't enough. We've already built the observational skills (Chapter 4), watched them work in real encounters (Chapter 5), and prepared for the worst-case scenarios (Chapter 6). Now we need to go deeper into the mechanics: what's happening in the brain and body during escalation, how crisis communication actually works at a neurological level, and why the approaches in this chapter succeed where the old habits fail.

That's where we go next. In Chapter 8 and beyond, we'll look at understanding crisis and communication: what happens in the brain when someone is overwhelmed, why emotion overrides logic, and how the specific tools of crisis communication (active listening, emotional labeling, paraphrasing, and the Behavioral Change Stairway Model) work to reverse that process. Because knowing what not to say is a start, but it's not a strategy. You need to understand why these mistakes hit so hard and why the alternatives work, so that the next time you're standing in front of someone whose world is falling apart, you're not reaching for a script. You're reaching for something real.

Notes

1. The term "amygdala hijack" was coined by Daniel Goleman in *Emotional Intelligence: Why It Can Matter More Than IQ* (New York: Bantam Books, 1995). Goleman described the process by which the amygdala can override the prefrontal cortex during perceived threat, triggering rapid emotional responses before rational thought can intervene.

2. For research on stress-impaired prefrontal cortex function, see Amy F. T. Arnsten, "Stress Signalling Pathways That Impair Prefrontal Cortex Structure and Function," *Nature Reviews Neuroscience* 10, no. 6 (2009): 410–422; see also Goleman, *Emotional Intelligence*.

CHAPTER 8:

UNDERSTANDING CRISIS AND THE POWER OF COMMUNICATION

In the last chapter, we looked at the ways well-intentioned professionals make things worse: telling people to calm down, explaining when they need validation, matching energy instead of managing it, minimizing, dismissing, and using language that sounds like accusation. Every one of those mistakes has something in common. The professional was responding to the situation without understanding what was happening inside the other person. This chapter changes that. To help us better communicate effectively with someone in crisis, we should have a basic understanding of what crisis does to a human being: how it reshapes their thinking, their emotions, their perception, and their capacity to hear anything we say. Once we understand that, the tools we've been building since Chapter 3 may start to make a better kind of sense.

Before we go further, a necessary disclaimer. I am not a mental health professional or a doctor, but I am a training consultant for the New York State Office of Mental Health, where I've contributed to the development of their Fundamental Crisis Intervention Skills for Law Enforcement curriculum, and help teach that across New York State. That work, combined with nearly three decades of encountering and communicating with individuals in crisis, has given me a deep respect for the complexity of what people carry into the encounters we face every day. I am not asking you to diagnose anyone's condition. In many tense situations, there's no time for that anyway, and it isn't your role. But in the majority of encounters that can be slowed down, where communication still has a chance to work, having some understanding of what the other person might be going through, living with, or suffering from can help in ways that matter. It can help you adjust your communication approach, so your words actually land instead of bouncing off a wall of emotion. It can help you recognize that the behavior in front of you isn't personal, even when it feels that way. It can help you understand why someone can't process what you're saying, no matter how clearly you say it. It can help you know when patience matters more than solutions. It can help you avoid the very responses we covered in Chapter 7 that make things worse. And it can help you identify what resources to look for and use, whether that means a family member who has information about the person's history, a doctor or clinician who can provide guidance, or a crisis team that can offer specialized support.

Emotional Distress

Understanding what emotional distress looks like is the first step. Understanding what contributes to it is the next. In FC2C training, we identify four contributing factors that can push someone into a state of emotional distress: mental illness, substance use, medical conditions, and situational stress. These aren't diagnoses. They're categories that help us make sense of what we may be observing so we can adjust our approach accordingly.[1]

The first is mental illness. An exacerbation of a mental health condition can cause a person to be in a state of emotional crisis. This is where assumptions become dangerous, so let me be direct about something: the vast majority of individuals with mental illness aren't violent, and the vast majority of individuals who are violent have no history of mental illness. These are facts, not opinions, and they matter because the moment we equate mental illness with danger, we've already failed at Professional Sincerity before we've said a word.[2]

The second is substance use. Alcohol or other drug use can impact how a person thinks, acts, feels, and interacts with others. Sometimes people under the influence become emotionally distressed, and the combination of impaired judgment and heightened emotion can make encounters unpredictable in ways that have nothing to do with intent.

The third is medical conditions. Symptoms of certain medical conditions can precipitate emotional distress or mimic those of mental illness entirely. A person experiencing a diabetic emergency, a traumatic brain injury, or a seizure disorder may present in ways that look like a behavioral crisis but have a purely physiological origin. This is one of the reasons we observe and we do not assume.

The fourth is situational stress. This is something everyone experiences at one time or another. When a person is confronted with stress that they perceive as overwhelming, they may go into a state of emotional distress. The key word there is "perceive." Stress is both subjective and cumulative. What looks manageable from the outside may be the last pebble in a backpack that has been filling up for years. It comes down to how well or how effective one copes with it.

The Backpack Analogy

Consider the backpack analogy: at the start of your life, you're given a backpack to carry around and collect rocks representing all of your problems. Small problems, like getting stuck in traffic or stubbing your toe, are small pebbles. Bigger problems bring bigger rocks. A death in the family, a divorce, financial problems, job loss. Sooner or later, that backpack fills up, and at some point, it either bursts because of something catastrophic or overflows from the smallest pebble that rolls out because there's simply no more room. That's the moment when a person's coping ability is exceeded, and they lose control.[3]

Individuals in Crisis

When any combination of these four factors overwhelms someone's capacity to cope, we're looking at what's properly called an individual in crisis. An individual in crisis may exhibit symptoms of known, suspected, or perceived mental conditions, including but not limited to mental illness, intellectual or developmental disabilities, or co-occurring conditions such as substance use disorders. It's an extremely broad category, and intentionally so, because it allows us to approach a wide range of encounters with the same foundational respect and the same communication tools. Having an identified condition, or for that matter an unidentified one, doesn't mean a person is necessarily in crisis. It does, however, mean that we should consider it and respond with heightened sensitivity. [4]

How do we determine that someone may be an individual in crisis? Through self-reporting, through information provided by witnesses or family members, through our own observations, or through previous knowledge of the individual. Every one of those sources connects back to the situational awareness skills we built in Chapter 4 and the behavioral observation we practiced in Chapter 5.

When Emotions Override Everything Else

When someone is in a state of emotional distress, all the normal ways people think, feel, and act can become distorted. Stress steals the brain's ability to process clearly. Fear, trauma, anxiety, mental illness, substances: any of these can push a person into a state where their reactions are faster and much less predictable. That's why we prepare our exits, stay situationally aware, and keep others informed, because emotional distress doesn't always look like distress until we're already in the middle of it. By the time we recognize the warning signs, we may already be deep into a deteriorating situation where our options have narrowed considerably.

Emotional distress manifests across multiple dimensions of human functioning and understanding these different manifestations helps us recognize when someone's capacity to cope is slipping away. From a behavioral perspective, the person may act in ways that seem unusual or inappropriate: pacing, withdrawing, invading personal space, or shifting rapidly between cooperation and resistance. Their movements might become erratic or unpredictable. They might fixate on certain objects or repeatedly check exits. These behavioral changes are the body's way of responding to an internal alarm system that's gone into overdrive.

From an emotional standpoint, they may show sudden mood swings that seem disproportionate to the situation at hand. They might display extreme anger or sadness, or conversely, show almost no emotion at all when the situation clearly calls for it, which can feel particularly unsettling to those around them. This emotional volatility or complete shutdown may signal that the person's normal emotional regulation systems have been overwhelmed. From a cognitive perspective, they may appear confused, disoriented, distracted, or lost inside their own thoughts, unable to follow directions or process what's being said. They might repeat themselves, struggle to track the conversation, or fixate on a single detail while missing everything else. Their problem-solving abilities have collapsed, leaving them unable to see options or solutions that might be obvious to someone thinking clearly.

And from a perceptual angle, the person may be experiencing things that aren't there: sights, sounds, or sensations their brain is generating under pressure. Hallucinations and misperceptions become their reality in that moment, and arguing with that reality only deepens their distress. Agreeing with them can be even more unproductive. What they're experiencing feels completely real to them, regardless of what we can observe from the outside.

All of these are human responses to overload. None of them automatically mean danger, but they absolutely mean we need to pay attention and adjust how we communicate. This is where our skills begin to matter. Everything we built in Chapters 4 and 5, the situational awareness, the behavioral observation, the ability to read what's unfolding, feeds directly into what we do next. And the Five Pillars from Chapter 3, especially Regulation and Validation, become the foundation for how we respond. When we can recognize these signs early and respond appropriately, we create opportunities to guide someone back from the edge before their capacity to cope collapses entirely.

What Is a Crisis?

If we're going to communicate effectively with individuals in crisis, if we're going to rely on verbal de-escalation techniques instead of physical force or retreat, we must first understand what's happening inside that person's mind during a crisis. A crisis occurs when someone is no longer able to cope with what's happening with them, or to them. They've slipped off of their normal functioning level because something, whether sudden or building over time, has overwhelmed their ability to think clearly, regulate their emotions, and make calm decisions.

A crisis is a situation where a person's emotions or stress surpass their ability to cope, resulting in impaired decision-making or behavior.[5]

Their thinking becomes impaired, their judgment becomes clouded, and their behavior no longer matches the situation around them. What might appear to us as a solvable problem can feel, to them, like a threat they can't escape. In that internal experience, options disappear. Logic disappears. The world narrows down to whatever emotion has taken control (fear, panic, anger, despair) and every response becomes driven by that feeling instead of clear thought. That's the moment when a problem becomes their crisis, and that's when they need us to step in with calm, patience, and the communication tools that bring emotions down and rationality back up toward a normal functioning level, as safety allows.

The Seesaw of Crisis: Emotionality vs. Rationality

Most of us live our daily lives at or near that normal functioning level. Even in this very moment, every one of us has stress, problems, and challenges lurking in the background of our minds, but we've developed stable and healthy ways to cope with those things. We can still think rationally, solve problems, and manage our emotions. We function despite the weight we carry because we've built the psychological infrastructure to handle normal stress loads. But when something pushes a person beyond what they can handle, that balance collapses.

As emotions rise (fear, anger, confusion, panic) rationality drops. The higher the emotional intensity, the lower the person's capacity to reason, communicate clearly, or follow direction. Picture it like a seesaw: on one side sits emotionality, on the other sits rationality. When emotions shoot up, rational thinking plummets. The brain can't hold both at maximum capacity simultaneously. This isn't a character flaw or a choice. It's basic human neurology. The emotional centers of the brain literally inhibit the functioning of the prefrontal cortex, the area responsible for reasoning, planning, and impulse control.[6]

Our job in those moments is to help restore that balance. Through communication and by applying the Five Pillars, Professional Sincerity, and the G.U.I.D.E. Elements we introduced in Chapter 3, we influence the person's emotional state. We want to help bring those emotions down so their rational thinking can rise again. We become the counterweight on that seesaw, helping shift the balance back toward a place where the person can think, process, and cooperate.

That shift, from overwhelmed and reactive back to grounded and manageable, is where influence happens. It doesn't happen by force. It doesn't happen by demanding compliance. It happens when we help the person regain enough control of themselves to choose cooperation. We create the conditions where their brain can start functioning normally again, where options become visible, and where solutions become possible.

When Time is Not on Our Side: A True Crisis

A crisis is usually temporary. It may last minutes, hours, or days. But while it's happening, it demands immediate attention because safety, wellbeing, or even someone's life may be at stake. Think about the types of encounters where we can't simply slow things down and talk through solutions: a house that's burning with people still inside, an active shooter scenario where people are already injured, or a person behaving in a way that's very likely to cause serious harm to themselves or others if nothing changes. Those are situations where time isn't on our side, and we must act quickly while still doing everything we can to preserve life. These are *true* crises.

Picture an emergency room nurse rushing to a patient room where a woman has just learned her teenage son didn't survive the car accident that brought them both in thirty minutes ago. The mother is screaming, hyperventilating, and has begun striking her own head repeatedly against the wall. Two family members are trying to physically restrain her while she fights them. Her vital signs are spiking dangerously. This isn't a moment for a twenty-minute conversation. This is a moment where the medical team must immediately intervene to protect the mother from harming herself. Sedation may be necessary, physical safety measures must be implemented, and mental health crisis services must be activated. The mother's capacity to cope has completely collapsed in the face of unimaginable trauma. Communication will come, but first, her safety must be secured.

To each individual, their crisis isn't defined by how dramatic the situation looks from the outside; it's defined by the individual's capacity to cope in the moment. When that capacity is overwhelmed, regardless of what caused it, normal functioning breaks down. Communication becomes difficult, rational thought disappears, emotions overwhelm judgment, and instinct takes over. That's when our role shifts. We must recognize the true urgency of the moment and intervene with a combination of safety, influence, and rapid decision-making to prevent the situation from getting worse, or withdraw from the situation entirely.

Crisis or Problem? A Critical Distinction

Now let's look at situations that *feel* like crises to the people experiencing them but don't require urgent tactical intervention: failing an exam or class, breakup with a significant other, bullying, being a victim of a crime, peer pressure, job loss, loss of benefits, loss of housing, inability to afford housing, child and family issues. These life situations, losing a job, losing housing, struggling to afford the basics, relationship breakdowns, academic failure, bullying, victimization, pressure at home or school, they're deeply painful. They can shake someone's confidence and stability. They can strip away control, dignity, and hope.

To the person experiencing them, it may feel like the sky is falling and that they're alone with no way out. These are the kinds of moments that keep people awake at night, that fill every waking thought with fear, shame, or uncertainty about what tomorrow will look like. They're problems that can absolutely *feel* like a crisis from the inside. The emotional experience is real, the suffering is genuine, and the sense of being overwhelmed is completely authentic. But from our professional standpoint, these stressors don't necessarily require an urgent or tactical response. There's usually no immediate threat to life or safety because someone has failed a class or is going through a breakup. The emotional weight is heavy, but there's still time. There's time to talk, to plan. There's time to calm the situation and help the person regain footing. The urgency is emotional, not physical.

Think about a case manager at the Department of Social Services sitting across from a single mother of three who is sobbing uncontrollably. The woman's voice cracks as she explains that her SNAP benefits were reduced due to a paperwork error, and she doesn't know how she'll feed her children this week. She's convinced this is the final blow, that she's failing as a mother, that the system has abandoned her, that there's no way forward. To her, in this moment, it feels like a crisis. Her world is collapsing. The case manager recognizes something essential: this isn't a burning building. There's no imminent physical danger. What this mother needs is someone who can help her see past the emotional storm to the solutions that exist. The case manager speaks calmly: "This sounds incredibly overwhelming right now. Let's take this one step at a time together. There are emergency food resources we can connect you with today, and we're going to fix this paperwork issue." Within minutes, the mother's breathing slows. Her tears begin to ease. She's still scared, but she's no longer drowning. The problem remains, but it's becoming manageable because someone helped her find solid ground and didn't minimize *her* crisis.

This is where our mindset matters. When we encounter someone who is convinced they're in a crisis, pacing, crying, overwhelmed, maybe shouting, maybe frozen, we must remember that we're seeing the world through *their* distress. Their logic circuits are shutting down. Their fear is taking over. And even though the situation is technically a problem with solutions, they can't see any of those solutions in the moment. They're drowning emotionally, and they need someone who can anchor them long enough to take a breath.

When we remain calm, composed, and grounded, when we recognize the difference between a true crisis and a painful problem, we give ourselves the ability to influence the situation instead of being controlled by it. We can be the steady presence that helps someone step back from the edge, lowers the emotional temperature, and brings rational thinking back online. That ability, turning a perceived crisis back into a manageable problem, is what de-escalation is built on. It's also why Regulation, the first of the Five Pillars, starts with us and not with them.

Let's put everything into context by asking a question that matters: do we have a crisis, or do we have a problem? One of the core principles of de-escalation is the concept of time. Specifically, whether we have the time to slow a situation down, influence emotions, and guide behavior before it escalates into a scenario where force, or even deadly force, becomes necessary. Our decision-making in those first few moments is shaped by our ability to determine whether the situation demands immediate action or whether there's room to communicate and calmly resolve what's happening.

At the heart of that decision is the distinction between crises and problems. A crisis demands urgent intervention because safety is at stake. A problem, on the other hand, lacks that urgency. It may be frustrating, inconvenient, or emotionally charged, but no one is in immediate danger. The truth is that many of our encounters aren't crises at all. They're problems. They feel like crises to the people involved, but they don't require a rapid tactical response. They require patience, professionalism, and perspective.

When we allow ourselves to get drawn into someone else's problem emotionally, when we match their frustration or take it personally, we risk making the situation worse and creating unnecessary conflict. Before we let that happen, we can pause, step back, take a slow breath, and remind ourselves that problems have solutions. They don't require us to rush. They don't require us to lose control of our own emotions. They only require that we remain the calmest person in the room. When we maintain that presence, we give ourselves the time we need to influence the moment instead of being consumed by it. We need to look at an individual's crisis as a problem. Because what can we do with a problem? We can help them solve it.

Consider a security officer at a major department store who spots a teenage girl concealing makeup items in her purse. Following protocol, the officer approaches calmly and asks the girl to accompany her to the security office. The moment the door closes, the girl breaks down. She's fifteen, scared, and begins hyperventilating. "My parents are going to kill me. I'm going to jail. My life is over. I can't breathe." To this teenager, her world just ended. The security officer has seen this dozens of times. She knows this isn't a life-threatening emergency. It's a scared kid who made a bad choice and is now overwhelmed by the consequences. Instead of lecturing or rushing to call police, the officer pulls up a chair, sits at the girl's level, and speaks quietly: "Take a breath with me. Good. Again." After a minute, the girl's panic starts to ease. "This feels like the end of the world right now," the officer continues, "but we're going to figure this out together. Your parents will need to be called, but before that happens, help me understand what's going on."

What could have escalated into a traumatic event instead becomes a moment where the officer helps a young person find her footing. The problem, the theft, still needs to be addressed. But by recognizing that time was on her side, the officer transformed a crisis mindset into a collaborative problem-solving conversation.

Even when someone feels overwhelmed and unable to cope, there are usually paths forward, and our role is to help them find those paths by lowering the emotional intensity and restoring their ability to think. But we have to be very careful, because the truth is that *we* can be the ones who turn a problem into a crisis. The wrong tone of voice, a dismissive comment, a rushed command, a lack of patience, unnecessary confrontation, or even just standing too close can send a person further into panic. The moment we escalate emotionally, whether through sarcasm, frustration, or forceful language, we contribute to the collapse of their ability to cope. A problem that could have been solved collaboratively becomes a crisis we now have to control. That's why our professionalism, our emotional regulation, and our communication style matter so much. We aren't just responding to the situation. We're influencing what the situation becomes. This is Professional Sincerity in its most fundamental form: showing up with credibility, consistency, and genuine investment in a better outcome. We can't fix the crisis itself, but many times we can help solve the problem.

Empathy and Legitimacy

So, if we accept that many of the situations we encounter are problems, not true crises, then the question becomes: how do we begin to influence them without making them worse? We gave some examples in Chapter 7, now let's expand on that. The answer isn't speed, authority, or control. It starts with how we show up as human beings in the first moments of the interaction. In Chapter 3, we called this Professional Sincerity: the ethical standard of credibility, consistency, and respect that allows authentic communication even in the worst moments. Before we try to fix anything, before we offer solutions or set boundaries, we have to address the emotional temperature of the room. People who feel overwhelmed aren't refusing to cooperate. They're struggling to cope. If we want time on our side, if we want space to slow things down and guide behavior, we first have to reduce the emotional intensity that's driving the situation. That begins with empathy.

Empathy isn't agreement, and it isn't weakness. It's a deliberate choice to acknowledge what someone is experiencing so their nervous system can settle enough for thinking to return. When we do that well, we reinforce our legitimacy in their eyes, and legitimacy is what allows communication to work at all. This approach is part of maintaining legitimacy, the foundation of trust between us and the people we serve. When someone is overwhelmed and struggling, legitimacy means demonstrating empathy, compassion, and patience in the moment. It means recognizing that their feelings are real to them, even when their reactions seem exaggerated or unreasonable to us. It means labeling the emotions we're seeing so the person feels understood instead of dismissed. And above all, it means treating them the same way we would want a member of our own family to be treated if they were the ones having a hard time: with dignity, respect, and a sincere intention to help. When people feel valued and believed, their defensiveness drops, their fear eases, and their willingness to cooperate rises. That simple shift in how we show up can prevent a problem from becoming a crisis and a crisis from becoming a tragedy.

Simply put, empathy is the ability to understand what someone is feeling without having to feel it yourself.[7]

A church usher notices a man in his thirties sitting alone in a back pew long after the Sunday service has ended. The man is rocking back and forth slightly, hands clasped tightly together, tears streaming down his face. Other volunteers have already left, but the usher approaches slowly, sitting down two seats away, close enough to show presence but far enough to avoid overwhelming the man. "It looks like you're going through something really hard right now," the usher says quietly. No demands. No rush. Just witnessing. The man looks up, startled, then begins to speak in broken sentences. He lost his job three weeks ago. His wife left last week. He hasn't slept in days. He came to church because he didn't know where else to go. To him, everything has fallen apart. The usher doesn't try to fix it all. He doesn't minimize his pain or offer quick platitudes. He simply says, "That sounds incredibly overwhelming. I'm glad you're here. You don't have to be alone in this." He offers to call the church's pastoral care team, connects him with community resources, and most importantly, he sits with him until he feels steady enough to leave.

The usher didn't solve the man's job loss or marital crisis. But by showing up with empathy and patience, he helped him move from complete emotional collapse back to a place where he could begin to think about next steps.

The Currency of Patience

In Chapter 3, we introduced the Power of Two Minutes: the idea that giving someone even a brief window to be heard can fundamentally change the trajectory of an encounter. Here's where that principle meets reality, because patience is one of the most valuable tools we have when dealing with people in crisis, and it's also one of the hardest to maintain. We all come into this work with our own frustration, stress, and fatigue. We listen to the same complaints day after day. We handle the same arguments, the same excuses, the same drama. We all have our own personal problems, our own heavy backpacks, and sometimes we show up already close to our limit. So, when someone else is falling apart in front of us, patience doesn't always come naturally. And I want to be honest with you. I can teach you communication strategies, influence, I can teach you how to recognize what someone is going through. But the one thing I can't give you is time. You're busy. You have multiple cases, multiple clients, multiple fires burning all at once. You're overworked, understaffed, underpaid, and expected to solve problems faster than they can be created. I recognize that and I respect that.

But here's the reality: just a little patience can prevent a situation from spiraling into something dangerous. Most people in these moments don't need you to solve their entire life. They don't need a miracle. They need a chance to release pressure. They need someone to witness their frustration instead of shutting them down. If we give them the space to vent, even when their words are messy or repetitive or feel like a waste of our time, their emotions begin to settle. Their breathing slows. Their thinking becomes clearer.

Imagine a patient access representative at a community health clinic facing an angry man who's been waiting forty-five minutes past his appointment time. He's raising his voice, gesturing wildly, telling the representative how incompetent the whole system is, how nobody cares, how he took time off work for this. Other patients are watching. The representative feels his own frustration rising. He didn't make him wait, he's not a doctor, and honestly, he's heard this complaint five times already today. But he pauses. Takes a breath. And instead of defending or dismissing, he says: "You're absolutely right to be frustrated. Forty-five minutes is a long time to wait when you've arranged your whole day around being here. I can hear how stressful this is for you." The man stops mid-sentence. His shoulders drop slightly. "Yeah," he says, quieter now. "Yeah, it is." That's it. Thirty seconds of acknowledgment. The rep didn't fix the wait time. He didn't change the schedule. But he gave him a moment to be heard, and it changed everything. Two minutes later, the patient is sitting calmly in the waiting area because someone finally saw his frustration as valid.

If you can give them thirty extra seconds, great. If you can give them a full minute, even better. But if you can give them two minutes, two uninterrupted minutes to talk, to express emotion, to say what they need to say, that's the gold standard. Even if you're ultimately going to hand them off to someone else. Even if you know there's nothing more you can personally do for them. Those two minutes may be the difference between an escalation and a breakthrough. Patience isn't just kindness. It's tactical. It buys you space. It buys you safety. And it helps them regain enough control to meet you in a better place.

Moving Forward

Next, we put everything so far into practice. We'll take the tools we've been building, Professional Sincerity, the Five Pillars, and G.U.I.D.E., and apply them to the mechanics of crisis communication: how we use our voice, how we listen, how we set boundaries, and how we move someone from crisis back toward a place where problem-solving becomes possible.

Notes

1. These four categories are drawn from crisis intervention training frameworks used across law enforcement, mental health, and social services, including Crisis Intervention Team (CIT) curricula and the New York State Office of Mental Health's Fundamental Crisis Intervention Skills for Law Enforcement program. They are adapted here as part of the FC2C training methodology.

2. See Swanson et al., "Violence and Psychiatric Disorder in the Community: Evidence from the Epidemiologic Catchment Area Surveys," *Hospital and Community Psychiatry* 41, no. 7 (1990): 761–770; Heather Stuart, "Violence and Mental Illness: An Overview," *World Psychiatry* 2, no. 2 (2003): 121–124. Stuart concludes that "mental disorders are neither necessary nor sufficient causes of violence" and that the major determinants of violence remain sociodemographic and economic factors.

3. The backpack analogy is a widely used teaching metaphor in crisis intervention education and training. Variations of it appear across CIT curricula, counseling programs, and stress management instruction. The version presented here is adapted for FC2C training.

4. Chicago Police Department, Special Order S04-20, "Recognizing and Responding to Individuals in Crisis" (Chicago: CPD, 2023), issued pursuant to *Illinois v. City of Chicago*, No. 17-cv-6260 (N.D. Ill. Jan. 31, 2019), https://www.chicagopolice.org/policy-review/recognizing-and-responding-to-individuals-in-crisis-draft-directives/.

5. This working definition draws on Caplan's foundational crisis theory, which describes crisis as a state in which an individual's customary problem-solving strategies are overwhelmed, resulting in disrupted equilibrium and impaired functioning. See Caplan, *Principles of Preventive Psychiatry* (New York: Basic Books, 1964). The phrasing used here is the FC2C adaptation of this concept.

6. On the reciprocal inhibition between emotional arousal and prefrontal cortex function, see Goleman, *Emotional Intelligence*; Arnsten, "Stress Signalling Pathways That Impair Prefrontal Cortex Structure and Function," *Nature Reviews Neuroscience* 10, no. 6 (2009): 410–422.

7. This is the FC2C working definition, distinguishing empathy from sympathy. Empathy involves cognitive understanding of another person's emotional state without requiring the observer to share in or absorb that emotion.

CHAPTER 9:

COMMUNICATION IN PRACTICE: PROFESSIONAL SINCERITY AND G.U.I.D.E. IN ACTION

In the last chapter, we explored what crisis does to a human being; how emotional distress reshapes perception, narrows thinking, hijacks rationality, and leaves people operating from the survival centers of the brain rather than the decision-making parts. We examined the seesaw between emotionality and rationality and distinguished true crises from problems that feel like crises. And we established that empathy, legitimacy, and patience aren't soft skills or luxuries. They're the entry points for influence.

All that understanding matters, but understanding alone doesn't de-escalate anyone. Knowing why someone is upset doesn't calm them down. We still need to do something. We still need to communicate in a way that reduces emotional intensity, builds trust, and opens the door to cooperation. We've discussed bits of how to validate feelings and to let someone vent but now let's put it all together.

This chapter is where we do that. Everything we've built since Chapter 3, the Five Pillars, Professional Sincerity, and G.U.I.D.E., comes together here as a working system. Not as theory or as a checklist to memorize, but as a living, adaptable framework you can apply under pressure, in the heat of the moment, when the person in front of you is angry, afraid, confused, or hostile.

We're going to go deep into the mechanics of using your voice, because the way something is said is essential. We're going to give Professional Sincerity the depth it deserves, because it's the ethical standard that makes everything else work. We're going to walk through G.U.I.D.E. as the operational model that turns credibility into direction. And we're going to connect boundaries, active listening, and emotional regulation to the framework so you can see how all these pieces fit together in real encounters.

That's what this chapter is built around: the practical application of everything we've developed, in the real conditions where it matters most.

Communication: The Heart of De-Escalation

Communication isn't just part of the de-escalation process. It's at the heart of it. There are many ways to reach a de-escalated outcome, heavily influenced by the actions of the person you're encountering, and sometimes the safest choice is to disengage, create distance, or remove yourself from the situation entirely. But when we can communicate effectively, it becomes our most powerful tool for fostering the conditions needed for a calm resolution. Every word, every choice of tone, every moment of patience helps reduce emotional intensity and brings the person closer to a state where they can think instead of react. Communication is what turns chaos into cooperation, crisis to calm.

Effective communication in a crisis also serves as our primary intelligence-gathering tool. When a person speaks, they give us insight into their motivations, their fears, their needs, and their intentions. The more they share, the more we can listen for the hooks and the barbs, the emotional words and themes that reveal what matters most to them and what may be driving the crisis. When we identify those hooks and barbs, we can better understand what outcome they might accept and how to influence the direction of the conversation.

We want the other person talking. When they're talking, chances are they aren't hurting you, themselves, or someone else.

Communication is also a tool for reading intent. We've talked about hostile intent, recognizing when someone is preparing for aggression. How someone speaks, the changes in their tone, their fixation on certain topics or people, and how their body responds while speaking can all give us early warning signs. By listening and observing, we can identify risk and act before the situation becomes dangerous.

Through communication, we make informed decisions. We're constantly evaluating whether we can safely continue the conversation in its current form or whether the situation requires a shift in strategy. We may need to call for additional resources, reposition ourselves to maintain safety, create distance, or even leave. Those decisions are guided not by guesswork, but by the information we gather through conversation and observation.

And ultimately, communication gives us influence. When someone feels heard, understood, and respected, they're far more willing to work with us. Cooperation becomes possible. We can guide them toward safer behavior, give them options, and move toward a resolution that protects everyone involved. Influence doesn't come from controlling the person. It comes from connecting with them. Communication is how we earn that connection.[1]

If we want safer encounters, if we want to reduce risk, reduce force, and resolve more situations peacefully, communication is the tool that helps get us there. It's the anchor, the bridge, and the lever that moves the encounter from crisis to calm.

Your Voice Is Your Number One Tool

Our voice is the tool we use more than anything else. Long before we set boundaries, offer options, or take any physical action including leaving a situation, we communicate through speech. And the way we say something can be far more powerful, and far more dangerous, than the actual words coming out of our mouth. Tone, volume, pacing, and emphasis all communicate attitude, and attitude is what people react to first.

When someone is in emotional distress, their brain is operating in survival mode. The emotional centers have taken over and impulse control is impaired. In this state, the person isn't processing our words the way they would in a calm conversation. Their responses become unpredictable. Some may scan for threats, reading our tone, our body language, our facial expression, and making split-second decisions about whether we're safe or dangerous. Others may shut down entirely, unable to hear or respond to anything we say. Others may run, lash out, or react in ways that have nothing to do with us and everything to do with a nervous system that has been pushed past its ability to cope. What they're almost never doing is thinking clearly. That's why how we show up in that moment matters so much, because we may be the only stable point in an environment their brain has decided is threatening.

Our voice may be the first signal they receive. It tells them everything they need to know about our attitude and our intentions before they've even processed the meaning of our words. That's why the way something is said can be many times more important than what is said.[2]

Tone: The Attitude Behind Your Words

Tone is often the very first thing a person responds to, even before they understand the words we're saying. It communicates intention. It tells the other person whether we're angry, annoyed, impatient, sarcastic, dismissive, or genuinely there to help. Someone in crisis may already be scanning the environment for danger, and if our tone even slightly suggests that we're frustrated or fed up, they will immediately interpret that as a threat.

Their emotional brain reacts long before their rational brain can assess the situation. This is why even neutral words delivered with a sharp, clipped, or commanding tone can escalate a moment faster than shouting ever could. Tone must match our goal: steady, calm, and grounded, the sound of someone who is in control of themselves and therefore able to help someone else regain that control. When our tone demonstrates respect and patience, it becomes a powerful signal of safety, and safety is the first step toward influence.

Think about your own family. Your spouse, your kids, your parents. They know when you're irritated before you say a single sentence. They hear it in your voice. They see it in your posture. People in crisis are even more attuned to this because their survival instincts are heightened. They're watching and listening for any sign that we're annoyed, overwhelmed, or dismissive. And if they pick up on that, their defenses go up, their emotions intensify, and cooperation becomes much harder.

Let's be specific about what tone actually is. It isn't just volume. It's the attitude our voice conveys, the subtle emotional coloring that tells the other person how we feel about them and the situation. A sharp, clipped tone tells them they're an inconvenience. A singsong, overly sweet tone tells them we're being fake. A flat, monotone delivery tells them we couldn't care less about what happens to them. But a steady, warm, grounded tone tells them we're present, we're listening, and we're going to work through this together.

Consider a phone call to an auto insurance claims office. A man has just picked up his car from the shop after a fender bender and is staring at a $3,000 repair bill he assumed his policy would cover. When the claims representative answers, the man is already frustrated: he has been on hold for twenty minutes, transferred twice, and now he is hearing for the first time that his claim has been denied because the damage falls below his deductible. The representative has delivered this same explanation dozens of times this week. She's behind on callbacks. Her instinct is to get through the call efficiently: "Your deductible is $2,500, and the approved estimate came in at $2,400, so the claim doesn't meet the threshold. You can file an appeal if you'd like, but I want to be upfront with you about where it stands."

Technically, those words aren't wrong. They're clear, they're factual, and they even offer a next step. But delivered with a rushed, flat tone, the kind that says this call is one of fifty and she is already thinking about the next one, the man hears something entirely different: your problem is routine, your frustration is inconvenient, and I am trying to get you off this phone. His frustration turns to anger. He starts demanding a supervisor. His voice gets louder. The representative feels her own tension rising. What started as a claims question is becoming a hostile call.

Now imagine those same words delivered with a different tone. Her pace slows. Her voice warms. She pauses briefly after the numbers to let them land instead of plowing through to the next sentence. The information hasn't changed. The policy hasn't changed. But the man hears something different this time: someone who recognizes that $3,000 out of pocket isn't a small thing, someone who isn't rushing to get rid of him, someone who is being straight with him because she respects him enough to be honest. He's still unhappy. But the emotional intensity drops just enough that the conversation stays productive instead of adversarial.

That's the power of tone. It's not manipulation, it's showing through your voice that you see the person, you recognize their struggle, and you're there to help, not to argue.

Inflection: The Meaning Behind Your Words

The inflection of our voice is also critical. Inflection is the rise and fall of our voice, the melody of how we speak. When we raise the pitch at the end of a sentence, we can turn a statement into a question without meaning to. That creates uncertainty, undermines confidence, and makes it sound like we don't know what we're doing. Conversely, if we flatten our inflection when asking a question, the person may hear it as a command and react defensively. We have to match our vocal inflection to our intention so the meaning is clear and so we don't accidentally escalate an already unstable moment.

Enunciation and emphasis matter as well. How we shape each word can change the meaning entirely. Here's a classic example: Mary had a little lamb. We would normally look at that sentence from a nursery rhyme and see five words, one simple sentence, one meaning. But think about how we say it. How we emphasize and articulate each word. We can quickly start to give it five different meanings.

If we emphasize "Mary," it sounds like Mary had one, not Jeff. If we emphasize "had," it suggests she doesn't anymore. If we emphasize "a," it means she only has one. If we emphasize "little," now size is the issue. If we emphasize "lamb," maybe we're contrasting it with a puppy. Same sentence. Completely different meanings based solely on which word we choose to highlight.

When someone is in crisis, their brain is already struggling to interpret the world around them. If we change the meaning with poor emphasis or sloppy enunciation, we can accidentally send a message that increases fear or confusion. You might think you're asking a helpful question, but if your inflection is wrong, they hear it as criticism or accusation.

Here's a real-world example. A social services case manager is meeting with a client who missed three appointments. The case manager wants to understand what's happening, so she asks: "Why didn't you come to your appointments?" Same seven words. But depending on where she places the emphasis, the client will hear two completely different messages.

If she hits the word "didn't" hard, with a flat, downward tone, "Why *didn't* you come to your appointments," it lands as an accusation. The client hears: You're irresponsible. They get defensive. They shut down.

But if she leads with a softer emphasis on "why" and lets her voice rise slightly at the end, "*Why* didn't you come to your appointments?" it becomes a genuine question. The client hears: I want to understand what happened. Now they're more likely to open up.

We don't want to be fake; we want to be intentional. People pick up on that. We're using our voice to signal that we're asking out of curiosity and concern, not judgment.

Rate and Pacing: Slowing Down the Moment

Our pacing, the rate at which we speak, is a very underestimated part of communication. When emotions are high and adrenaline is flowing, our speech naturally speeds up. That rush can feel like pressure, and pressure fuels panic. We want the opposite. We want to slow the moment down. When we slow our speech, we slow the encounter which may slow the person's breathing and thinking. Like a good barbecue, low and slow, we take our time. We think about what we're saying. We deliver our message with calm, controlled confidence. That pacing helps the other person mirror our emotional state instead of pulling us into theirs.[3]

Picture a teacher managing a student who is escalating in the classroom. The student is pacing, voice raised, refusing to sit down. Other students are watching. The teacher feels the pressure to resolve this quickly before it disrupts the entire class. Her instinct is to speak quickly and firmly: "You need to sit down right now. I'm not going to ask you again."

Fast speech. Clipped tone. The student hears a threat, their brain registers escalation, and the situation gets worse.

Now imagine the same teacher with FC2C training. She slows everything down, takes a breath, lowers her voice slightly and speaks slowly, deliberately: "Hey, you're really upset right now. That's okay. Let's take a minute. You don't have to sit down this second. But I do need you to help me out here. What's going on?"

Slow speech. Calm tone. The student's brain registers something different: safety. Not immediate threat. There's space and time. The pacing itself de-escalates because it communicates that the teacher isn't panicking, which means maybe the situation isn't as dire as it feels. That shift, from urgent to steady, is often the turning point.

Our voice isn't just a way to communicate information. It's the primary instrument we use to influence emotion and behavior. When we control our voice, that's part of our self-regulation, which helps us influence the outcome of the encounter. When we lose control of our voice, we lose control of the outcome. We have to project sincerity, or no one will acquiesce to a behavioral change. And that brings us to the concept that ties everything in this chapter together.

Professional Sincerity: The Ethical Standard of Influence, Credibility, and Respect

Sincerity is the core of trust. It's the belief the other person forms about whether we're genuinely here to help or just going through the motions. People can feel insincerity instantly. They see it in our face, hear it in our tone, and pick it up in the way we rush past their concerns. And when they sense we don't truly care, they shut down cooperation because they don't feel safe being influenced by someone who isn't invested in their well-being. Influence requires permission, and sincerity is how we earn that permission.

That's why we take sincerity even further in this work. Professional Sincerity is the professional behavior we display when it matters most, particularly when emotions are high and the situation feels unpredictable. It starts with how we sound, long before it's ever understood through the words we choose. It combines authenticity with strategic communication in the high-stakes environments encountered by professionals in people-oriented roles. While everyday sincerity implies deep personal connection or emotional investment,

Professional Sincerity is more nuanced. It's grounded in genuine communication, alignment between words and actions, and a commitment to ethical standards. In a professional context, especially in roles that involve managing conflict or crisis, sincerity takes on a functional dimension.

In those moments, people aren't evaluating our intentions, résumés, or training certificates. They're evaluating our presence. They're making rapid, instinctive judgments: "Do I trust you? Do you respect me? Are you going to make things better, or are you going to make things worse?" Their brain decides in a fraction of a second whether we're a credible and safe person to engage with. That decision happens before logic, before reasoning, and long before cooperation takes place, which is why Professional Sincerity becomes the foundation for influence. Without it, our expertise, our instructions, and even our best intentions often fall flat.

The chain works like this: credibility comes first. When credibility is present, trust becomes possible. When trust opens the door, cooperation is now an option. Cooperation leads directly to increased safety, for us, for our colleagues, and for the very person whose behavior is challenging. That entire chain depends on how we show up in the first moments of contact. We can't wait for things to calm down. We must be the reason the interaction begins to calm.

The Five Principles of Professional Sincerity

Professional Sincerity is built on five observable principles, each working together to communicate that we're trustworthy, capable, and committed to a fair and safe solution. These five principles define what Professional Sincerity looks, sounds, and feels like in the real world. They're intentional behaviors, not emotions and not internal beliefs. They are: Trust and Credibility, Authentic Presentation, Purposeful Communication, Ethical Influence, and Boundaries and Safety.

Trust and Credibility are earned not in what we say but in what we consistently demonstrate. Credibility is a professional currency. It grows slowly and can be lost in a single moment of sarcasm, condescension, inconsistency, or dismissal.

Authentic Presentation is about showing up as a real person, not a scripted robot or an uncaring authority figure. When our words don't match our tone and behavior, people instinctively distrust everything that follows.

Purposeful Communication means every word we choose, and the way we choose to say it, is designed to move the situation toward a safer outcome. We aren't trying to win. We're trying to resolve.

Ethical Influence means we align our actions with what's honorable, fair, and transparent. No trickery, no hidden motives, no false promises. If we mislead someone, even with the best of intentions, trust is destroyed and resistance skyrockets.

Boundaries and Safety serve as the framework that protects both people and the process. When boundaries are predictable, people feel less fear and more fairness. We protect others by providing clarity, and we protect ourselves by upholding it.

You may have noticed that some of the Five Principles overlap with the Five Pillars and the Five Elements of G.U.I.D.E.. That's by design. Validation appears as a Pillar and shows up again in how we practice empathic engagement. Boundaries live in the Pillars and also in how we maintain ethical limits on influence. The frameworks aren't isolated systems running on parallel tracks. They're interconnected layers of the same philosophy, each reinforcing the others from a different angle. The Pillars tell us what to prioritize. The Principles tell us how to show up. The Elements of G.U.I.D.E. tell us how to move through the encounter. When they overlap, it's because many of the truths about effective crisis communication are important enough to appear in every frame.

Together, these five principles form a behavioral profile that communicates competence, fairness, and respect. They're not internal attitudes. They're visible choices. A person watching us should be able to say, "I may not like the situation, but I can tell this person is trying to help and will treat me decently." That's the essence of Professional Sincerity.

Here's what Professional Sincerity looks like when the stakes are at their highest, not in a de-escalation setting, but in a criminal investigation, one of thousands I worked on over my career. Both environments share the same truth: dealing with a person in crisis.

In December of 2014, while assigned as an Investigator in the New York State Police Troop G Major Crimes Unit, I responded with a county sheriff's office to a reported kidnapping in a very rural, small town. An eight-year-old boy had supposedly been taken from the front steps of his home by someone wearing a black ski mask and driving a black van. As the investigation progressed, the person who had reported the kidnapping began to change her story. Eventually, during an interview with a deputy and me, she said, "I don't remember what he did that set me off, but I grabbed him by the neck..." and then described, in graphic detail, what she had done to him. His body had already been found, though she didn't know that at the time.

When I recount this case in training, I often ask: why would she confess? Why would someone reveal something that would ultimately result in spending the rest of her life in prison? The most common answer I receive is guilt. Perhaps. But guilt alone doesn't explain cooperation of that magnitude.

What allowed that conversation to move forward was Professional Sincerity. Not a script or a trick.

Did we like her? No. She sure wasn't our friend. We certainly didn't agree with her actions or excuse what she had done. But we treated her with respect. We listened. Her *emotional* experience was acknowledged without validating or condoning her *behavior*. There was no deception involved, no false promises, no manufactured rapport. The interaction was grounded in influence rather than manipulation.

Influence generated by validating her emotions.

In that interview, the emotions behind her actions were acknowledged. The actions themselves weren't excused. We didn't say, "I don't blame you, I would have done the same thing." We did say, in substance, that she must have felt overwhelmed and didn't know how to handle what she was experiencing. "I don't blame you for *feeling* that way." People are entitled to their emotions, no matter what they may be. They aren't entitled to harm others because of them. Recognizing that difference allows professionals to validate without compromising accountability.

That's Professional Sincerity in practice.

Strategic Detachment

To stay professional in these difficult moments, we utilize strategic detachment, which helps us avoid taking the other person's emotion personally. Their fear or frustration is almost always about their situation, not about us as individuals. When we internalize the emotion aimed at us, we tend to respond impulsively. When we recognize that the emotion isn't about us, we respond with skill. Strategic detachment gives us the space to lead and the leverage to de-escalate.

When I was an investigator, there were many times where I sat across from a murderer or a child molester and I allowed them to cry on my shoulder or gave them a hug. I went home wanting to jump in the shower right away and burn my suit. It was Professional Sincerity that allowed me to strategically detach myself from that situation, from that individual, and from the horrific things that they did, in order to bring about the behavioral change that I desired. That required separating my personal feelings from my professional responsibility. It's not easy. It never is. But it works.

And that's why, when you look back at the earlier examples, the pattern becomes clear: the patient's pain is real even if their behavior is unacceptable; the client's situation deserves understanding even if their honesty is questionable; the parent's care is genuine even if their approach is problematic; and even a person who has committed the unthinkable still has emotions that can be acknowledged without excusing what they've done. Professional Sincerity focuses on the part that's true and uses it to lead.

Ethical Influence vs. Manipulation

Professional Sincerity draws a hard line between influence and manipulation, and that line isn't just ethical. It's tactical. Manipulation attempts to control through distortion or pressure, and while it may momentarily force a direction, the long-term effect is resentment, defiance, or complete disengagement. Deceit may produce temporary compliance, but it destroys credibility the moment it's discovered, and once credibility is gone, cooperation becomes significantly harder to restore. Influence, by contrast, is rooted in respect. It seeks to align the person's needs with the path toward a safer outcome. Influence grows trust, which strengthens cooperation, which improves safety. Manipulation shortcuts that process and nearly always leads to increased resistance and future conflict.

The distinction is concrete, and it often comes down to a single word. Deceit is the use of lies, omission, or misrepresentation to control or trick someone into an action or belief. It's self-serving and it results in the collapse of credibility. An example of deceit in an encounter would be condoning the behavior: "I would have done that too. I don't blame you for doing it."

Influence, on the other hand, is the use of trust, communication, empathy, and logic to guide someone toward a desired outcome. It's collaborative and it leads to cooperation, informed consent, and sustainable change. An example of ethical influence in the same encounter, just like I mentioned before: "You must have felt very upset. I don't blame you for *feeling* that way."

See the difference? The first statement condones the action. It crosses a professional and ethical line by telling the person their behavior was acceptable. The second statement validates the emotion without approving the behavior. It acknowledges the person's experience without endorsing what they did. That single word change, from "doing" to "feeling," is the line between deceit and influence, between manipulation and professionalism.

Validation and Understanding

This is why validation matters so much. People instinctively defend their emotional experience, even when the facts aren't in their favor, because their feelings represent their reality in that moment. When those feelings are dismissed, minimized, or debated, the brain interprets that as a threat to identity or dignity, triggering a rise in defensiveness and emotion. When we validate the emotion, not the behavior, the brain interprets that as safety. That sense of safety lowers defensive posture and makes cooperation more likely.

Validation sounds like "This must really mean a lot to you," or "That sounds like a difficult situation." These statements don't give in to demands or excuse negative behavior. They simply communicate that we're listening and that their concerns matter enough to be recognized. When people feel understood, they're more willing to understand in return. When they feel respected, they're more open to respecting the process and the boundaries we set. Validation and understanding are what transform conflict from a personal battle into a problem-solving conversation.

What Professional Sincerity Does Not Require

It's equally important to clarify what Professional Sincerity doesn't require. It doesn't require agreement or liking someone. It doesn't require approving of their choices, sympathizing with their actions, or excusing behavior that violates rules or safety. We can disagree completely with someone's behavior while still recognizing their emotional state and communicating respectfully. We separate the person's humanity from their behavior, supporting the former while managing the latter. As in the case above, we can validate a feeling without validating the action. We simply need to communicate in a way that keeps influence available.

Let me be clear: Professional Sincerity doesn't mean you have to like or even care about the person you're dealing with. Now, I get that that sounds harsh. We must treat people equally and compassionately and do our jobs to the best of our ability for *everyone*, but outside of normal human compassion and not wanting something bad to happen to someone else, we really don't have to care. We often don't remember people's names, circumstances, and don't form friendships or intimate relationships with people we serve and don't follow up most times after an encounter.

Professional Sincerity means you must communicate in a way that feels sincere to them. If you don't come across as genuinely caring, your ability to influence their behavior is diminished. Maintaining Professional Sincerity is essential to defusing tensions and achieving positive outcomes, whether you're handling a customer service complaint, a high-stress confrontation, or even a hostage negotiation.

Boundaries: Where Professional Sincerity Meets Safety...Again

Professional Sincerity also has a protective side. It allows us to stay empathetic while still expecting reasonable behavior in return. That's where boundaries become essential. We've discussed them earlier in this book, but they deserve a closer look in the context of real-time communication.

Boundaries aren't walls. They're lanes that help us keep the interaction safe and productive. They reduce uncertainty, which is calming for people in distress, because clarity helps stabilize emotion. Boundaries communicate what happens when behavior stays within the lane and what happens when it drifts outside it. And importantly, they show the person that their behavior has influence, that they can help move the situation forward by making better choices.

Boundaries protect dignity on both sides. They allow us to stay compassionate without being pushed into chaos or disrespect. They define what we can participate in and what we can't, and we communicate those limits in a way that preserves the relationship rather than tearing it down. When boundaries are done well, the person feels respected, not punished. Guided, not controlled. Included, not dismissed.

Boundaries must be behavior-focused, not personality-focused. We aren't judging the person. We're shaping the moment. There's a simple structure that makes boundaries clear and effective: affirm the goal, state the limit, offer a path forward. It sounds like this: "I want to help, but not like this, here's how we continue." That formula accomplishes three things simultaneously. It reaffirms our commitment to helping, which preserves rapport. It names the specific behavior that needs to change, which gives the person clarity. And it provides a constructive alternative, which gives them a way forward without losing face. And remember, "I" statements are effective and appropriate in setting boundaries.

Non-Verbal Boundaries

Non-verbal boundaries happen first, because our body language always speaks before our mouth does. Stepping back even slightly can reduce tension. Turning to a slight angle reduces a sense of confrontation. Keeping your shoulders relaxed and your hands visible signals safety without giving up authority. You're sending the message: "I'm calm, and you can be too."

Verbal Boundaries

Then we support those non-verbal boundaries with well-crafted verbal boundaries that focus on behavior, not blame. We validate what the person feels, then clearly explain what keeps the conversation productive. We avoid threats, we avoid judgments, and we absolutely avoid escalating statements like "Calm down." What we do instead is provide a path forward that still gives them choice.

Consider an example where someone keeps interrupting or showing signs of verbal escalation. The boundary might sound like: "I want to understand, and I will. Let me finish this thought first, then I'll listen to your response." Notice how we reinforce cooperation without shame or threat, keeping momentum toward the shared goal.

Or consider a more aggressive encounter where someone is yelling, cursing, or trying to intimidate in a public-facing role. The boundary might be: "I'm here to help. I can do that, but only if we talk respectfully." That's Professional Sincerity with guardrails. Supportive tone, clear condition, safety and dignity protected for everyone.

When Boundaries Become the Priority

There are specific situations where boundaries shift from a communication tool to a safety imperative. When safety is immediately threatened, when someone is displaying pre-attack indicators, when the situation is seconds away from becoming physical, this isn't the time for options. Clear direction is appropriate: "Stop. Step back. Don't touch that." Your boundary protects everyone present, including the person who is escalating.

When the behavior violates non-negotiable rules, when someone is harassing other people, damaging property, or creating a genuinely unsafe environment, you don't offer them options about whether to stop.

You tell them firmly that the behavior stops now. You might offer options about what happens next, but the boundary itself isn't negotiable.

And sometimes, the person is so dysregulated that choices overwhelm them further. You see this with severe panic attacks, with certain trauma responses, with extreme distress. In those moments, gentle directive language like "Let's sit down together" works better than options because you're reducing cognitive load rather than adding to it.

Many people do this backward. They lead with boundaries and authority because it feels more efficient, and they only try options after resistance has already built up. But resistance is much harder to overcome than prevention. When you start with options in situations where options are appropriate, you build cooperation from the beginning. When you save boundaries for moments that genuinely require them, they carry more weight and meet less resistance.

G.U.I.D.E.: From Influence to Direction

Everything we've talked about up to this point, tone, patience, empathy, listening. Professional Sincerity. It's how we show a person that we see them, that we respect them, and that we're there to help, not harm. Professional Sincerity opens the door. G.U.I.D.E. is what moves us through it.

Professional Sincerity focuses on the person. G.U.I.D.E. focuses on the problem. Both are necessary, and both must work together. If we stay stuck on the problem without keeping the person engaged, we lose rapport and increase risk. If we focus only on the person without guiding a solution, we prolong the crisis and allow emotions to rise again. We first stabilize the emotions, even if only by ten percent, and that's our window to begin guiding safer choices. Professional Sincerity makes the encounter human. G.U.I.D.E. makes the encounter successful.

G.U.I.D.E. stands for five elements: **G**round Yourself, **U**nderstand Emotion, **I**dentify Shared Goal, **D**irect the Interaction, and **E**nsure Safety and Support. These elements aren't linear steps that we check off in order. They function more like adaptable gear. We select the element that meets the need of the moment, and if the interaction shifts, which they often do, we shift with it. G.U.I.D.E. is built to be dynamic because the situations we face are dynamic. Emotions change fast, and we return to whichever element protects influence right now.

G: Ground Yourself

Grounding begins with controlling our own presence to maintain influence. When tension increases, the pressure to respond instinctively rises with it. The other person's urgency, blame, fear, or disrespect can quickly pull us into a reactive posture. Grounding interrupts that pull. It's a conscious choice to project calm, stability, and confidence so that we don't become a second source of escalation.

Grounding is both physical and internal. Physically, we manage our pace, our stance, our voice level, and our facial expression. We make sure our hands are visible, our posture is balanced, and our breathing is controlled. These are the signals the human brain uses to assess safety. Internally, grounding is a reminder that their emotion isn't about us personally, it's about their experience and perception of the moment. The more we detach from personal offense, the more we're able to influence the outcome.

It begins with the approach. The person comes to you, you go to them, it doesn't matter. This is the opening of the encounter, and it often sets the stage for everything to follow. Before we say anything, our body language has already delivered a message. Standing tall with shoulders back and an open posture communicates confidence and authority, while a stable stance grounded in the environment shows we're secure and in control of ourselves. Steady, appropriate eye contact signals attention without aggression, and controlled gestures reinforce thoughtfulness rather than nervous energy.

I typically initiate my approach with someone using steady eye contact, a genuine smile, and a small nod that acknowledges their presence and humanity. My hands are held out in front of me with my palms open. That posture communicates two important things at the same time: first, that I am not a threat, and second, that I am open to communication and willing to listen. Open palms are a universal signal of cooperation. They show that I am not hiding anything, and they help the other person feel a little safer just by seeing that. At the same time, this position isn't passive. It lets me keep my hands ready and available if I need to react. It invites connection and conversation while also giving me a safe, prepared posture. It's Professional Sincerity in action: calm communication on the outside, tactical readiness underneath.

Then I speak. My opening line is almost always the same: 'Hey, I'm Jeff, what's going on?' It sounds simple, and it is. That's the point. I lead with my first name because it humanizes me immediately. I learned this the hard way early in my state police career.

It was so long ago that I don't even remember the kind of call or encounter it came from, but I remember the words and the lesson very well. Someone asked me my name, and I responded, "Trooper Scholz." Appropriate, had it been left at that. Then, the person asked me what my first name was, and I said, "Trooper." It didn't go over well, and it shouldn't have. It was rude, unprofessional, and I was lucky that the person, annoyed as they were didn't make a complaint. Even worse though as I look back on it now, I probably damaged their perception of police by being a wiseguy.

I was ultimately embarrassed by my behavior, and it made me realize that I was never going to make connections with people like that. I started using my first name whenever I could. Unless in a very official capacity, like in court, I tried to stay away from "Trooper Scholz," and just became "Jeff." I mean, why not? They already knew I was the police. Big hat, gun belt, purple tie. Why not be just Jeff?

I'm not a badge, a title, or an authority figure. I'm Jeff. That one word closes distance. It tells the person they're dealing with a human being, not a system. It became my opening line in the vast majority of my encounters. "Hey, I'm Jeff, what's going on?" Then I follow it with an open-ended question designed to do one thing: get them talking. Not 'Are you okay?' which they can shut down with a yes or no. Not 'What's your problem?' which puts them on the defensive. Just 'What's going on?' It's an invitation to tell their story, and the moment they start talking, I'm gathering information, reading emotion, and building the connection I need to influence what happens next.

I'll say it again, the more they talk, the less likely it is that they're hurting you, themselves, or someone else.

Our bodies broadcast stress long before our words reveal it. Controlled breathing helps suppress adrenaline and prevents visible signs of anxiety such as shaking hands, flushed skin, or trembling voice. A neutral but attentive facial expression shows engagement without judgment. If we start to feel overwhelmed, taking one calm, intentional pause is far more professional than pushing forward while visibly losing composure.

But grounding isn't just about how we appear to the other person. It's also about managing what's happening inside us. Here's the part of this work that traditional programs almost never address: what do you do when you're the one who is escalating emotionally? When your heart is pounding, when you're frustrated, when you're scared, when you're angry because this is the fifth time today you've dealt with someone yelling at you?

You're human. You've got your own stress, your own limits, your own emotional responses, and when you walk into a crisis encounter already close to your limit, your ability to influence someone else drops dramatically. FC2C acknowledges this reality and teaches you how to regulate your own nervous system in real time so you don't become a second source of escalation. Before you can influence someone else's emotional state, you have to manage your own. This isn't abstract. It's physical. Here are a few things to think about:

Breath control. When adrenaline spikes, your breathing becomes rapid and shallow. That signals your brain that you're in danger, which intensifies your stress response. Consciously slow your breathing, inhale deeply through your nose, exhale slowly through your mouth. That sends a countersignal to your nervous system: "I'm okay. I'm in control." You don't need to take ten deep breaths. One or two is enough to lower your physiological arousal just enough that you can think clearly.

Physical grounding. Feel your feet on the ground. Notice your weight. When you're grounded physically, your brain gets feedback that you're stable, which reduces the fight-or-flight response.

The Self-Check

Before and during an encounter, run a quick self-check. How is my breathing? If it's shallow or rapid, slow it down. How is my posture? Am I tense? Relax your shoulders. What's my tone? Am I sounding impatient or sharp? Adjust. Am I taking this personally? If yes, reset. This is about them, not you.

This takes no more than three seconds, and it can be the difference between escalating and de-escalating.

When You Need to Step Away

Sometimes the most professional thing you can do is recognize that you aren't in the right state to handle the encounter and you need support. Maybe you had a terrible day. Maybe this person reminds you of someone who hurt you. Maybe you're dealing with your own crisis and you just don't have the emotional bandwidth.

Asking for help isn't weakness. It's professionalism. It's recognizing your limits and protecting both yourself and the person you're trying to help. "I need to step away for a moment. My colleague is going to continue this conversation with you," or, "I'm going to get my supervisor involved because I want to make sure we handle this correctly." That's not giving up, it's being strategic.

U: Understand Emotion

We focus on the meaning behind the behavior. Human behavior, especially escalated behavior, is rarely driven by the surface-level issue being argued in the moment. People escalate to protect something important to them: control, fairness, dignity, time, respect, or safety. If we try to change behavior without understanding what that behavior is protecting, resistance increases. If we acknowledge the underlying meaning, defensiveness decreases and communication reopens.

Understanding doesn't require agreement or approval, as we already discussed with Professional Sincerity. It's simply recognizing and acknowledging the emotion and the need behind it. When a person feels unheard or dismissed, they begin to defend themselves more aggressively. When they feel understood, even briefly, cooperation becomes possible again.

This means being intentional about the words out of our mouth from the very start. Most of us have heard, or even used, questions that accidentally put the person on the defensive: "What's wrong with you?" or "What's your problem?" or "Why are we here again?" Even if we don't mean harm, those kinds of statements imply that the individual is the problem. And the moment someone feels judged or blamed, their walls go up and we've just created a brand-new barrier.

Instead, we shift the focus to the situation rather than the person. A simple reframe makes all the difference: "What happened today?" or "What brought us here today?" Those questions communicate collaboration. They show that we're working with the individual to understand the issue, not accusing them of being the issue. When we ask about what happened instead of what's wrong, we create a space where the person can share their story rather than defend themselves. And once they feel heard instead of judged, de-escalation has already begun.

A phrase I really try to avoid in crisis situations is, "How are you doing?" or "How's it going?" Both are a perfectly natural thing to say, a common social greeting. In a friendly environment, it's harmless because we're all on the same emotional playing field. But when someone is in crisis, that question lands very differently. We already know they aren't doing well. So asking "How are you doing?" can feel like poking the exact wound they're already struggling with. Instead, I shift to something more useful, like that opening line: "Hey, what's going on?" or "Tell me what happened today." These aren't just nicer phrases. They're strategic communication tools that guide the person toward telling their story, and storytelling is where we discover hooks and barbs, pieces of information, emotion, or motivation we can connect to. When we replace casual greetings with purposeful, curiosity-based questions, we're no longer focusing on their suffering. We're focusing on their experience.

I: Identify a Shared Goal

Conflict is fueled by the belief that we're working against each other. When we identify a shared goal, we shift the dynamic into partnership. The shared goal doesn't have to be large or complicated. It can be as simple as wanting the situation over quickly, wanting to avoid trouble, wanting the interaction to stay respectful, or wanting privacy. Shared goals remind both parties that movement is possible and that cooperation benefits everyone involved.

Naming shared goals out loud reduces the emotional distance between us and the person we're communicating with. It sends the message that we aren't the obstacle, that we're part of the path forward. We need the individual in crisis onboard with us. We try to motivate rather than use commands. We want this person to see us as an ally, someone focused on assisting them out of their situation. We aren't overcoming them or defeating them, and that's an important distinction to realize. We're working to keep them engaged and collaborating with us.

A probation officer is conducting a routine check-in when her client, a man in his late twenties, becomes increasingly agitated. He's convinced she's there to violate him over a missed appointment, and his voice is rising with every exchange. He starts pacing, arms crossed, repeating that the system is set up to fail him and that nothing he does matters. The officer could defend the process, correct his assumptions, or remind him of the consequences of non-compliance. Any of those responses would feel like confirmation that they're on opposite sides of this conversation. Instead, she takes a breath and says: "Here's what today looks like from where I'm standing: you walk out of here with no violations and your supervision intact. That's the goal. That's what this visit is for." The man stops pacing. She continues: "So let's talk about that missed appointment, because if something is going on that needs to be worked around, now is the time, and handling it now keeps things moving forward for both of us."

The shared goal, avoiding a violation, was already there. It belonged to both of them. She just said it out loud. In doing so, she shifted the frame from confrontation to problem-solving, and the conversation that followed was entirely different from the one it had been threatening to become.

D: Direct the Interaction

Once alignment exists, the situation needs momentum. Stagnation increases anxiety. When people feel forced, trapped, or stuck, they resist to regain control of themselves and their immediate environment. Direction is how we restore movement with respect. We provide options, choices that preserve dignity and autonomy while moving toward the needed outcome. When people have choice, they feel a sense of control, and that feeling reduces resistance dramatically.

Directing the interaction isn't about giving orders. It's about shaping a path with professional guidance. Option-based language such as, "Here are two ways we can go with this," or "Which of these works better for you right now?" keeps both clarity and respect intact. Direction breaks the circular conversation and creates forward progress.

Don't hesitate to simply ask the person to consider the safe behavior we're working toward. We can direct toward a quicker outcome. Whether that means coming out of a room, putting down a knife, sitting down, or lowering their voice, sometimes the straightforward request is exactly what's needed. But that request must be paired with a genuine, credible assurance that they will be treated with dignity and not harmed. It isn't enough to say the words. Your tone, your posture, your pacing must all communicate sincerity. We're asking them to trust us at a moment where they may feel they have no reason to trust anyone.

One time, I was a secondary negotiator on a barricaded subject call that went on for four hours. Four hours of the primary negotiator talking, building rapport, working through the emotions. When the situation finally resolved safely, we debriefed the subject, as we always do, and asked him what the negotiator said that made him decide to come out. His answer: 'He asked me to.' Four hours, and the turning point was the ask. Could it have happened sooner if we had simply asked earlier? Maybe. The lesson here is straightforward: don't be afraid to ask. Some of the longest, most complex incidents are resolved with the simplest turning point. Think about that. All the tactical skill, all the communication effort, and what ultimately mattered was the ask. Sometimes that's all it takes: one sincere invitation at the right moment, backed by respect and calm.

We also have to respect resistance. If they say no, fine. We don't fight them on it. We let it sit and then come back to it later, once rapport has built and emotional activation has come down. The door stays open, even if they aren't ready to walk through it yet.

E: Ensure Safety and Support

Throughout the entire interaction, safety must remain our priority, for everyone involved. Emotional safety and physical safety are intertwined.

You saw boundaries in Professional Sincerity as our baseline standard. Here, boundaries become the priority when safety is at risk. They set clear expectations and give the person a simple understanding of what must happen for the situation to remain controlled. Ensuring safety isn't aggressive, it's stabilizing. It communicates fairness and predictability.

Good boundary-setting is supported by situational awareness, paying attention to where we are, what's around us, and how the environment can either help or hurt our safety. I am aware of exits, obstacles, the person's positioning relative to me, and whether I have a safe path to disengage. Repositioning, adjusting my stance or location to create space, maintain a tactical advantage, and avoid being cornered, can drastically reduce risk without making the other person feel challenged.

We can also use physical barriers: tables, chairs, a desk, railings, a bus seat, anything that helps keep distance and slows down a sudden rush. These aren't shields for fighting. They're tools for stabilizing a dangerous moment and buying time for communication to work.

And when an immediate threat emerges, when volatility crosses into danger, boundaries become action. Professional Sincerity teaches us to influence behavior through connection, but it also includes removing ourselves when safety can no longer be maintained. Disengaging isn't failure. Disengaging is the correct decision when the situation demands it.

G.U.I.D.E. in Motion

Because emotions can change rapidly, G.U.I.D.E. is designed to change with them. At any point we can return to Grounding if our composure slips, to Understanding if the person feels unheard, to Direction if things become stuck, or to Ensure Safety when the situation is approaching a tipping point. The goal isn't to complete all five elements. The goal is to choose the right element for the right moment to keep influence alive.

Moving Forward

This is about understanding human behavior well enough to meet people in their moments of crisis with authenticity, skill, and the confidence to adapt when the textbook approach isn't enough.

In the next chapter, we take these tools and integrate them into the highest-stakes communication model in the world. The Behavioral Change Stairway Model, developed through decades of FBI hostage negotiation experience, provides a step-by-step framework for moving someone from emotional crisis to voluntary behavioral change. It builds directly on everything we've covered here, and it will show you how these skills layer together to produce outcomes that authority alone never could.

Remember this though: communication isn't about controlling someone else. It's about influencing the emotional environment so that cooperation becomes possible. It's about showing up as the calmest, most grounded person in the room, and using that presence to help someone else find their way back from the edge. That's the power of Professional Sincerity in action. That's what makes From Crisis to Calm different.

Notes

1. On the relationship between perceived procedural justice (including voice, respect, and trustworthiness) and cooperation with authority, see Tom R. Tyler, *Why People Obey the Law* (Princeton: Princeton University Press, 2006).

2. On the role of vocal prosody in threat detection and social bonding, see Stephen W. Porges and Gregory F. Lewis, "The Polyvagal Hypothesis: Common Mechanisms Mediating Autonomic Regulation, Vocalizations, and Listening," in *Handbook of Mammalian Vocalizations: An Integrative Neuroscience Approach*, ed. Stefan M. Brudzynski (Amsterdam: Academic Press, 2010), 255–264.

3. On emotional contagion and the tendency for people to unconsciously synchronize their emotional states, see Elaine Hatfield, John T. Cacioppo, and Richard L. Rapson, *Emotional Contagion* (Cambridge: Cambridge University Press, 1993); see also Stephen W. Porges, *The Polyvagal Theory: Neurophysiological Foundations of Emotions, Attachment, Communication, and Self-Regulation* (New York: W. W. Norton, 2011).

4. On active listening as a therapeutic and conflict-resolution tool, see Carl R. Rogers, *On Becoming a Person: A Therapist's View of Psychotherapy* (Boston: Houghton Mifflin, 1961); see also Michael J. McMains and Wayman C. Mullins, *Crisis Negotiations: Managing Critical Incidents and Hostage Situations in Law Enforcement and Corrections*, 5th ed. (New York: Routledge, 2014).

5. On listening retention and the gap between speaking speed and thinking speed, see Ralph G. Nichols and Leonard A. Stevens, "Listening to People," *Harvard Business Review* 35, no. 5 (September–October 1957): 85–92. Nichols and Stevens found approximately 50 percent retention immediately after listening, declining to roughly 25 percent over time. The thinking-speed range of 400–800 words per minute, compared with an average speaking rate of 125–175 words per minute, reflects the conservative end of estimates reported in listening research.

CHAPTER 10:

THE BEHAVIORAL CHANGE STAIRWAY MODEL

You can read the behavior. You understand how crisis reshapes the brain, how the amygdala hijacks rational thinking, and how emotional distress narrows perception until the world feels like it has collapsed to a single point of pain, fear, or rage. You know what Professional Sincerity looks like, and you've mastered the communication fundamentals: tone, inflection, pacing, active listening, validation, boundaries, and the self-regulation that keeps you from becoming part of the problem. You can work the G.U.I.D.E. framework, selecting the right operational behavior for the moment. And you can spot the difference between someone who is emotionally distressed and someone preparing to act on hostile intent.

But here's the question that ties it all together: How do you actually move someone from crisis to calm? How do you take all of those individual skills and string them into something that works when it matters most, when someone is dysregulated, overwhelmed, and teetering on the edge of a decision that could go very wrong?

The answer comes from one of the most high-stakes environments imaginable: FBI hostage negotiations.

The Origins of the Behavioral Change Stairway Model

In Chapter 2, we traced how de-escalation was born from tragedy, from Attica to Munich to those early NYPD hostage standoffs that gave us the world's first negotiation team under Dr. Harvey Schlossberg and Lieutenant Frank Bolz. We saw how the philosophy of "Talk to Me" replaced the instinct to rush in with force and we examined dynamic inactivity, the Three Keys of Contain, Isolate, and Negotiate, and how those principles evolved into the Three C's of Contain, Control, and Communicate as they spread from law enforcement to healthcare, education, social services, and every other profession where people face individuals in crisis. That history is the foundation under everything we're about to finish building.

In 1974, the FBI recognized the value of the NYPD approach and adopted it, expanding and enhancing the model through its own field training program at Quantico, Virginia.[1] Early FBI negotiation pioneers gathered experiential data from around the country and abroad, building an increasingly sophisticated understanding of crisis communication. The curriculum spread quickly across the United States and eventually overseas.

But the early negotiation model still had limitations. It was largely transactional, built around a quid pro quo framework: you give me something, I give you something. That approach worked well enough with instrumental hostage-takers, people who had specific demands, wanted money, wanted a getaway car, wanted a prisoner released. But the FBI quickly learned that most crisis situations didn't involve instrumental demands at all. The vast majority of people they encountered weren't career criminals with a calculated plan. They were individuals in crisis, people with poor coping skills reacting to challenging life events. They were impulsive, overwhelmed, and often had no idea what they actually wanted. When asked for demands, many simply said, "Go away and leave me alone." That's not a substantive demand you can negotiate around. It's an emotional plea from someone whose world has narrowed to a point of desperation.

In 1990, this realization drove a fundamental shift. Gary Noesner, who would become the first chief of the FBI's Crisis Negotiation Unit, implemented a major change in the FBI's approach by centering the entire program on active listening skills drawn from the mental health counseling field pioneered by American psychotherapist Dr. Carl Rogers.[2] Rogers had demonstrated that when people feel genuinely heard and understood by another person, they become more open, more willing to engage, and more capable of moving toward change. Noesner took that insight and operationalized it for crisis negotiation, giving FBI and police negotiators clearly defined tools to use in their communications with a wide range of highly emotional and expressive individuals. The positive results were overwhelming.

To better illustrate this crisis intervention approach and to give negotiators a clear framework for how these skills translate into behavioral outcomes, Noesner created the Behavioral Change Stairway Model[3] (BCSM). The BCSM demonstrated that the influence negotiators sought to gain cooperation didn't come automatically because of rank or authority. It came through sincere and genuine empathic engagement. Active listening allowed negotiators to understand the emotion driving dangerous behavior, and that understanding eventually earned them the right to present alternatives to violence based on the positive relationship they had created.

The results spoke for themselves. The FBI statistically determined that the approach achieved a success rate in the mid-to-high ninetieth percentile. Few things in law enforcement, or in any professional field, achieve that kind of outcome.

Then came Waco. In 1993, the standoff between the FBI and the Branch Davidians at their compound in Mount Carmel, Texas, ended in a fire that killed seventy-six people. The tragedy exposed a devastating disconnect between negotiation and tactical operations. After Waco, the FBI created the Critical Incident Response Group and transformed the negotiation program into the Crisis Negotiation Unit, which continues to operate today as one of the premier crisis communication programs in the world.[4]

The BCSM was designed for extreme, life-threatening situations: barricaded subjects, suicidal individuals, armed standoffs, hostage crises. But here's what makes it so powerful for everyone else: the same principles that work when someone has a gun also work when someone is standing in your reception area shouting about a denial letter, or refusing to leave a hospital room, or melting down in a classroom, or blocking your exit during a home visit. The neuroscience doesn't change. The stress response doesn't change. The way human beings move from emotional reactivity back to rational thinking doesn't change. What changes is the stakes. But the process stays the same.

The Five Steps: A Progressive Framework

The BCSM is a five-step progressive framework: **Active Listening, Empathy, Rapport, Influence, and Behavioral Change.** Each step builds on the one before it. Here, you can't skip steps and you can't rush them. You absolutely can't force someone up the stairway faster than their nervous system can handle.

It's important to understand that the BCSM is both progressive and fluid. We may need to cycle back through earlier steps depending on how the person responds. The key is that the process gives us direction: start with human connection, earn trust, understand the story, and then guide behavior. The ultimate goal is to use communication to build enough trust and connection that the person chooses a calmer, safer path, not because they're forced into compliance, but because they believe we're an ally, helping them get there. That's Professional Sincerity again.

In this chapter, we're going to walk up these stairs together, slowly, deliberately, and not just going over what each step is, but why it works and how to apply it across difficult encounters you might face.

Step One: Active Listening

Active listening is the foundation of the BCSM, not because it's the easiest step, but because nothing else works without it. You can't build empathy with someone who doesn't feel heard. You can't establish rapport with someone who thinks you're just waiting for your turn to talk. And you definitely can't influence someone who believes you're ignoring what matters most to them.

Beyond Just Hearing

Now let's talk about one of the most misunderstood communication skills in existence: active listening. Traditional training will tell you what it is. Pay attention. Make eye contact. Nod. Paraphrase what they said. That's all true and covered in FC2C as well. But that's the mechanics, the surface-level actions. FC2C teaches you why it works and how to do it authentically when every fiber of your being wants to interrupt, defend, or shut the conversation down.

Most of us think we're good listeners. Guess what? We're not. Research consistently shows that people retain only about half of what they hear immediately after a conversation, and that number drops to roughly 25 percent over time. Part of the reason is physiological. We think at roughly 400 to 800 words per minute, but the average person speaks at about 125 to 175 words per minute.[5] That gap between speaking speed and thinking speed is enormous, and our brain fills it with distractions, judgments, rebuttals, and whatever else happens to be competing for our attention. We aren't listening. We're waiting for our turn to talk. We hear something that triggers a thought, and we throw it in before the other person has even finished their sentence. We interrupt and redirect. We make the conversation about us. We've all done it, and we've all had it done to us. It's a deeply human habit, and in everyday conversation it's annoying but survivable. In crisis communication, it can be the difference between cooperation and catastrophe.

There's also an important distinction between hearing and listening that most people never think about. Hearing is passive. It's a biological function. Sound enters your ears whether you want it to or not. Listening is something entirely different. Listening is an intentional act. It requires focus, presence, and the discipline to set aside your own agenda long enough to actually absorb what the other person is saying. When someone in crisis is talking, they aren't just sharing information. They're telling you what they need, what they fear, and what it will take to bring them back from the edge. If we're only hearing them, we miss those signals. If we're truly listening, we catch the hooks and the barbs, the words and themes that reveal what matters most and give us the leverage to influence the outcome. In a crisis, listening isn't a courtesy. It's a required skill, and it's one of the most important tools we have.

In crisis situations, active listening isn't about collecting information. It's about lowering emotional temperature. When someone feels heard, truly heard, it signals safety, so their nervous system begins to calm. The act of being listened to without interruption, without judgment, and without immediate problem-solving sends a powerful message: "You matter. Your experience is valid. I'm not your enemy."

That message is what opens the door to cooperation. But here's where it gets tricky: active listening under pressure requires you to manage your own emotional response while fully absorbing theirs. You have to hear their anger, their fear, their accusation, and not react defensively. You have to sit with their discomfort without rushing to fix it and resist the urge to explain, correct, or defend yourself even when they're saying things that aren't fair or accurate.

Let's break this down into practical components that you can apply even when your own stress is high.

Physical attention. Face the person. Make appropriate eye contact, not a stare-down, but enough to show you're engaged. Two to four seconds is good. Nod. Tilt your head to convey understanding without saying it. Put down your phone. Stop what you're doing. Even if you can only give them sixty seconds, make those sixty seconds count by giving them your full attention. People can tell when you're half-listening, and partial attention feels like dismissal.

Verbal acknowledgment. Use small verbal cues that show you're tracking: "Mm-hmm." "I hear you." "Okay." These aren't interruptions. They're breadcrumbs that let the person know you're still with them. Without these cues, people sometimes escalate because they aren't sure you're actually listening.

Resisting the urge to interrupt. This is the hardest part. When someone is venting, especially if they're saying things that are inaccurate or unfair, your instinct is to jump in and correct them. Don't. Let them finish. Let the pressure release. Interrupting to correct details sends the message, "Your feelings don't matter as much as the facts." That shuts down cooperation instantly.

Consider a retail manager dealing with an angry customer who received the wrong order. The customer is furious, talking rapidly, rehashing every detail of how inconvenient this has been, how incompetent the company is, how many times they've tried to resolve this. The manager knows the mistake wasn't her store's fault. It was a warehouse error. She is tempted to interrupt and explain that, but she doesn't. She listens. She nods. She lets the customer finish. And when there's finally a pause, she says: "I can absolutely see why this has been so frustrating. You ordered something specific, it's important to you, and we didn't deliver what we promised. Let's make this right."

She didn't agree that the company is incompetent or accept personal blame. She validated the customer's experience, and because the customer felt heard, they're now willing to work with her to find a solution. That's the power of active listening, and that's Professional Sincerity at work.

The 85/15 Rule

Many people are familiar with the 80/20 listening-to-talking rule, which suggests we should be listening about eighty percent of the time and talking only twenty. In everyday communication, that balance already gives us a tremendous advantage in understanding others.

But in a crisis situation, I take that even further: 85/15. That means eighty-five percent of the interaction is me listening, observing, and gathering information, and only fifteen percent is me speaking. And that fifteen percent isn't there for me to lecture, direct, or dominate the conversation. I am using my small share of talking strategically, to ask open-ended questions, to make supportive statements, and to keep the other person talking. The more the person speaks, the more they reveal: their fears, their wants, their pain points, their hopes, and the hooks we can use to guide them toward a safer resolution. And, say it with me: if they're talking, they probably aren't hurting you, themselves, or someone else.

In crisis communication, silence isn't a void. It's a tool. When we discipline ourselves to say less, we create the space for the other person to say what we actually need to hear. The listener in a conversation holds more power, because the listener gathers the information while the talker reveals it.

The Sub-Skills of Active Listening

Active listening isn't a single technique. It breaks down into several interconnected sub-skills, each of which serves a specific purpose in lowering emotional intensity and gathering the information you need to guide the encounter toward safety. You won't always use every one of these all the time, but you'll always use at least one. And it's important to note that none of these are interruptions. They are actually encouragers, aimed at getting the person to tell you more as their emotions and rationality level out.

Emotional Labeling. This is where validation and emotional acknowledgment becomes a specific, operational skill inside the BCSM. This is where you listen past the words and start paying attention to the emotional current underneath what the person is saying. People rarely come right out and tell you their true emotional state, especially in a crisis. They show it through tone, pacing, volume, word choice, and the way they describe what happened. Your job is to pick up on those clues and give that emotion a name. When you say something like, "It sounds like you're really rattled by this," or "You seem like you're carrying a lot right now." You aren't telling them how they should feel. You're showing them you're paying close attention to how they do feel.

The label doesn't have to be perfect. It just has to be sincere and in the ballpark. Use the Emotional Labeling sheet from the Appendix to help when you're having trouble putting a word to the feeling. When you listen closely, you'll often notice that there's more than one emotion sitting underneath the surface. Someone may sound angry, but once they've talked long enough, you may also hear disappointment, fear, or hurt woven into the story. That's when you might expand the label: "It sounds like you're angry, and maybe you're feeling really hurt as well." What happens next is important. Most people will correct you, clarify, or add more detail, and that's exactly what you want. It opens the door and keeps them talking. And it shows them that you're actively trying to understand their experience instead of dismissing or challenging it.

Here is a big rule that people violate all the time: don't tell the person you understand what they're going through. You don't. Even if you've lived through the same category of event, the same loss, the same type of crisis, the same kind of setback, you didn't live their version of it. You don't know their circumstances, their history, or the thousand private variables that shape how this moment feels to them. What you can understand, and what you should respond to, is the emotion you're hearing. You can say, "I can hear how painful this is," or "It sounds like this really shook you," because now you're speaking to the emotional truth, not claiming expertise over their experience.

I use an example of a person whose dog just died. If your dog died a few years ago, that doesn't give you the right to say, "Oh, my dog died too. I know what you're going through." No, you don't. You know what you went through. Their loss and grief is theirs and theirs alone. They're going to manifest the experience differently than you did. What they need from you isn't a matching story. It's the recognition of the emotion behind their story.

Paraphrasing. Paraphrasing serves two purposes at the same time. First, it confirms that you actually understand what the person is telling you, not what you think they said, not what you're guessing they mean, but the message they're actively trying to get across. Second, it shows the person that you're genuinely paying attention. When you paraphrase, you're taking their words, their meaning, their perspective, and putting it back in front of them in a clear, concise way. You aren't adding anything, you aren't fixing anything, and you aren't judging anything. You're simply demonstrating that their message landed with you.

For example, if the person says, "He's always busy talking and doesn't want to listen to anything I have to say," a simple paraphrase might be, "So he doesn't really pay attention to what you're trying to tell him." It's straightforward, it's accurate, and it reflects their experience back to them. For some people, this might be the first time anyone has ever acknowledged their frustration in a direct, non-judgmental way.

And that's why paraphrasing matters so much: it gets them talking more. When someone feels heard, truly heard, they will almost always keep going. They might add details, vent, explain, clarify, and reveal what's really driving their behavior. Paraphrasing keeps them in that talking space, and the more they talk, the more influence you gain over the direction of the encounter.

Mirroring and Reflecting. This is where a lot of people get tripped up. We've already established that you never mirror or reflect a person's behavior. If they're yelling, you don't yell back. If they're pacing, you don't pace with them. If they're agitated, you don't match that energy. Behavior mirroring in a crisis is gasoline on a fire.

What we do mirror and reflect is what they say and how they feel about it. When someone says, "She never listens to me and what I have to say, and it really makes me angry," a reflective response might be, "It makes you angry." You're taking the essence of what they expressed and handing it back to them in a calmer, clearer form. When you reflect the emotion underneath the statement, you're showing them that you aren't just hearing the words but understanding the impact those words carry for them.

Chris Voss, a former FBI lead international hostage negotiator, describes a study in his book *Never Split the Difference* that perfectly illustrates why reflecting is so effective.[6] The study involved waiters and waitresses trained to respond to customers in one of two ways. One group used positive reinforcement, things like "Great choice!" or "Absolutely!" or really talked up the choice. The other group used simple mirroring, repeating back the last few words of what the customer said in a natural, conversational way. The servers who mirrored their customers received dramatically higher tips than those who used positive reinforcement. The reason had nothing to do with flattery. It had everything to do with connection. The customers felt more listened to and more understood, and that moment of recognition nudged them into a more trusting, collaborative interaction. If this technique can increase tips in a restaurant, imagine its power in a crisis, where feeling understood can be the difference between escalation and cooperation.

Reflecting in your own words also slows the tempo of the conversation. It shifts the tone away from the person's heightened emotional pace and into something steadier and safer. It models calm speech, which often helps bring their intensity down without them even realizing it.

Open-Ended Questions. Using open-ended questions is another tool that keeps people talking, gives you more information, and lowers the sense of threat in the interaction. They revolve around the basics: who, what, where, when, why, and how. They expand the conversation instead of shutting it down.

But each of these carries a different weight, and "why" is the one that can get you into trouble if you aren't careful. "Why" questions tend to sound like accusations. In a crisis, "why" can hit the ear like "Explain yourself." Even when you don't mean it that way, people often hear it as judgment. "Why did you do that?" "Why are you upset?" "Why are you acting like this?" To an escalated person, those questions don't feel curious. They feel critical.

It isn't that you can never use "why." It's that you have to translate it into something less loaded. Instead of "Why did you do that?" try "What happened right before this?" Instead of "Why are you so angry?" try "What's going on that's hitting you this hard?" Same intent. Same goal. Completely different impact.

Using "how" and "what" questions are also one of the strongest tools you have for saying "no" without ever actually saying the word. Instead of delivering a flat denial, which usually hits like a brick wall, these questions redirect the conversation back to the other person, shift the mental load onto them, and keep the dialogue open and collaborative. Instead of "No, we can't do that," you redirect with something like, "What other options do you think might work here?" Instead of "No, you can't stay here," you say, "How can we work together to find a solution to move on from here?" The boundary hasn't changed, but the way you deliver it changes everything. People handle problem-solving far better than rejection.

Minimal Encouragers. These are small verbal cues, simple phrases like "okay," "really," "I understand," or even a quiet "mm-hmm," that signal to the person that you're fully present, tracking what they're saying, and not drifting off. They may be small, but they play a big role in keeping the person talking. People can sense when the listener is distracted or mentally somewhere else, and that usually makes them shut down or escalate. Consistent, well-timed encouragers tell them that you're still engaged, still listening, and still following their train of thought.

Summarizing. Summarizing brings together everything the person has told you in a way that shows you have genuinely been tracking their story and their emotions from start to finish. When you summarize, you're putting their experience into your words, not changing the meaning, not adding judgment, just offering a clear overview of what they've expressed so far. Periodic summaries help anchor the conversation. People in crisis often talk in circles, jump between topics, or lose their own train of thought because of the emotional overload they're experiencing. When you step in with a calm, accurate recap, it organizes their narrative and reassures them that you haven't missed the important pieces.

Effective Pauses. Silence makes most people uncomfortable. But in crisis communication, that discomfort is exactly what makes it powerful. Effective pauses create space. They slow the moment down, they let emotions settle, and they open the door for the person to keep talking. Most people feel compelled to fill a silence, especially during a tense or emotional conversation, and that often leads them to reveal more, explain more, or clarify what's really going on underneath the surface. A pause before or after something meaningful helps focus the person's attention. It signals that the moment matters, that something significant was said, or that you're giving them room to think. Pauses are also especially useful when someone is angry. When a person is fired up, anything you say, even something reasonably phrased, might be taken as argumentative or dismissive. A moment of silence, however, can keep you from stepping into their emotional momentum.

What Happens When Active Listening Works

When you're using active listening skills consistently, certain outcomes appear reliably. The person starts giving you more information. They open up, fill in details, elaborate on what's really going on. That happens because they feel heard, validated, and understood, and when people feel that way, they naturally keep talking. And while they're talking, they aren't acting out. They're processing instead of reacting. They're engaging their prefrontal cortex, even if just barely, instead of operating purely from their amygdala.

You may notice their speech changes. The volume drops. The pace slows. The pitch lowers. These are physiological indicators that the emotional brain is losing its grip and the thinking brain is beginning to reengage. They might start talking about personal issues, what's really hurting them, what they're worried about beneath all the anger or fear. People don't volunteer personal truths unless they feel some degree of safety, so when the conversation shifts from defensive venting to genuine sharing, you know active listening is working.

Active listening isn't magic, and it doesn't work on everyone. There will always be people who refuse to engage or situations where the emotional intensity is too high to rely on communication alone. And when you're confronted with an immediate threat, active listening isn't your tool. Safety comes first. But in the majority of encounters, especially those where you have time and space to practice these skills, active listening becomes incredibly effective. It isn't about being soft. It's about gaining information, reducing tension, and guiding the encounter to a safer outcome.

When Active Listening Meets Resistance

Here's what traditional training won't tell you: sometimes active listening doesn't work on the first try. You listen. You validate. You paraphrase. And the person keeps escalating. They accuse you of not really listening. They repeat themselves louder. They get angrier, not calmer.

This is where most people give up on de-escalation and assume the person is just irrational. But FC2C teaches you to ask yourself a different question: Why isn't this working?

Usually, it's one of three reasons. First, they don't feel heard yet because their emotional intensity is still too high. You haven't listened long enough. They need more time to vent the pressure. Your job is to keep listening, keep validating, and give them the space to exhaust the emotion. It might take five minutes, it might take ten, it might take more but rushing them will only restart the cycle.

Second, your body language or tone might be contradicting your words. You might be saying, "I'm listening," but your arms are crossed, you're looking at your watch, or your tone sounds impatient. The person picks up on that mismatch, and it feels like fake empathy. This is where Professional Sincerity matters. You have to be genuine, or they will sense the performance and reject it.

Third, the person needs something specific, and listening alone won't give it to them. Maybe they need information, maybe they need action, maybe they need to hear that someone is going to do something concrete. In this case, you transition from listening to directing the encounter. You acknowledge what they've said, validate their experience, and then offer a clear path forward.

Active listening isn't a magic incantation. It's among the first, most critical steps in earning the trust that makes the next steps possible. When it meets resistance, we don't abandon it. We adjust, we adapt, and we draw on the other tools in our framework.

Step Two: Empathy

Active listening gets the person talking. Empathy is what helps them feel understood, sometimes for the first time in a very long time.

When someone is in crisis, their world has usually narrowed to pain, fear, anger, shame, or confusion. Empathy helps widen that world just enough for them to breathe again. Your goal isn't to fix their story or approve of it. Your goal is to let them feel that another human being actually sees what they're going through.

As we established in Chapter 8, and again in Chapter 9 with the kidnapping/murder case and the distinction between validating emotions and condoning behavior, empathy isn't agreement. It isn't approval. It's a tool that keeps the conversation calm instead of combative, and it's the second step of the BCSM for a reason: without it, the stairway stalls.

The Hole Analogy

Empathy is not simply "I'm sorry."

Saying "I'm sorry" doesn't get anyone out of a crisis, and it doesn't move a dangerous or emotionally charged situation toward safety. That's sympathy. It acknowledges what happened, but it doesn't help. Think about it this way: you and I are walking down a path, and you fall into a hole. I look down and say, "Oh no, you fell in that hole. I'm sorry." That does absolutely nothing for you.

Jumping into the hole with you doesn't help either. That's identifying with the problem, feeling everything you're feeling right alongside you. Now we're both stuck. Your problem has become my problem. I don't need your problems added to mine, and you don't need me trapped next to you.

Real empathy is neither of those things. Real empathy is me staying grounded at the top while I figure out how to help: "Oh no, you fell in that hole. I'm going to get a rope and pull you out." That's operational empathy. You aren't taking on their pain, and you aren't dismissing it. You're acknowledging the emotion, not the experience, and positioning yourself as someone who can help them move forward. You maintain your stability so you can actually be useful instead of becoming another person who needs rescue.

And remember the distinction between a crisis and a problem? The crisis is that you fell into the hole. I can't change that. The problem is getting you out. That's what we can work on.

Empathic Stems: The Language of Understanding

In actual conversation, that "hole" is the crisis. The "rope" to help you out of the problem is delivered through empathic stems: short, simple statements that validate emotion without condoning behavior. These stems show the person you recognize their emotional reality while still keeping control of the interaction.

"You were really hurt by that." "That sounds frightening." "It sounds like you've been really stressed." "It's hard for you to know what to do." "Right now, you feel like there's no hope." "You wish things were different."

When you say things like this, you're recognizing and validating the emotional reality they're communicating. This is what takes the edge off. People in crisis often feel unseen, dismissed, or misunderstood. When you label what they're experiencing, it creates a moment of alignment, a sense that someone finally "gets it." That alignment lowers defensiveness and increases cooperation.

These stems also give the person new language for what they're feeling. Someone might be rambling, angry, overwhelmed, or scattered, and when you reflect back a concise emotional truth, it organizes their emotions in a way that helps them calm down. You aren't fixing anything. You're helping them make sense of it.

Even longer stems show that you listened, understood the context, and can clearly state the emotional impact: "You're frustrated because this has been going on a long time and you're not getting straight answers." "It makes sense that you're angry. You've been trying to get help and you feel unheard." That's what people respond to. They don't calm down because you tell them to calm down. They calm down because they feel heard.

No "I" Statements

Take a close look at those empathic stems. Notice anything missing? There are no "I" statements. That's intentional.

We've talked about this throughout the book, in the Five Principles, in the communication fundamentals, in the G.U.I.D.E. framework. It keeps coming up because it keeps mattering. The moment you start a sentence with "I think" or "I feel" or "I understand," the focus shifts away from the person in crisis and onto you. And in those moments, they don't care about you. They care about being heard, understood, and taken seriously. When you use "I," it can sound like you're centering your own perspective, or like you're trying to make the conversation about your reaction instead of their experience. Even if you mean well, it comes across as self-focused, and self-focus is the opposite of empathy.

People in crisis need to feel that they're the center of your attention. That's why our language has to reflect it. When you say, "You're really overwhelmed," or "It sounds like you've been carrying this for a long time," you keep the spotlight exactly where it belongs: on them, their emotions, and their experience.

In FC2C, our "you" statements do something entirely different from the traditional crisis-communication approach. Traditional programs have historically taught "you" statements that come across as directive or judgmental: "You should try to relax." "You need to take a breath." "You've got to work with us here." Even when well-intentioned, those kinds of statements center authority over empathy, and they almost always escalate the very behavior they're meant to stop. We use non-threatening "you" statements that reflect emotion, not behavior. We aren't telling someone what they're doing wrong. We're acknowledging what they're feeling. That shift is everything.

There are exceptions. When you're personally offering assistance, "I" becomes responsibility-centered, not ego-centered: "I'm right here with you." "I'll make sure to keep you informed." "I'm going to work with you on this." These statements aren't about you. They're about what you're offering them. And when you're personally attacked or extreme outbursts occur, "I" becomes a boundary tool: "When you do that, I can't help you." These are operational "I" statements. They serve the person, not your ego. They preserve Professional Sincerity, reinforce your role, and keep the interaction safe and functional.

Empathy Plus Emotional Labeling: The Neuroscience

Earlier in the book we explored how the amygdala hijacks rational thinking during crisis and how emotional distress narrows perception. Here's the science that explains why everything we've been building actually works at the neurological level. When we combine empathy with emotional labeling, we can interrupt that hijack. We can figuratively flip a switch in the brain and help transfer control back from the amygdala to the prefrontal cortex. This isn't magic. It's neuroscience. In 2007, Dr. Matthew Lieberman at UCLA ran an experiment that changed how we understand emotional regulation.7 Participants were placed in fMRI scanners and shown images designed to trigger emotional responses. When the subjects simply looked at the emotionally charged images, the amygdala lit up intensely, exactly what you would expect during stress or threat. But when the subjects were asked to simply label the emotion, "("fear," "anger," "confusion," "sadness") the activity in the amygdala dropped, and the right ventrolateral prefrontal cortex, a region associated with cognitive control, lit up. When they named the emotion, their brain shifted from pure reaction to controlled processing.

Lieberman called this "affect labeling." In crisis communication, we call it emotional labeling, and we pair it with empathy. When we say to someone, "It sounds like you're overwhelmed," or "You're angry because you feel ignored," we're essentially performing the emotional labeling for them. Their brain recognizes the label as accurate, which allows the prefrontal cortex to come back online and dial down the amygdala response. It doesn't fix their problem, but it gives them enough cognitive control to talk, listen, and make safer decisions. Daniel Goleman's work on emotional intelligence supports the same conclusion: one of the most effective ways to interrupt an emotional hijack is through emotional acknowledgment.[8]

This is why empathy combined with emotional labeling can feel almost like magic, not because we're manipulating anyone, but because of how powerful the psychological shift is. You're not forcing anything. You're helping their brain transition out of panic mode and back into thinking mode. When the amygdala stands down and the prefrontal cortex steps in, everything gets easier: people talk more, fight less, and think more clearly. And that's the moment behavioral change becomes possible.

When people feel seen, they stop fighting to be seen. So much of crisis behavior, the anger, the defensiveness, the escalation, is a battle for acknowledgment. Empathy helps end that battle. The moment a person feels understood, something shifts. Their shoulders drop, their breathing changes, the intensity eases. The fight drains out because its purpose has already been satisfied. And that's exactly the opening we need to build rapport.

Step Three: Rapport

They've told you their story. You showed empathy by naming what they're feeling and acknowledging the weight of it. The person feels heard and understood. Now comes the step that makes influence possible: rapport.

Rapport is trust built through connection, and it's the moment when the person shifts from seeing you as a threat or an obstacle to seeing you as someone who might actually be there to help. It isn't friendship. You aren't trying to become buddies or create some deep personal bond. It's simply enough trust to move forward together, enough connection to make cooperation feel safer than resistance.

Without rapport, everything else stalls. You can listen perfectly, reflecting back every emotion with textbook accuracy. You can label feelings flawlessly, hitting every empathic stem exactly right. But if the person doesn't trust you, if they still see you as "the system," "the enemy," "just another person who doesn't care about what happens to me," they won't follow your lead, they won't accept your guidance, and they won't cooperate.

Rapport grows out of one simple truth: every single person has something they want to talk about. And I mean everyone. I've talked to drug dealers, murderers, scammers, hardened criminals; people who swear they will never say a word end up talking because the need to be understood, even in a tiny way, is one of the most powerful forces in human psychology. Your job is to locate what they care about, what matters to them, what has weight in their world, and then use that as the connection point.

Hooks and Barbs

In crisis negotiation, we talk about "hooks" and "barbs." We introduced this concept in Chapters 5 and 9 as part of the intelligence-gathering purpose of communication. Here's where we put them to work. Barbs are the complaints, the insults, the distractions, the grievances. They're the things people say when they're venting, when they're defensive, when they're trying to push you away or test whether you're really listening: "You people never help." "This system is broken." "Nobody cares about people like me."

Barbs aren't productive. They don't move the conversation forward. But you can't ignore them, and you can't argue with them. If you get defensive or try to prove them wrong, you lose rapport instantly.

What you can do is acknowledge the barb without getting stuck on it, redirect the conversation, and then look for the hook**.** Hooks are the things that matter to the person: their values, their fears, their hopes, their priorities. The things they actually care about underneath all the noise. A parent saying, "You people never help" might really be saying, "I'm scared my kid is going to fail and I don't know what to do." A patient saying, "Nobody cares" might really be saying, "I'm in pain and I feel invisible."

And once you find the hook, that's what you focus on. "It sounds like you're really worried about your child." "You're in pain, and that's been going on way too long." Now you're talking about what actually matters. The barbs lose their power because you've moved past them to the real issue.

Sometimes a barb isn't an insult or a complaint. It's a painful detail that the person drops into the conversation, something that's feeding their crisis rather than helping them move through it. If someone tells you they just got out of the hospital after a mental health evaluation, that experience may be the very thing that has them escalated right now. Staying on that topic keeps them anchored to the pain, the shame, or the anger that came with it. Your job isn't to explore that experience with them. Your job is to gently move the conversation somewhere more productive. You acknowledge what they shared without digging into it: "That sounds like it was really tough. I'm glad you're here now. Tell me what's going on today." You've validated the weight of what they went through, and shifted the focus forward, toward the present, toward something you can actually help with. The hospital is the barb. What you need right now is the hook.

Finding the Doorway In

Hooks don't just come from words. They come from everything around the person. Think about walking up to someone's house to conduct an interview and spotting a classic car in the driveway. I don't know anything about cars, not beyond turning mine on and putting gas in it. I don't need to. But, if that car means something to them, then it instantly becomes valuable to me, because it's now a doorway into their identity.

So I ask about it. Not with a script. Not with fake enthusiasm. Just Professional Sincerity and part of my 15% of the talking used strategically: "How long have you had it? Is that the original paint? Did you restore it yourself or send it out? Is it tough finding parts for something that old?" And then I might finish with: "You must be really proud of it."

What happens next is predictable and powerful: they start talking. And once they start talking, my questions become easier. Their answers give me material to work with, more details, more personal meaning, more clues about who they are and how they see the world. Every minute they keep talking, two things happen simultaneously: they're getting more comfortable with me, and they're forgetting that they're talking to someone in a professional role. They're just talking to a person who seems genuinely interested in something that matters to them.

This is rapport. Not charm or manipulation and not friendliness for its own sake. It's the deliberate use of human connection to lower defenses, reduce threat perception, and create a space where communication can actually happen.

Beyond conversation, there are countless visual cues and small gestures that can build rapport. A superhero shirt, an anime hoodie, a band T-shirt, a team on a hat. These are instant openings if you're paying attention. A bracelet with meaning, a tattoo, a unique pair of sneakers, a phone case. Offering a glass of water when someone has been waiting a long time. Sitting down so you're at eye level instead of standing over them. Slowing down your pace instead of rushing through the interaction. Each of these communicates respect and attention, and people respond. They soften. They engage. They start to see you as someone who might actually care about what happens to them.

Understanding why this works is worth taking a moment to explore, because when you understand the mechanism, you can apply it more deliberately and under more pressure.

When someone wears a band shirt, a sports jersey, or carries any visible marker of personal interest, they're making an identity declaration. They're saying, in effect: this is part of who I am. Social identity theory, developed by Henri Tajfel and John Turner, establishes that people derive a significant portion of their self-concept from group memberships and shared affiliations, and that having those memberships recognized produces a measurable positive emotional response.[10] When a person in crisis is feeling invisible, dismissed, or dehumanized, an identity acknowledgment does something profound. It says: I see you as a person, not as a problem.

There's also a dynamic that plays out when you ask someone to teach you something they know well: you place them in the role of expert. You are, in that moment, voluntarily subordinate. For someone who feels out of control, that shift is profoundly disarming. Chris Voss, drawing on his FBI negotiation experience, describes a version of this when he writes about questions designed to give the other person a sense of control and authority over the conversation.[11] The underlying principle is the same: when you invite someone to be the authority, they almost always accept the invitation.

There's something else at work here too, something social psychologists refer to as the Benjamin Franklin Effect. Jon Jecker and David Landy documented the observation that asking someone to do you a favor actually increases their positive feelings toward you, because people rationalize their own behavior.[12] When you ask someone to share their expertise with you, they're doing you a favor. The act of explaining the band or the car or the tattoo creates cognitive consistency in the speaker: I'*m telling this person about something I love, therefore I must feel comfortable with this person.* The rapport doesn't just precede the conversation. It's created by the conversation itself.

The Hook Is a Rapport Tool, Not a De-Escalation Tool

Here's something that's easy to miss and missing it is why the technique sometimes fails in the field: the hook isn't an opening move. It's a rapport tool, and rapport tools don't work during de-escalation. They work in the transition out of it.

When someone is yelling, flooding with adrenaline, and cycling through grievances at full volume, walking in with "Hey, is that a Megadeth shirt?" is going to land like a non-sequitur at best and an insult at worst. The hook requires the person to shift their attention outward, to engage something external to their emotional state. That capacity is exactly what gets shut down under peak emotional arousal. You can't reach through the amygdala and tap someone on the shoulder. You have to wait for the neurological conditions that make reaching through possible.

What you're actually waiting for isn't a behavioral milestone like "they stopped yelling," but a neurological one: the moment when the person's nervous system has discharged enough activation that the prefrontal cortex begins coming back online, even briefly. Crisis communication researchers and trauma-informed practitioners sometimes refer to this as the window of tolerance, a concept developed by Daniel Siegel to describe the zone of arousal in which a person can process input without either flooding into overwhelm or shutting down completely.[13] The person doesn't have to be calm. They just have to be slightly less flooded than they were thirty seconds ago. That's enough of a window to work with.

The Bridge: What You're Doing Before the Window Opens

Before the hook is available, there's a phase of the encounter that most people leave unnamed. Let's call it the bridge. The bridge is everything that happens between full escalation and the moment the window opens, and it isn't a passive waiting period. It's an active discipline.

The cardinal rule of the bridge phase is this: you aren't solving anything. You're creating the conditions for the window to open. Every time someone says, "if you'll just calm down, I can explain," they're demonstrating the instinct to solve, and they're demonstrating exactly what not to do. The instinct to explain, clarify, justify, or offer options during peak escalation is nearly universal and almost always counterproductive. Content closes windows. Presence opens them.

What you're doing in the bridge phase is validating emotion without agreement, holding silence strategically, and managing your own nervous system. We've covered all three of these tools in depth in this book, and this is where they earn their keep. "That sounds incredibly infuriating," doesn't mean you agree with anything. It means you received what was just communicated to you, and that reception is often the only thing that begins moving someone from flooding back toward regulation. Silence, as covered in the effective pauses sub-skill of this chapter, creates a mild but real pull for the person to re-engage on different terms. And your own regulated presence isn't just professionally appropriate. It's actively doing regulatory work on the person in front of you through co-regulation, the interpersonal neurobiological process by which one person's regulated nervous system helps stabilize another's.[14]

While you're managing the bridge, you're also scanning the environment for the hooks that will be available when the window opens. The Megadeth shirt is something you noticed in the first thirty seconds. You file it. You continue doing bridge work. When the window signal appears, the hook is already loaded.

Reading the Window

The window doesn't announce itself. It appears in behavioral signals that are observable and learnable once you know what to look for.

The first is a pause that's qualitatively different from a pause to reload. People who are still in full escalation pause to breathe and then re-engage. The pause that signals a window is slightly longer and slightly less purposeful. The person looks away, or down, and isn't composing their next salvo. Something has shifted internally and the outside is catching up.

The second is a drop in volume without a corresponding drop in emotion. The person may still be angry, still telling you exactly what they think, but the decibel level comes down a notch without you forcing it. That drop is the nervous system doing its work. It isn't resolution. It is reduction, and reduction is all you need.

The third is a question directed at you, even a hostile one. When someone shifts from declarative statements to questions, even adversarial ones, they have implicitly acknowledged that you exist in the interaction as someone worth engaging. "You people don't even care, do you?" is an invitation, however disguised. The willingness to ask means something has shifted. Any question is a window signal.

The fourth is physical reorganization. Maybe the person sits down when they were standing, shifts their weight, rubs their face. Any physical repositioning signals re-orientation to the environment rather than being driven purely by internal state. Their attention, even briefly, has moved outside their own emotional experience.

The fifth is a minimal acknowledgment of something you said. If you've been using validation and minimal encouragers and you get back a quiet "yeah" or even a slight nod, the window is beginning to open. They have started processing input rather than only generating it. That's the moment you've been waiting for.

These signals rarely arrive alone. More often a window opens because two or three signals cluster within a short span: the person sits down, exhales, and says quietly, "I'm just so tired of this." When that happens, the window isn't cracking open. It's swinging wide open.

Exploiting the Window: Getting the Hook to Land

Recognizing the window is a perceptual skill. Exploiting it is an execution skill. They're different, and knowing the first without the second is like being able to read a weather forecast but not knowing whether you're getting wet or staying dry.

The most common failure at this stage isn't missing the window. It's deploying the hook too abruptly. A person sits down, exhales, and the responder immediately says: "Hey, is that a Megadeth shirt?" The timing is technically correct. The delivery is wrong. There's been no landing, no matching of the new energy, no shared moment of stillness. The hook arrives like a non-sequitur and the window closes.

The principle that fixes this comes from motivational interviewing, where practitioners are trained to pace with a person's current state before attempting to lead them toward a new one.[15] In a crisis context it means something very practical: if the person just went quieter, you go quieter too. If they just sat down, you adjust your posture to be less formal. If they just exhaled, you slow your own speech down. You're matching the landing, not the launch.

This match is followed by what I think of as a landing phrase: a brief, low-stakes, low-content utterance that occupies the space just long enough that the hook which follows feels organic rather than premeditated. A soft "yeah" or a quiet "take your time" or even just a slow nod. Something completely non-crisis-related: "It's warm in here" or "Been a long day." If they said something like "I'm so tired of this," the landing might simply be: "Yeah. Tired." Quiet, unhurried, with no solution attached. Then the silence. Then, from inside that new register, the hook arrives almost as an afterthought: "Hey, is that a Megadeth shirt?"

What the person experiences is someone who moved *with* them rather than *at* them. The hook doesn't feel like a technique because it didn't arrive alone. It arrived after a moment of shared stillness, and by the time the question comes, the conversation has already quietly changed registers.

The rhythm to aim for is: the window opens, match the energy, land quietly, let the new silence sit, then the hook arrives as a natural observation. Slow everything down once the window opens. The hook should sound like something that just occurred to you, because the pace you've set makes it feel that way.

A Note on Awkwardness

I want to say something directly here that doesn't usually make it into books like this: this is going to feel awkward the first time you do it. Probably the second time too. Real awkward.

That's not a sign that the skill isn't working. It's a sign that the skill is being learned. Motor learning research describes three stages of skill acquisition that every learner passes through. Paul Fitts and Michael Posner identified these as the cognitive stage, where the person is consciously thinking through each step and performance is halting and effortful; the associative stage, where the steps begin to connect and errors become less frequent; and the autonomous stage, where the skill runs without conscious management.[16] The cognitive stage is supposed to feel exactly like what you'll experience the first time you try to match energy and deploy a landing phrase under real-world pressure. The gear grinding isn't failure. It is the mechanism of learning.

The analogy I use in training is driving again, just like in situational awareness. Nobody gets behind the wheel for the first time and nails a three-point turn. The instructor explained everything correctly, the mechanics are all there, but the execution is halting and self-conscious because the brain hasn't automated any of it yet. Given time and repetition, the three-point turn eventually runs without a single conscious thought. This skill is the same process, with higher stakes in the practice environment because there's a person in front of you instead of a parking cone, (which I highly recommend using rather than a Troop car when teaching your kids how to drive - never mind, long story).

The other thing worth knowing is that people on the receiving end of an awkward but sincere attempt are far more forgiving than you might expect. Research on social perception consistently shows that people evaluate intent more heavily than execution quality, particularly in emotionally charged situations.[17] A responder who stumbles through the hook but is genuinely curious and genuinely present will land better than a polished responder who delivers it smoothly but mechanically. Professional Sincerity covers a lot of rough edges, and that isn't a workaround. It's the point.

The Pivot: From Hook to Real Subject

A hook is never the point of the conversation. It's the doorway into the person. Once rapport is established through that doorway, you need to pivot toward the real subject. You don't abruptly cut the conversation off and announce that it's time to get down to business, because that would undo everything you've just built.

Instead, you wait for a natural pause, a moment where they've just finished talking about something they care about, and then you link that energy to the situation you actually need to address. Here's what that looks like:

A security guard finds an intoxicated patron in an unauthorized area behind the stage. The man is agitated, yelling, and not interested in cooperating. Instead of leading with authority and demanding that he leave, the guard asks him what he thought of the set. The patron lights up. He starts talking about the band, the songs, the energy of the crowd. For a minute or two, the guard just listens, nods, keeps him talking. The agitation drops. The yelling stops.

Then comes the pivot. The guard waits for a natural pause and says, "Sounds like a hell of a show. Let's get you back out there, so you don't miss the encore."

No confrontation. No command. The guard used the hook to bring the emotional temperature down, then linked the patron's own enthusiasm back to the outcome that needed to happen. The patron doesn't feel managed. He feels heard. And now he's walking willingly instead of being escorted.

What you've done in that moment is use the hook as a bridge, reinforcing their sense of identity and tying that positive identity to the kind of conversation you now need. The pivot feels seamless because it honors the rapport instead of shattering it.

A pivot won't always land cleanly. People can suddenly shut down, get suspicious, or pull back the moment they sense the conversation moving toward something uncomfortable. When that happens, recovery begins by stepping back into rapport rather than pushing forward into content. You simply return to whatever part of the earlier conversation felt natural and genuine. You're signaling: I'm not here to trick you, I'm not here to rush you, and I'm not here to corner you. When someone sees that you don't abandon rapport the second you hit resistance, their trust in you grows. They relax again. They reopen. And when they talk the second time, they usually talk even more freely than before.

This is where Professional Sincerity becomes indispensable. You aren't pretending to like the person. You aren't lying to them. You're choosing to show up as someone who is steady, grounded, and able to work with whoever is in front of you regardless of who they are or what they've done. Rapport also requires consistency. If your words say "I'm here to help" but your body language screams impatience, they will sense it instantly. When the presentation is authentic, something shifts. The person starts to see you not as someone working against them, but as someone working with them.

And once you have rapport, you start to have influence.

Step Four: Influence

If you've been following the progression of this book, you already know what influence is and what it isn't. We defined it in the Five Pillars. We grounded it ethically in Professional Sincerity and we operationalized it in G.U.I.D.E.. The reason it keeps appearing is because influence isn't a single moment. It's the cumulative result of everything you've done on the steps below. Every time you listened without interrupting, labeled an emotion accurately, every time you found the hook instead of reacting to the barb, you were building toward this step. The person is now willing to hear you because you've proven you're willing to hear them. That's influence, and it was earned long before you ever open your mouth to guide the conversation forward.

Options: The Language of Influence

Once you've got influence, the question becomes how you use it. The answer, in almost every case, is options. Options are the gentle steering wheel of influence. They pop up all over FC2C and they work because they give the individual just enough control to prevent defensiveness while still moving them toward the outcome you need.

A person in crisis already feels their world collapsing inward. Their choices feel reduced, their coping mechanisms offline, and their sense of power gone. When you offer two or three structured options, you aren't just helping them decide what to do next. You're restoring autonomy.

Collaboration Is Key

That's why options don't sound like orders. They sound like collaborations.

Another reappearing part of FC2C, collaboration is the thread that ties the entire options strategy together. When you frame the interaction as a shared effort rather than a confrontation, everything in the person's physiology changes. Their shoulders drop. Their voice softens. Their defensiveness eases. Collaboration interrupts the "me versus you" dynamic that fuels escalation and replaces it with "you and I versus the problem." Even if the actual options you're offering are limited, the experience of collaboration is what matters most to the person in crisis, because it restores a sense of agency they thought they had lost.

A person who feels cornered will fight for control because that's all their nervous system knows how to do in that moment. But a person who feels included in the process will fight with you instead of against you. You're shifting their internal narrative from "I'm being told what to do by someone who doesn't understand my situation" to "I'm being helped toward something I can actually manage by someone who's trying to work with me."

"It's okay to feel upset, but let's figure this out. Let's take a few breaths here or step outside, and then we can solve this together. What would you like to do?" You aren't telling them how to behave. You're giving them a controlled space in which to choose calm. Either option is acceptable, because whichever they choose, the emotional temperature drops and they move with you, not against you.

"You seem really upset, let's talk. We can talk here or step aside to a quieter space where you feel more comfortable. What works for you?" These kinds of choices are carefully structured to move the person into a safer, more cooperative lane. Standing still? Good. Stepping aside? Also good. Either way, they're following you, on their own terms.

How to Present Options

Keep it simple: two or three choices maximum. A person in crisis has limited cognitive capacity. Their prefrontal cortex is struggling and their working memory is reduced. Two choices is ideal. Three is acceptable if the situation truly requires it. More than three and you risk overwhelming them, which defeats the entire purpose.

Make both options acceptable. Every option you present needs to be a path you're genuinely willing to take. You aren't trying to steer them toward the "right" choice by making one option clearly terrible. That isn't offering options. That's issuing an ultimatum disguised as a choice, and people sense it immediately.

Frame options around their needs, not your authority. Notice how effective options are framed around what might help the person, what might make them more comfortable, what might meet their needs, not around what you need or what your policy demands. Less effective: "I need you to either sit down or leave the area." More effective: "You might feel better if we sat down to talk, or if you'd rather have some space, we could step outside for a minute. What sounds better?" Same outcome. Completely different tone.

Use "you" language, not "I" language. Just as we avoid "I" statements in empathy because they shift focus away from the person in crisis, the same principle applies to options. Keep the spotlight on them: "You can talk to me about what's going on, or if you want, you can take a walk and we'll connect in a few minutes. Up to you."

The Ethical Line

We drew this line clearly in Chapter 9, and it hasn't moved. The brain resists force but responds to choice. When you offer options, you're engaging the part of their brain that wants control, stability, and dignity. Professional Sincerity is what keeps this ethical. When done correctly, people follow your lead not because you forced them but because you created conditions where choosing the safer path became the most logical, dignified, and human option available to them.

Step Five: Behavioral Change

Now we arrive at the final step in the Behavioral Change Stairway Model: behavioral change itself. Everything we've done up to this point has been about moving a person out of their crisis-thinking brain and back into a place where reasoning, options, and cooperation are possible.

Behavioral change is what we've been building toward since the first step. It's the moment when the person actually does something different: lowers their voice, puts down the weapon, comes out of the locked room, agrees to the plan, accepts the help, follows the direction. Sometimes they get there willingly. Sometimes they don't. But the model is designed to give you the best possible chance of achieving the change without needing force, and to set conditions that make any force that does occur shorter, safer, and less destructive.

In some professions, law enforcement, corrections, security, healthcare, crisis intervention, behavioral change sometimes has to occur with or without the person's voluntary agreement. The presence of a possible use of force doesn't negate the value of the model. It simply means the stakes are higher and the need for good communication is even more critical. The purpose of everything leading up to this point, listening, empathy, rapport, options, is to create the conditions where voluntary compliance is more likely, because voluntary compliance is safer for everyone involved.

When a person feels understood, respected, and given choices, their emotional intensity decreases, their reasoning improves, and the odds that force will be necessary dramatically decline. But if force does become necessary, the same groundwork still matters. A person who feels heard is far less likely to fight. A person who has been offered choices is less likely to view intervention as a humiliation. A person who believes you're trying to help them is less likely to escalate. By the time you reach behavioral change, you've already reduced the person's perception of threat, increased their cognitive functioning, and created an environment where compliance feels less like surrender and more like the next logical step.

Signs Behavioral Change Is Happening

The shift in the other person is rarely sudden or dramatic. It shows up in small, reliable signs that the crisis is loosening its grip. You might notice their language starts to change. The violent, hostile, or chaotic content in their speech begins to soften. They aren't talking in threats or absolutes anymore, not stuck in that narrow tunnel of "I have to" or "someone's going to." Instead, they're talking like someone who is starting to reengage with the world instead of fighting it.

They also start talking more, and that increased talking is one of the clearest indicators that things are moving in the right direction. Not necessarily calmly at first, they might still be venting, still working through the emotional backlog, but more consistently, with more detail, and for longer stretches at a time. You will hear it in the pace of their speech too. Their words come slower, their pitch drops, the volume settles into something that doesn't feel like it's vibrating with adrenaline. These are physiological indicators that the amygdala is losing steam and the prefrontal cortex is beginning to reassert control.

Another clear sign is when the person shifts from defending their position to revealing what matters beneath it: what they've lost, what they're afraid of, what they wish could be different. That kind of disclosure doesn't happen when someone still sees you as a threat. It happens when rapport has taken hold. The moment they go from talking at you to talking with you, you know the stairway is working.

And the threats decrease. They don't disappear all at once, and you shouldn't expect them to vanish completely, but they become less frequent, less intense, and less credible. The posture shifts from aggressive to neutral. The emotional temperature drops from boiling to something closer to a simmer.

BCSM and Professional Sincerity: How They Work Together

The Behavioral Change Stairway Model is the psychology. It's the map that shows you how people move from emotional crisis back to rational thinking. Professional Sincerity is the ethical foundation that ensures you're guiding that journey with authenticity instead of manipulation. Together, they create a framework where influence happens without trickery, where boundaries are maintained fairly, and where behavioral change occurs because the person chooses it rather than being forced into it.

The BCSM is where Professional Sincerity becomes operational. Active listening becomes honest attentiveness and validation, not performative nodding while you wait for your turn to talk. Empathy becomes authentic reflection and emotional acknowledgment, not fake sympathy or empty reassurances. Rapport becomes trust built through mutual respect and consistency, not manufactured friendliness that collapses the moment you set a boundary. Influence becomes collaboration and validation that guide toward cooperation, not commands disguised as suggestions. And behavioral change happens in a place that feels safe and respected because of all those validated feelings and all that genuine understanding built along the way.

This is why FC2C insists on Professional Sincerity as the ethical core: you can't fake your way through the Stairway. You can't perform these steps like a memorized script while your tone and body language broadcast that you don't actually mean any of it. People sense inauthenticity, and when they do, every step collapses. The listening feels hollow, the empathy feels manufactured, the rapport never takes root, and influence becomes impossible. But when you show up sincerely, when you listen because you want to understand and validate because you genuinely see their struggle even when you disagree with their choices, the stairway works. Not every time. Not with everyone. But more often than not. And in crisis work, "more often than not" is the difference that matters.

Connecting BCSM to G.U.I.D.E.

The BCSM and G.U.I.D.E. work hand in hand. Think of it this way: Professional Sincerity opens the door. G.U.I.D.E. walks you through it. The BCSM is the stairway beyond the door. It's the psychology of what's happening as you walk.

When you Ground Yourself, you're preparing to engage in active listening without letting your own emotions hijack the encounter. When you Understand Emotion, you're applying empathy and emotional labeling to see what's really driving the behavior. When you Identify a Shared Goal, you're building rapport by showing the person you're both working toward the same outcome. When you Direct the Interaction, you're using influence and options to guide them toward safer choices. And when you Ensure Safety and Support, you're creating the conditions where behavioral change can actually happen.

They aren't separate systems. They're the architecture of From Crisis to Calm. The Five Pillars tell you what to prioritize. Professional Sincerity and its Five Principles tell you how to show up. G.U.I.D.E. and its Five Elements tell you how to move through the encounter. And the BCSM puts it all together, the psychology underneath the process. Every layer reinforces the others, and together they give you something no single model can provide on its own: a complete, adaptable system for moving people from crisis to calm.

Putting It All Together: The Stairway in Action

In a very simplified way, let's look at what the BCSM looks like in practice across different professional settings.

Outpatient Clinic

A woman walks into a community health clinic visibly shaking. She has just been told that her insurance denied coverage for the medication she has been on for two years. Without it, she knows what happens. She has been through withdrawal before. She isn't yelling, but her voice is tight, her hands are trembling, and she is talking fast, repeating herself, circling back to the same words: "They can't do this to me."

The intake coordinator steps out from behind the desk and sits in the chair next to her.

Active Listening: "You've been on this medication for two years and now they're telling you it's not covered. That's a lot to process all at once."

Empathy: "It sounds like you're scared about what happens next, and that makes complete sense."

Rapport: "How long have you been dealing with this? Walk me through what they told you."

Influence: "Here's what I'd like to do. I can get our patient advocate on the phone right now to start working the appeal, or I can connect you with the prescriber to talk about a bridge supply while we sort this out. Which would help you most right now?"

Behavioral Change: Her hands stop shaking. She takes a breath. "The advocate. I need someone to fight this with me."

The coordinator didn't fix the insurance denial. He didn't override the system. But he moved the woman from spiraling panic to a concrete next step by walking her up the stairway.

Social Services Home Visit

A case manager arrives at a client's home for a scheduled visit. Before he can even introduce himself, the client is in the doorway, arms crossed, voice rising. His SNAP benefits were cut two weeks ago with no explanation. He has two kids, an empty refrigerator, and a letter from the state that reads like it was written by a machine. He isn't interested in being managed. He is interested in someone telling him why his family can't eat.

Active Listening: "Your benefits were cut two weeks ago and nobody's explained why. That's two weeks of trying to figure out how to feed your kids."

Empathy: "That sounds terrifying. You're doing everything you're supposed to do and the system pulled the rug out."

Rapport: "Are those pictures of your kids? You must be very proud of them."

Influence: "Here's what I'd like to do. I can call the eligibility office right now from your kitchen table and find out exactly what happened, or I can set up an emergency appointment for tomorrow morning so we can sit down with a supervisor together. Which one works better for you?"

Behavioral Change: His arms uncross. He steps back from the doorway. "Call them now. I need to know what happened."

The case manager didn't restore his benefits on the spot. He didn't have that power. But he moved the client from ready to slam the door to sitting at his own table while someone fought alongside him. That's the stairway.

Church Office

A woman comes into the church office unannounced on a Tuesday afternoon. She is asking to speak with the pastor, but he isn't in. The office administrator tells her he is available Thursday, and the woman's composure breaks. She starts crying, then shifts to anger, saying nobody in this church actually cares, that she has been coming here for three years and when she finally needs help, nobody is around. Her voice is getting louder. Other staff are starting to look.

Active Listening: "You came here today because you needed to talk to someone, and finding out he's not here feels like one more door that closed on you."

Empathy: "It sounds like something happened that brought you here today, and the weight of it's hitting you all at once."

Rapport: "You said you've been part of this church for three years. This place matters to you. Tell me what's going on."

Influence: "I want to make sure you get the support you came here for. I can sit with you right now and listen, or I can call Pastor Murray and see if he can speak with you by phone this afternoon. What would help most?"

Behavioral Change: She wipes her eyes. Her breathing slows. "Can you call him? I just need to talk to someone who knows me."

The administrator wasn't a counselor. But she didn't panic, she didn't dismiss, and she didn't hide behind a scheduling policy. She walked the woman up the stairway, one step at a time.

When the Stairway Does Not Work

Let's be honest: the BCSM doesn't work on everyone. Nothing is 100 percent. There will always be people who refuse to engage, situations where the emotional intensity is too high, moments where communication simply isn't enough, or an immediate threat presents itself.

When you're confronted with an immediate threat, someone displaying hostile intent with means, opportunity, and intent all present, the BCSM isn't your tool. Safety comes first. Disengage. Get help.

Remember the discussion of hostile intent from earlier chapters. When someone has transitioned from crisis behavior to predatory behavior, when their goal is violence rather than emotional release, options aren't going to help. A person who has decided to hurt someone isn't looking for a way out. They aren't seeking validation or autonomy or control over their choices. They've moved past the point where communication tools are effective. If you're seeing pre-attack indicators that cluster, you aren't in an options conversation anymore. You're in a safety response situation.

Even when the stairway doesn't result in voluntary compliance, the groundwork still matters. A person who has been listened to, validated, and offered choices is less likely to fight when force becomes necessary. The encounter is shorter. The resistance is lower. The outcome is safer for everyone. So even when the BCSM "fails" to produce voluntary behavioral change, it hasn't truly failed. It has created conditions that make whatever comes next less dangerous and more dignified than it would have been otherwise.

The BCSM Is a Journey, Not a Checklist

Here's the final thing I'd like you to understand about the Behavioral Change Stairway Model: it's not a checklist you complete and move on from, and it's not a linear script you follow rigidly without variation. Like any journey involving real people in real crisis, it can be messy and unpredictable and rarely follows the clean path you would draw on paper.

Remember, people are unpredictable. Sometimes you'll move up the stairs quickly because the person was just on the edge of crisis and your listening pulled them back almost immediately. Sometimes you'll spend a long time on one step because that's where the person is stuck and they need to stay there until they're ready to move. Sometimes you might move up two steps and then drop back down one because the person's emotional state shifts. Something triggers them, a memory surfaces, their fear spikes again, and you have to rebuild rapport before you can regain influence. That's okay. That's what working with human beings looks like.

The stairway gives you direction and a map, showing you where you're trying to go and what each phase of the journey requires. But how you get there, the specific words you use, the pace you move at, the moments when you pause and the moments when you push gently forward, that's where your professional judgment, your authenticity, and your experience come in.

Moving Forward

The FBI created the BCSM for life-and-death negotiations, for situations where getting it wrong meant someone died. But the reason it works across every profession, from healthcare to education to social services to retail to loss prevention, is because it's based on how human beings actually work: how our brains respond to stress, how our nervous systems regulate, how we move from emotional reactivity back to rational thinking. That's universal. That doesn't change whether you're a hostage negotiator, a nurse, a teacher, a social worker, a retail manager, or a police officer.

Learn the stairway. Practice it and trust in it. And then make it your own, adapting it to your environment and your professional context while keeping the core psychology intact. When you combine the psychology of the BCSM with the ethics of Professional Sincerity, the operational framework of G.U.I.D.E., the communication fundamentals, and the behavioral recognition skills you've developed, you become someone who can actually move people from crisis to calm. And you do it the right way, through understanding, connection, and genuine skill.

That's From Crisis to Calm. That's the Behavioral Change Stairway Model. In the next chapter, we will take everything we've built, every framework, every skill, every principle, and look at how they come together in the real world, where encounters don't follow textbook patterns and every situation demands that you think, adapt, and respond with everything you have.

Notes

1. For the FBI's adoption of crisis negotiation, see Gary Noesner, "Fifty Years of FBI Crisis (Hostage) Negotiation," *FBI Law Enforcement Bulletin*, August 6, 2024.

2. For Carl Rogers's foundational work on active listening, see Carl R. Rogers and Richard Evans Farson, *Active Listening* (1957; repr., Mansfield Center, CT: Martino Publishing, 2015). See also Noesner, "Fifty Years of FBI Crisis (Hostage) Negotiation."

3. For the origins and application of the Behavioral Change Stairway Model, see Gregory M. Vecchi, Vincent B. Van Hasselt, and Stephen J. Romano, "Crisis (Hostage) Negotiation: Current Strategies and Issues in High-Risk Conflict Resolution," *Aggression and Violent Behavior* 10, no. 5 (2005): 533–551. See also Gary Noesner, *Stalling for Time: My Life as an FBI Hostage Negotiator* (New York: Random House, 2010).

4. For the post-Waco reorganization, see Noesner, *Stalling for Time*; and Noesner, "Fifty Years of FBI Crisis (Hostage) Negotiation."

5. Ralph G. Nichols and Leonard A. Stevens, "Listening to People," *Harvard Business Review* 35, no. 5 (September–October 1957): 85–92. Nichols and Stevens found approximately 50 percent retention immediately after listening, declining to roughly 25 percent over time. The thinking-speed range of 400–800 words per minute, compared with an average speaking rate of 125–175 words per minute, reflects the conservative end of estimates reported in listening research.

6. Chris Voss, *Never Split the Difference: Negotiating As If Your Life Depended on It* (New York: Harper Business, 2016). The original study Voss references is Rick B. van Baaren, Rob W. Holland, Bregje Steenaert, and Ad van Knippenberg, "Mimicry for Money: Behavioral Consequences of Imitation," *Journal of Experimental Social Psychology* 39 (2003): 393–398.

7. Matthew D. Lieberman, Naomi I. Eisenberger, Molly J. Crockett, Sabrina M. Tom, Jennifer H. Pfeifer, and Baldwin M. Way, "Putting Feelings into Words: Affect Labeling Disrupts Amygdala Activity in Response to Affective Stimuli," *Psychological Science* 18, no. 5 (2007): 421–428.

8. Daniel Goleman, *Emotional Intelligence: Why It Can Matter More Than IQ* (New York: Bantam Books, 1995).

9. For the distinction between ethical influence and manipulation in crisis negotiation, see McMains and Mullins, *Crisis Negotiations: Managing Critical Incidents and Hostage Situations in Law Enforcement and Corrections*, 5th ed. (New York: Routledge, 2014). See also Tom R. Tyler, *Why People Obey the Law* (Princeton, NJ: Princeton University Press, 2006) on procedural justice and voluntary compliance.

10. On social identity theory and the psychological significance of group membership recognition, see Henri Tajfel and John C. Turner, "An Integrative Theory of Intergroup Conflict," in *The Social Psychology of Intergroup Relations,* ed. William G. Austin and Stephen Worchel (Monterey, CA: Brooks/Cole, 1979), 33–47; and Henri Tajfel, *Human Groups and Social Categories: Studies in Social Psychology* (Cambridge: Cambridge University Press, 1981).

11. Voss, *Never Split the Difference,* especially Chapter 7, on calibrated questions as a tool for restoring a sense of control and authority to the other party.

12. Jon Jecker and David Landy, "Liking a Person as a Function of Doing Him a Favour," *Human Relations* 22, no. 4 (1969): 371–378.

13. On the window of tolerance and its neurobiological basis in affect regulation, see Daniel J. Siegel, *The Developing Mind: Toward a Neurobiology of Interpersonal Experience* (New York: Guilford Press, 1999), 281–282. See also Daniel J. Siegel, *Mindsight: The New Science of Personal Transformation* (New York: Bantam Books, 2010).

14. On co-regulation as an interpersonal neurobiological process, see Stephen W. Porges, *The Polyvagal Theory: Neurophysiological Foundations of Emotions, Attachment, Communication, and Self-Regulation* (New York: W. W. Norton, 2011). See also Porges and Lewis, "The Polyvagal Hypothesis," cited in note 2 of Chapter 9.

15. On the directing, guiding, and following communication style framework that underlies this principle, see William R. Miller and Stephen Rollnick, *Motivational Interviewing: Helping People Change,* 3rd ed. (New York: Guilford Press, 2013), Chapter 1. The authors describe a guiding style that sits between directing and following, matching the person's current state before moving them toward change.

16. Paul M. Fitts and Michael I. Posner, *Human Performance* (Belmont, CA: Brooks/Cole, 1967). The three-stage model, cognitive, associative, and autonomous, is the foundational framework in motor learning research and has been applied broadly to professional skill acquisition across many disciplines.

17. On the primacy of perceived intent in interpersonal evaluation, see Fritz Heider, *The Psychology of Interpersonal Relations* (New York: John Wiley & Sons, 1958), especially Chapter 4, "The Naive Analysis of Action," which establishes intentionality as the foundational criterion by which people judge the behavior of others. For a contemporary structural elaboration, see Bertram F. Malle, Steve Guglielmo, and Andrew E. Monroe, "A Theory of Blame," *Psychological Inquiry* 25, no. 2 (2014): 147–186.

CHAPTER 11: PUTTING IT ALL TOGETHER

From Theory to Practice

You have the pieces. Now let's see how they work together in real encounters from beginning to end, and talk about what to do when things don't go as planned.

Complete Encounter: Social Services Home Visit

Sarah, a DSS eligibility worker is conducting a home visit to assess a benefits application. The client has been difficult to reach, has missed previous appointments, and the worker is required to complete this assessment to process the application.

The Setup

The worker arrives at the address and knocks. Through the window, she can see someone moving inside, but no one comes to the door. She knocks again and identifies herself clearly: "Ms. Johnson? I'm Sarah from Social Services. We had an appointment scheduled for today about your application."

After a long pause, the door opens partway. A woman in her 30s stands in the doorway, not making eye contact, arms crossed, body partially blocking the entrance. The worker is already reading the scene. Defensive body language, crossed arms, blocking the doorway, no invitation inside despite the scheduled appointment. The environment visible through the door shows clutter but nothing alarming. No signs of substance use or immediate safety concerns. The woman appears tired and wary, but not aggressive.

Her shoulders are tense. Her jaw is tight. She is standing in a position that could quickly close the door if needed. These are protective behaviors, not aggressive ones. She is guarding, not attacking.

Sarah processes all of this in seconds. This person is stressed and defensive, maybe expecting judgment or carrying bad experiences with "the system." The missed appointments may not have been defiance. Maybe Ms. Johnson was overwhelmed or just avoiding it. The underlying need is probably help, but the barrier is fear, maybe of judgment, maybe of past negative experiences with authority figures. And both the worker and the client actually want the same thing, to get this assessment done so benefits can be processed. The client just doesn't realize that yet.

Sarah takes a breath, notices her own frustration about the missed appointments and the difficult caseload, and consciously sets it aside. She makes her call: lead with human connection, not authority or policy.

The worker speaks, keeping her voice calm and warm: "Ms. Johnson, I appreciate you opening the door. I know today might not be the easiest day for this." She pauses, lets the acknowledgment land. "I'm here because you applied for assistance, and I want to make sure we get that moving for you. Can we talk for a few minutes?"

Ms. Johnson's posture softens slightly. She still doesn't make eye contact, but she opens the door a bit wider. "I guess. But the house is a mess."

"That's completely okay. Making sure you and your kids are safe and getting you the support you need is all that matters."

Ms. Johnson steps back and lets her in.

Walking Up the Stairway

Sarah sits down at the kitchen table, pulling out paperwork but not diving into it immediately. She knows that if she goes straight to bureaucratic questions, she will lose the fragile trust she just started building.

"Before we get into the paperwork," the worker says, "can you tell me what's been going on that made you apply for assistance? Help me understand your situation."

Ms. Johnson hesitates, then starts talking. She has been out of work for three months. Her car broke down, which made it impossible to get to her job. She couldn't afford to fix it. She lost the job. Now she is behind on rent, her utilities are about to be shut off, and she has two kids to feed. She applied for assistance, but the process feels impossible. So much paperwork, so many appointments, people asking the same questions over and over. She missed the last two appointments because she didn't have childcare and couldn't bring the kids with her on the bus.

The worker listens. When Ms. Johnson pauses, she responds: "That sounds absolutely exhausting. You've been dealing with one thing after another, and every time you try to get help, it feels like the system just makes it harder."

Ms. Johnson's eyes well up. "Exactly. I'm trying. I'm really trying. But it feels like nobody cares."

The worker doesn't say "I understand what you're going through." Instead: "It's been a fight to hold this together, and every time you reach out for help it feels like you hit another wall. That's exhausting."

Something shifts. Ms. Johnson wipes her eyes and looks directly at Sarah for the first time. "Can you actually help me, or is this just more paperwork that goes nowhere?"

"Here's what we can do," Sarah says, leaning forward and nodding slightly to signal engagement. "There's no guarantee you'll be approved for everything you applied for. But this assessment gets completed today so your application moves forward. Everything gets documented correctly so there are no delays. And if there are resources available, food banks, utility assistance, job placement, we'll check into that information before we're done. That's what today can look like. Does that sound helpful?"

Ms. Johnson nods. "Yeah. Okay."

Now the worker can start directing the interaction toward the specific information she needs for the assessment. She does it through options, not commands. Worth pausing here for a moment: that was also a strategic use of the word "but." Remember before how we talked about "but" negating everything that comes before it? Here is a great placement of it, to take away from the only negative sounding part of what Sarah is saying, that there's no guarantee Ms. Johnson will be approved for everything. It's a potential barb that's been dealt with very effectively.

"Let's get through this assessment so we can move your application forward," the worker says. "I need to verify some information and ask about your household situation. We can go through the paperwork question by question together, or if it's easier, you can tell me your situation in your own words and I'll fill in the forms based on what you tell me. Which would feel better?"

Ms. Johnson chooses the second option, telling her story while the worker fills in forms. It feels more like a conversation than an interrogation.

Throughout the assessment, the worker continues using options whenever possible:

"We'll need to see documentation of your income and expenses. Do you have those handy now, or would you rather gather them while I ask these other questions and we'll come back to that?"

"For this section, I can explain what they're asking for first, or if you'd rather just read it yourself and ask questions, that works too. What's easier?"

Small choices. Each one preserves dignity and autonomy while moving the assessment forward.

Forty-five minutes later, the assessment is complete. Ms. Johnson has provided all necessary information, Sarah has documented everything clearly, and they've moved from defensive standoff to collaborative problem-solving.

"Okay," the worker says, "here's where we are. Your application is complete. It'll go to review within the next week, and you should hear something within ten to fourteen days, maybe sooner. While you're waiting, here's a list of food pantries in your area that don't require appointments, here's the contact for the emergency utility assistance program, and here's the number for a job placement service that specifically helps people who have transportation issues."

Ms. Johnson takes the paper, looks at it. "Thank you. Seriously. I didn't think anyone was going to help."

Ms. Johnson showed up for future appointments because the worker also said, "I know getting here's hard. If you need to reschedule the follow-up, call me directly and we'll figure something out." Sarah got what she needed professionally, and Ms. Johnson got treated like a human being instead of a problem.

That's FC2C from start to finish, every element working together.

Complete Encounter: Hospital Emergency Behavioral Health Crisis

Different context, higher volatility, tighter time constraints. Same framework.

The Setup

A man in his late 20s was brought to the ED by police on a mental health hold. He is pacing in the behavioral health room, talking rapidly, making poor eye contact. The nurse entering the room immediately begins reading the situation.

He is agitated but not aggressive. He is pacing in a pattern, window to door, window to door. Talking to himself but not screaming. Hands visible, no weapons. Responding to internal stimuli, possibly hallucinating, but still aware of the external environment. He looks up when the nurse enters. This is crisis behavior, not predatory behavior. He is dysregulated, possibly psychotic, but not hunting for a target. The pacing is self-regulation, not attack preparation.

The nurse processes her assessment: this person is in severe distress, likely experiencing symptoms he can't control, and probably terrified. The police transport could have felt like being kidnapped. He isn't trying to hurt anyone. He is trying to survive whatever his brain is telling him is happening. She decides on a slow approach, calm presence, active listening to understand what he is experiencing, and options to restore some sense of control.

The nurse takes a breath at the doorway, checks her own fear response. This patient is larger than her and is agitated. He could become dangerous. She acknowledges that reality without letting it drive her behavior. Her goal is assessment and stabilization, not control through dominance.

She observes the pacing, the rapid speech, the hypervigilance. This looks like terror being managed through movement. Both she and the patient actually want the same thing, for him to feel safer. But he doesn't know that yet. The police brought him against his will. He probably thinks the hospital is part of whatever threat he is perceiving.

The nurse stays in the doorway, doesn't enter his space yet. She keeps her hands visible, her posture open. "Hi, I'm Amanda. I'm one of the nurses here. Looks like you had a pretty rough night. Do you mind if I come in and we talk for a minute?"

The man stops pacing, looks at her warily. "You're going to lock me up."

Amanda doesn't lie. "Right now you're in the hospital because the police brought you here. My job is to make sure you're safe and figure out what's going on. Can I sit down over there or should I talk from here?" She points to a chair near the door, not blocking his exit path.

He nods slightly. She sits. He continues pacing but less frantically.

"I need to ask you some questions so I can understand what's been happening and figure out how to help. But before I do that, I want to make sure you're okay. Do you need water?" (Pause) "Are you hungry?" (Pause) "Are you in any physical pain?"

Active Listening and Empathy Combined

"Can you tell me what happened tonight that brought you here?"

He launches into a story that's partly coherent, partly delusional. Someone is following him. His phone is tapped. They sent the police to get him. The hospital is probably part of it. But woven through the paranoia are real details: he hasn't slept in three days, he stopped taking his medication two weeks ago because he couldn't afford the refill, and he lost his housing.

Amanda listens without challenging the delusions. She focuses on the emotional truth and the factual details she can work with.

"It sounds like you've been terrified that someone is trying to hurt you, and on top of that you haven't slept in three days, and you've been without your medication. That's a lot to deal with."

"I haven't slept because if I sleep, they'll get me." His agitation spikes slightly.

"Okay. So, sleep feels dangerous right now because of what you think might happen. Here's what I need to know. Have you been safe? Have you hurt yourself or anyone else?"

"No. I'm not the dangerous one. *They're* the dangerous ones."

"Okay. That's important for me to know. Here's what we need to figure out: you need sleep, you need your medication, and you need to be somewhere safe while your brain settles down. That's what I can help with. How we do that, whether you're comfortable staying in this room, whether you'd feel better in a different space, whether you want me to contact anyone who can support you, we can talk about that. But the basic plan is get you safe, get you stabilized, and figure out the next steps. Does that make sense?"

Outcome

He doesn't magically become asymptomatic. But he stops pacing. He accepts water and a sandwich. He agrees to stay in the behavioral health area while they wait for psychiatry to evaluate him. He takes his medication when it arrives because the nurse frames it as "this might help you feel less on edge while we figure things out" rather than "you're mentally ill and need treatment."

What to Do When Things Are Not Working

Sometimes you do everything right and the encounter still escalates. Sometimes the person isn't responsive to communication. Sometimes you run out of time or space or options. This is where understanding when and how to shift approaches becomes critical.

Recognizing When Your Approach Is Not Landing

Pay attention to behavioral feedback. If you're using active listening and empathy but the person is getting more agitated rather than less, if their speech is getting faster and louder despite your calm presence, if their body language is becoming more threatening instead of relaxing, your current approach isn't working.

This doesn't mean you did something wrong. It might mean the person is too dysregulated for communication to work right now. Their amygdala is fully in control and no amount of good communication will bring the prefrontal cortex back online yet. They might need space, time, or medical intervention before words will help. It might mean you're missing something about what they actually need. Maybe you're validating frustration when the real emotion is fear. Maybe you're offering autonomy when what they need is clear direction. Maybe there's a physical need, pain, hunger, exhaustion, that's overriding everything else. It might mean there's a factor you don't know about that's driving the behavior: a medical issue, intoxication, severe mental illness, a trauma trigger, a cultural misunderstanding, something that changes the equation in ways you can't see. Or it might mean that time has run out and the situation requires a different response because the environment has become unsafe or the window for communication has closed.

When you notice things escalating despite your best efforts, there are several ways to shift:

Pass the encounter to someone else. Sometimes a different voice, a different gender, or a different role changes everything. The person who couldn't talk to you might talk to your supervisor, your partner, someone from a different department. That isn't failure. That's strategy. Don't let ego prevent you from using the most effective tool, even if that tool is someone else. There were many, many times during my career that I handed the torch to another officer.

Change the environment. Sometimes the location is the problem. Too many people watching. Maybe you're in an area that's too confined or too exposed. Offering to step outside, move to a different room, go somewhere with more privacy or more space can completely shift the dynamic. The change of scenery interrupts the escalation pattern and gives both of you a chance to reset.

Slow everything down. Sometimes you unconsciously match the person's urgency, and that actually makes things worse. Intentionally slowing your speech, taking longer pauses, suggesting a brief break can interrupt the escalation cycle. "Let's both take a breath here" isn't weakness.

Bring in additional support before you need it. Don't wait until things are dangerous to call for backup. If your gut tells you a situation is deteriorating, get more people involved while you still have communication and cooperation, not after things have gone physical. Additional presence can be calming, or it can be escalating depending on how it's introduced. "How about bringing in my supervisor to help us figure this out?" lands differently than "I'm calling security because you're out of control."

Set clearer boundaries. Sometimes empathy and options have created the impression that there are no boundaries at all, and the person is testing to see what they can get away with. When that happens, you shift from influence to clear direction: "I've been trying to work with you on this, and I'm noticing we're not getting anywhere. Here's what we need to do now." The boundary itself becomes the structure that helps them regulate.

When Communication Is No Longer the Right Tool

Remember what we covered in Chapters 4 and 6 about hostile intent. If someone crosses from crisis behavior into predatory behavior, if you see the M.O.I., the means, opportunity, and intent, the time for talking is over and safety becomes the only goal. Create distance. Get barriers between you and the threat. Get help. Disengage if possible. Keeping in mind that you're responsible for your actions, use whatever force is necessary and legally justified if disengagement isn't possible.

This isn't a failure of the framework. This is appropriate recognition that you're in a different situation than you thought you were in, and different situations require different responses.

Practical Realities That Make or Break Encounters

We've covered the frameworks, the skills, and the science. Most of what follows has been touched on throughout this book. But there are a few practical realities worth emphasizing here because they're the things that separate professionals who are good in the classroom from professionals who are effective in the field.

The first is flexibility. The ability to adjust your approach, to try different angles, to pivot when something isn't working, that's a sign of skill, not indecision. Rigid adherence to one method when it's clearly not working is what gets people hurt.

The second is face-saving. This one doesn't get enough attention in training. People need to be able to back down from escalated positions without feeling humiliated. If you corner them, embarrass them, or make them feel like they lost, you risk triggering a last-minute surge of aggression or resistance because saving face becomes more important than de-escalation. Always give them a way out that preserves some dignity. Let them exit the crisis without feeling defeated. Chances are you or someone you work with will encounter them again, and although you may not remember them, they will remember you and how they felt about that encounter.

The third is knowing when to leave certain topics alone. Religion and politics are emotional landmines in crisis situations, even when you think you agree with the person. People in crisis can flip positions rapidly, and what seemed like a connection point can become a dealbreaker in seconds. If they bring it up, let them vent about it, stay noncommittal, and redirect back to the immediate situation.

And the universal rule underneath all of it, as we've said throughout this book: be genuine. Everything works better when it's authentic, and everything becomes more damaging when it's paired with insincerity.

Knowing Your Limits

There's a mythology in helping people that you're supposed to be infinitely patient, infinitely compassionate, infinitely available. That if you're good at your job, you can handle anything, bounce back from everything, absorb unlimited trauma without it affecting you.

That mythology is dangerous. It burns people out, it breaks them. That makes them worse at their jobs, not better, because exhausted and dysregulated professionals can't regulate others effectively.

Let's talk honestly about limits.

You Can't Help Everyone

Some people are beyond your capacity to help in the moment. Maybe they're too escalated, maybe they're too intoxicated, maybe their mental illness is too acute, maybe they've decided on violence and communication is no longer effective. Maybe you don't have the training or the resources or the time to provide what they actually need. That isn't failure, it's reality.

Your job is to do what you can with what you have in the time available. Sometimes "what you can do" is stabilize the immediate situation, get the person connected to someone better equipped to help, or simply keep everyone safe until additional resources arrive.

You don't have to fix everything and you can't save everyone. You have to show up professionally, do your best, and know when your best isn't enough for the situation at hand.

You Are Allowed to Disengage

If a situation becomes dangerous, if your safety is genuinely threatened, if the person transitions from crisis behavior to predatory behavior, if the environment becomes untenable, outside of law enforcement, in most cases, you're allowed to leave. You're allowed to stop engaging. You're allowed to prioritize your own safety. It's not abandonment, it's survival. Dead heroes don't help anyone.

Know your agency's protocols for disengagement. Know when you're supposed to call for backup, when you're supposed to retreat, when you're supposed to switch to a purely defensive posture. And when those conditions are met, follow the protocol. Don't try to be a hero. Don't convince yourself you can handle it alone when every indicator says you can't.

The Check Engine Light

Your body and brain have warning systems that tell you when something isn't functioning correctly. Changes in sleep patterns. Irritability. Emotional numbness. Overreacting to small stressors. Difficulty concentrating. Withdrawing from relationships. Intrusive thoughts about cases. Nightmares. Physical symptoms without medical cause. The list goes on.

These are your check engine lights. They're telling you something is wrong and needs attention.

Most people ignore them. "I'm fine. I can handle it. It's just stress. It'll pass." Just like a real check engine light in a car. "Oh, it's just on because I hit 50,000 miles," or "I'll take care of it next week." And then they keep driving with the check engine light on until something breaks completely: the engine seizes, the catalytic converter fails, you've got a bad battery. Ignoring *your* check engine light might mean panic attacks, substance abuse, relationship collapse, getting hurt on the job because your judgment was impaired by exhaustion and unprocessed trauma.

Don't ignore your check engine light.

If you notice these symptoms in yourself, do something about it. Talk to someone you trust. Seek professional support if needed. Take time off if that's possible. Change your workload if you can. Address it before it becomes a crisis. You deserve the same quality of care you give to the people you serve.

And if you notice these signs in a colleague, say something. Ask if they're okay. Offer support. Sometimes people don't even realize how much something affected them until another person names it. Peer support is often the strongest safety net there is.

Practical Self-Care That Actually Works

Let's be honest: the phrase "self-care" has become almost meaningless, when what you really need is systemic change in how your job treats you. But there are concrete things that actually help with the cumulative impact of crisis work.

Sleep. Not just any sleep, regular sleep, enough sleep, like six to eight hours consistently. Sleep is when your brain processes trauma and emotional experiences. Without it, everything builds up and nothing gets resolved. Your cognitive function degrades and your emotional regulation suffers. Your judgment gets impaired. Sleep is a necessity.

Physical activity. It doesn't have to be intense exercise. Even short walks help. Movement processes stress hormones, regulates mood, and gives your body something to do with all the adrenaline that crisis work generates. Twenty minutes of walking does more for stress management than an hour of sitting and worrying.

Real separation between work and life. When you're off duty, be off duty. Don't live every moment waiting for the next crisis. Don't bring work stress home and let it bleed into every relationship and every moment of supposed rest. Be where your feet are. Be present with the people who matter to you outside of work.

Connection with people who aren't in crisis. Time with family, friends, colleagues where you aren't processing trauma or solving problems. Just being human with other humans. Laughing. Talking about normal things. Remembering that life exists outside of crisis response.

Professional support when needed. Therapy isn't weakness. Peer support groups aren't for people who can't handle the job. They're maintenance, like changing the oil in your car. You do it to prevent breakdown, not just to fix something after it's already broken. If you work in crisis response long enough, you will need professional support at some point. That isn't a character flaw, it's a predictable consequence of this difficult work.

The Long Game

Crisis work is a marathon, not a sprint. If you burn yourself out trying to save everyone, trying to be available 24/7, trying to handle more than any human can reasonably handle, you will flame out. And then you won't help anyone, including yourself, because you will be too broken to function.

The goal is sustainability. Show up professionally. Do good work. Take care of yourself. Set boundaries. Ask for help when you need it. Process what you're carrying. Rest when you can. And accept that you're human, which means you have limits, you will make mistakes, and you can't do everything.

Sustainability allows you to keep doing this work for years instead of months, to stay effective instead of burning out, to actually serve the people who need you instead of just adding yourself to the casualty list.

The Framework Is a Map, Not a Script

FC2C isn't a script to memorize and recite. It's a framework to internalize and adapt.

You take what you've learned and make it your own. You adapt it to your context, your population, your environment, your personality. You keep the core principles intact while being flexible about application.

Some encounters will move through the BCSM quickly. Some will take hours. Some will loop back through earlier steps multiple times. Some will require you to adjust on the fly because the situation doesn't allow for the full process. That's okay, and it's normal. That's how it works with real humans in real crisis.

The frameworks give you direction, not dictation. They tell you where you're trying to go and what psychological principles are in play, but *how* you get there depends on the specific encounter, the specific person, and your own professional judgment informed by training and experience.

Learn them, practice them, trust them, and then make them yours. That's From Crisis to Calm, and it's what this book has been building toward.

Now there's just one thing left to talk about: where you go from here.

CHAPTER 12:

WHERE YOU GO FROM HERE

You've got the framework, the science behind it, the ethics underneath it, and the skills to put it into practice. What happens next is up to you.

The temptation after finishing a book like this is to wait until you feel ready. To tell yourself you need more training, more practice, more confidence before you start applying what you've learned. That instinct is understandable, but it's wrong. You don't get good at this by studying it. You get good at this by doing it.

Here's what to expect. At first, you may feel like you've gotten worse. You will second-guess yourself, miss opportunities to use techniques you just read about, and fumble through moments you used to handle on autopilot. You may even feel like the techniques are too simple to work. That's normal. Psychologists call it conscious incompetence, the stage where you know what you don't know, and it's uncomfortable because you're hyper-aware of every mistake.[1] Most people quit here. They decide the techniques don't feel natural and go back to their old habits. Don't quit here.

Push through, and you will reach conscious competence, where the skills work but still require deliberate effort. You can do it well when there's time to think. You struggle when things move fast. Keep going. Eventually the frameworks disappear into your instincts, and you stop running through a checklist and start responding with fluency. That transition doesn't happen overnight, but it does happen.

Start small. You don't need a full-blown crisis to practice. Every interaction is an opportunity. The next time a colleague is frustrated about something you can't fix, validate the frustration without agreeing the policy is wrong. The next time you need information from someone, offer them a choice about how to provide it instead of issuing a directive. Practice listening a little longer before you respond. Pick one skill and use it on purpose. Then pick another.

The beauty of low-stakes practice is that mistakes cost you nothing. If you fumble an empathic response or offer options poorly, the worst that happens is a slightly awkward moment. But you learn, and next time you do it better. Over time, the individual skills stop being things you think about and become the way you operate.

You will also get it wrong sometimes in moments that matter. You will misread a situation, say the wrong thing, lose your composure, or realize halfway through an encounter that you should have taken a completely different approach. I've been doing this work for over thirty years, as a police officer, as a crisis negotiator, as a trainer, and I still learn from every difficult encounter. I still make mistakes. That isn't a sign that the training failed. That's the reality of working with real human beings in unpredictable situations. What matters is what you do after: adjust, learn from it, and show up better the next time.

One more thing. This work changes you. When you start paying attention to how people communicate under stress, you see it everywhere. You notice escalation patterns in everyday conversations. You catch yourself using the skills with your family, your friends, people in line at the grocery store. That isn't a side effect. That's the point. Crisis communication is really just communication, practiced with greater awareness and discipline. The better you get at it professionally, the better you get at it as a human being.

So go do the work. The people you serve are counting on you, even when they're yelling at you, shutting you out, or making your job as difficult as possible. Especially then. Because those are the moments that matter most, and you're now better equipped to meet them. If this book has given you tools to do that more effectively, then it has done what I intended.

From crisis to calm. You know how to get there.

Stay well and stay safe!

Notes

1. The conscious competence learning model is commonly attributed to Noel Burch of Gordon Training International, circa 1970s. The model describes the progression from unconscious incompetence through conscious incompetence, conscious competence, and finally unconscious competence.

BIBLIOGRAPHY

Arnsten, Amy F. T. "Stress Signalling Pathways That Impair Prefrontal Cortex Structure and Function." *Nature Reviews Neuroscience* 10, no. 6 (2009): 410–422.

Bolz, Frank, and Edward Hershey. *Hostage Cop*. New York: Rawson Associates, 1980.

Borum, Randy M., and Thomas Strentz. "The Borderline Personality: Negotiation Strategies." *FBI Law Enforcement Bulletin* 61, no. 8 (1992): 6–10.

Burch, Noel. Conscious competence learning model. Gordon Training International, circa 1970s.

California Bureau of Security and Investigative Services. "Training Requirements for Security Guards." Accessed February 12, 2026.

Centers for Disease Control and Prevention. "Emergency Department Visits for Mental Health Conditions and Substance Use Disorders." Analyses of National Hospital Ambulatory Medical Care Survey (NHAMCS) data, various years.

CIT International. "What Is CIT?" Accessed February 12, 2026. https://www.citinternational.org.

Coombs, W. Timothy. *Ongoing Crisis Communication: Planning, Managing, and Responding*. 5th ed. Thousand Oaks, CA: SAGE Publications, 2019.

Darling-Hammond, Linda, Roberta Furger, Patrick M. Shields, and Leib Sutcher. *Addressing California's Emerging Teacher Shortage: An Analysis of Sources and Solutions*. Palo Alto, CA: Learning Policy Institute, 2016.

Doyle, Arthur Conan. "A Scandal in Bohemia." In *The Adventures of Sherlock Holmes*. London: George Newnes, 1892.

Ekman, Paul. *Emotions Revealed: Recognizing Faces and Feelings to Improve Communication and Emotional Life*. 2nd ed. New York: Owl Books/Henry Holt, 2007.

Ekman, Paul. "Micro Expressions." In *The Oxford Companion to Emotion and the Affective Sciences*, edited by David Sander and Klaus R. Scherer. Oxford: Oxford University Press, 2009.

Ekman, Paul, and Wallace V. Friesen. "Constants Across Cultures in the Face and Emotion." *Journal of Personality and Social Psychology* 17, no. 2 (1971): 124–129.

Engel, Robin S., Nicholas Corsaro, Gregory T. Isaza, and Hannah D. McManus. "Assessing the Impact of De-Escalation Training on Police Behavior: Reducing Police Use of Force in the Louisville, KY Metro Police Department." *Criminology & Public Policy* 21, no. 2 (2022): 199–233.

Federal Aviation Administration. "Unruly Passengers." 2021 data. https://www.faa.gov/unruly.

Federal Bureau of Investigation. "Hate Crime Statistics." Annual reports.

Figley, Charles R., ed. *Compassion Fatigue: Coping with Secondary Traumatic Stress Disorder in Those Who Treat the Traumatized*. New York: Brunner/Mazel, 1995.

Fitts, Paul M., and Michael I. Posner. *Human Performance.* Belmont, CA: Brooks/Cole, 1967.

Florida Department of Agriculture and Consumer Services. "Class D Security Officer License Requirements." Accessed February 12, 2026.

Forbes, Stefan, dir. *Hold Your Fire*. IFC Films, 2021. Documentary.

Goleman, Daniel. *Emotional Intelligence: Why It Can Matter More Than IQ*. New York: Bantam Books, 1995.

Good, Ken J. *Got a Second? Boyd's OODA Cycle in the Close Quarter Battle Environment*. Progressive Combat Solutions. Accessed February 22, 2026. https://www.progressivecombat.com/pdfs/OODA.pdf.

Hatfield, Elaine, John T. Cacioppo, and Richard L. Rapson. *Emotional Contagion*. Cambridge: Cambridge University Press, 1993.

Heider, Fritz. *The Psychology of Interpersonal Relations.* New York: John Wiley & Sons, 1958.

International Association of Chiefs of Police (IACP). *National Consensus Policy and Discussion Paper on Use of Force*. January 2017, updated October 2020. https://www.theiacp.org/resources/policy-center-resource/use-of-force.

Jecker, Jon, and David Landy. "Liking a Person as a Function of Doing Him a Favour." *Human Relations* 22, no. 4 (1969): 371–378.

Joint Commission, The. "Workplace Violence Prevention Standards." R3 Report, Issue 30. June 18, 2021. https://www.jointcommission.org/standards/r3-report/r3-report-issue-30-workplace-violence-prevention-standards.

Kluge, P. F., and Thomas Moore. "The Boys in the Bank." *Life*, September 22, 1972.

Knowles, Malcolm S., Elwood F. Holton III, and Richard A. Swanson. *The Adult Learner: The Definitive Classic in Adult Education and Human Resource Development*. 8th ed. New York: Routledge, 2015.

Learning Policy Institute. "The Cost of Teacher Turnover." Research brief, September 2017. https://learningpolicyinstitute.org/product/the-cost-of-teacher-turnover.

Lieberman, Matthew D., Naomi I. Eisenberger, Molly J. Crockett, Sabrina M. Tom, Jennifer H. Pfeifer, and Baldwin M. Way. "Putting Feelings into Words: Affect Labeling Disrupts Amygdala Activity in Response to Affective Stimuli." *Psychological Science* 18, no. 5 (2007): 421–428.

Malle, Bertram F., Steve Guglielmo, and Andrew E. Monroe. "A Theory of Blame." *Psychological Inquiry* 25, no. 2 (2014): 147–186.

Mathieu, Françoise. *The Compassion Fatigue Workbook: Creative Tools for Transforming Compassion Fatigue and Vicarious Traumatization*. New York: Routledge, 2012.

McMains, Michael J., and Wayman C. Mullins. *Crisis Negotiations: Managing Critical Incidents and Hostage Situations in Law Enforcement and Corrections*. 5th ed. New York: Routledge, 2014.

Miller, William R., and Stephen Rollnick. *Motivational Interviewing: Helping People Change.* 3rd ed. New York: Guilford Press, 2013.

National Academies of Sciences, Engineering, and Medicine. *The Future of Nursing 2020–2030: Charting a Path to Achieve Health Equity*. Washington, DC: National Academies Press, 2021.

National Association of School Resource Officers. "School Safety and Threat Response Trends." 2022.

National Association of Social Workers. "Enhancing the Well-Being of Social Workers: Addressing Retention and Workforce Sustainability." March 2021. https://www.socialworkers.org.

National Center for Education Statistics (NCES). *Indicators of School Crime and Safety: 2022*. NCES 2023-092. Washington, DC: U.S. Department of Education, 2023. https://nces.ed.gov.

National Retail Federation. *2023 National Retail Security Survey*. https://nrf.com/research/national-retail-security-survey-2023.

New York State Division of Criminal Justice Services. "Security Guard Training in New York State." Accessed February 12, 2026.

New York State Special Commission on Attica. *Attica: The Official Report of the New York State Special Commission on Attica*. New York: Bantam Books, 1972.

Noesner, Gary. "Fifty Years of FBI Crisis (Hostage) Negotiation." *FBI Law Enforcement Bulletin*, August 6, 2024.

Noesner, Gary. *Stalling for Time: My Life as an FBI Hostage Negotiator*. New York: Random House, 2010.

Occupational Safety and Health Administration. *Guidelines for Preventing Workplace Violence for Healthcare and Social Service Workers*. OSHA 3148-04R 2015. https://www.osha.gov/sites/default/files/publications/osha3148.pdf.

OSHA. "Workplace Violence." U.S. Department of Labor. https://www.osha.gov/workplace-violence.

Ontario Police College, as cited in Toronto Police Service, *Chapter 15: Incident Response (Use of Force/De-Escalation) & Equipment*, Toronto Police Service Procedures (Toronto: Toronto Police Service, 2024). See also Ontario Police College, *Public-Police Interactions Training Aid Framework Document* (Aylmer, ON: Ontario Police College, 2023).

Porges, Stephen W. *The Polyvagal Theory: Neurophysiological Foundations of Emotions, Attachment, Communication, and Self-Regulation*. New York: W. W. Norton, 2011.

Porges, Stephen W., and Gregory F. Lewis. "The Polyvagal Hypothesis: Common Mechanisms Mediating Autonomic Regulation, Vocalizations, and Listening." In *Handbook of Behavioral Neuroscience*, vol. 19, 255–264. Elsevier, 2010.

Reaves, Brian A. "Private Security Guards: U.S., 2005." Bureau of Justice Statistics Special Report, NCJ 214915. Washington, DC: U.S. Department of Justice, 2008.

Reaves, Brian A. "State and Local Law Enforcement Training Academies, 2013." Bureau of Justice Statistics Special Report, NCJ 249784. Washington, DC: U.S. Department of Justice, 2016.

Reeve, Simon. *One Day in September: The Full Story of the 1972 Munich Olympics Massacre and the Israeli Revenge Operation "Wrath of God"*. New York: Arcade Publishing, 2006.

Ringstad, T. L. "Violence in the Workplace: A Study of Licensed Social Workers." *Social Work* 50, no. 4 (2005): 307–318.

Rogers, Carl R. *On Becoming a Person: A Therapist's View of Psychotherapy*. Boston: Houghton Mifflin, 1961.

Rogers, Carl R., and Richard Evans Farson. *Active Listening*. 1957. Reprint, Mansfield Center, CT: Martino Publishing, 2015.

Schlossberg, Harvey, and Lucy Freeman. *Psychologist with a Gun*. New York: Coward, McCann & Geoghegan, 1974.

Siegel, Daniel J. *The Developing Mind: How Relationships and the Brain Interact to Shape Who We Are.* New York: Guilford Press, 1999.

Siegel, Daniel J. *Mindsight: The New Science of Personal Transformation.* New York: Bantam Books, 2010.

Stamm, B. Hudnall. "The ProQOL Manual: The Professional Quality of Life Scale: Compassion Satisfaction, Burnout & Compassion Fatigue/Secondary Trauma Scales." 2010. https://proqol.org.

Strentz, Thomas. *Psychological Aspects of Crisis Negotiation*. 3rd ed. Boca Raton: CRC Press, 2017.

Substance Abuse and Mental Health Services Administration. *Key Substance Use and Mental Health Indicators in the United States: Results from the 2021 National Survey on Drug Use and Health*. HHS Publication No. PEP22-07-01-005, NSDUH Series H-57. https://www.samhsa.gov.

Tajfel, Henri, and John C. Turner. “An Integrative Theory of Intergroup Conflict.” In *The Social Psychology of Intergroup Relations,* edited by William G. Austin and Stephen Worchel, 33–47. Monterey, CA: Brooks/Cole, 1979.

Tajfel, Henri. *Human Groups and Social Categories: Studies in Social Psychology.* Cambridge: Cambridge University Press, 1981.

Texas Department of Public Safety. "Private Security, Training Requirements." Accessed February 12, 2026.

Theatro (a Motorola Solutions Company). *Retail Worker Safety Survey*. Conducted via Pollfish, March 23–24, 2024.

Tyler, Tom R. *Why People Obey the Law*. Princeton: Princeton University Press, 2006.

University of Memphis CIT Center. "Crisis Intervention Team (CIT) Programs." Accessed February 12, 2026. https://www.citinternational.org.

U.S. Bureau of Justice Statistics. "Law Enforcement Agency Census."

U.S. Bureau of Labor Statistics. "Census of Fatal Occupational Injuries (CFOI), Fatal Occupational Injuries by Event or Exposure." https://www.bls.gov/iif/.

U.S. Bureau of Labor Statistics. *Job Openings and Labor Turnover Survey (JOLTS)*. "Retail Trade: Annual Total Separations Rate."

U.S. Bureau of Labor Statistics. "Nonfatal Occupational Injuries and Illnesses Requiring Days Away from Work." Various years. https://www.bls.gov/iif/.

U.S. Children’s Bureau. "Child Welfare Workforce." In *Child Welfare Information Gateway*. Washington, DC: U.S. Department of Health and Human Services.

U.S. Children’s Bureau. "High Worker Turnover in Child Welfare Agencies." *Child Welfare Information Gateway* issue brief.

U.S. Department of Education, National Center for Education Statistics. *Teachers Threatened with Injury or Physically Attacked by Students: Indicator A05*. Washington, DC: NCES, 2023. https://nces.ed.gov/programs/coe/indicator/a05.

U.S. Department of Homeland Security. "Active Shooter: How to Respond." Washington, DC: DHS, 2008; updated 2017. https://www.cisa.gov/active-shooter-preparedness.

van Baaren, Rick B., Rob W. Holland, Kerry Kawakami, and Ad van Knippenberg. "Mimicry and Prosocial Behavior." *Psychological Science* 14, no. 1 (2003): 71–74.

Vecchi, Gregory M., Vincent B. Van Hasselt, and Stephen J. Romano. "Crisis (Hostage) Negotiation: Current Strategies and Issues in High-Risk Conflict Resolution." *Aggression and Violent Behavior* 10, no. 5 (2005): 533–551.

Voss, Chris. *Never Split the Difference: Negotiating As If Your Life Depended on It*. New York: Harper Business, 2016.

AFTERWORD:

Bringing From Crisis to Calm Into Your Organization

This book was written to reach beyond the classroom. Everything in these pages can be studied, practiced, and applied independently. But there is something that a book cannot replicate: the experience of practicing these skills in a live training environment, receiving real-time feedback, working through scenarios with colleagues, and building the kind of muscle memory that shows up when it matters most. That is what From Crisis to Calm training provides.

Practice with feedback. Reading about empathic stems is one thing. Using them in a role-play scenario while an experienced instructor coaches you through it is something else entirely.

Collaborative learning. Some of the most powerful moments in training happen when participants share their own experiences, the encounters that went well, the ones that did not, and the patterns they start recognizing once they have a framework for understanding them.

Customized content. Every training is adapted to the specific roles, authority levels, safety considerations, and organizational policies of the audience. The core curriculum is consistent, but the examples, scenarios, and applications are built around the work your people actually do.

Organizational impact. When an entire team trains together, they develop a shared language for talking about crisis encounters. That shared vocabulary improves debriefing, strengthens peer support, and creates a culture where de-escalation is valued as a professional skill.

Formats that work for you. From Crisis to Calm is available in multiple formats including full-day and multi-day programs, half-day focused sessions, and keynote presentations. Programs can be delivered on-site at your location or through other arrangements based on your organization's needs.

Talk to Me

If you are interested in bringing From Crisis to Calm to your organization, or if you would like to discuss how the training can be adapted to your team's specific challenges, I would welcome the conversation.

886 Consulting, LLC
Jeffrey G. Scholz
Owner and Lead Instructor
Website: www.886consulting.com
Email: jeff@886consulting.com

As a thank you for reading this book, I am offering readers an exclusive discount on From Crisis to Calm training services. Scan the QR code above to visit our website, where you can learn more about available programs and apply your reader discount when you reach out to schedule training for your organization.

Better communication. Safer outcomes.

APPENDIX

The following pages contain the core reference sheets used in From Crisis to Calm training. These are the same handouts provided to participants during live classes, designed to be practical, portable tools that reinforce the material covered throughout this book. Print them, copy them, keep them at your desk, or fold them into your pocket. They work best when they're within reach during the moments that matter.

RESPONDER HINTS

1) Listen Actively
- Give the person your full attention (eye contact, body language).
- Use minimal encouragers (nods, "I hear you," "Go on").
- Avoid interrupting or rushing them.

2) Validate Their Feelings
- Acknowledge their emotions without judgment ("It looks like this is really hard for you").
- Use empathetic statements:
- "That sounds overwhelming."
- "It makes sense that you feel this way."

3) Stay Calm & Regulate Your Own Reactions
- Keep your voice steady, slow, and neutral.
- Control your facial expressions and body language to remain non-threatening.
- Take a deep breath to keep yourself centered.

4) Provide Reassurance Without False Promises
- "You're not alone; I'm here to help."
- "We'll figure this out together."
- Avoid saying "calm down"; instead, offer guidance ("Let's take a deep breath together").

5) Give the Person Some Control

Offer choices:
- "Would you rather sit or stand while we talk?"
- "Do you want to talk here or somewhere quieter?"
- Let them set the pace of the conversation.

6) Ask Open-Ended Questions

Encourage them to express their thoughts:
- "Can you tell me what is going on?"
- "What is the hardest part about this for you?"
- Avoid "why" questions, which can feel accusatory.

7) Watch for Signs of Escalation
- Notice body language cues (clenched fists, pacing, rapid breathing).
- If the person escalates, give them space and consider removing yourself from the encounter.

BOUNDARY-SETTING CHEAT SHEET

These phrases help you maintain clear, respectful boundaries while demonstrating Professional Sincerity, empathy, and active listening. Use them to de-escalate, redirect, and retain control in challenging conversations.

Acknowledge + Redirect

- I hear that you're upset, and I want to help, but I can only do that if we keep this conversation respectful.
- I get that this is frustrating. I'm here to help you, but I can't do that while being yelled at.

Options-Based Boundaries

- Here's what I can do for you right now...
- You have a couple of options. I can explain them, and you can choose what works best.

Grounding the Conversation

- Let's focus on what we can do right now.
- I want to help, but I was hoping you could talk to me, not at me.

Personal Space / Safety

- I'm happy to continue this, but I'm hoping you could take a step back so we both feel safe.
- If you keep stepping toward me, I'll have to pause this conversation.

Time-Outs / Pauses

- Let's take a breath. I'm going to give us both a moment and check back in.
- We'll both get more out of this if we take 60 seconds to reset.

Respect-Based Framing

- I'll give you the same respect I ask in return. Can we agree on that while we talk?
- This space needs to stay safe for everyone. That includes you and me.

When Being Challenged or Dismissed

- You don't have to agree with me, but I need you to understand where I'm coming from.
- I'm not here to argue, I'm here to help solve this with you. Let's work together.

When Limits Are Reached

- I've done everything I can at this point. The next step is...
- I want to keep helping, but if this continues, I'll have to involve someone else.

When Someone Is Escalating Emotionally

- Your feelings are valid, and I want to support you. Let's find a way to talk about it that doesn't put us both on edge.
- It seems like you're feeling overwhelmed. I can stay here and talk, or I can give you space, your choice.

Emotional Labeling Feelings Words

Anger upset, irritated, mad, ticked off, pissed off, heated, fired up, agitated, worked up, bent out of shape, steamed, hot under the collar

Fear scared, afraid, nervous, worried, anxious, spooked, uneasy, on edge, shaken up, freaked out, panicked, rattled

Disgust sick of it, repulsed, turned off, grossed out, fed up with, can't stomach it, revolted by, done with, over it, appalled by, offended by, put off by

Sadness hurt, down, bummed out, heartbroken, crushed, devastated, lost, empty, defeated, heavy-hearted, low, broken

Frustration stuck, fed up, at your wit's end, exhausted, worn down, overwhelmed, discouraged, blocked, spinning your wheels, hitting a wall, beaten down, drained

Contempt disrespected, dismissed, looked down on, brushed off, belittled, put down, discounted, snubbed, blown off

www.ingramcontent.com/pod-product-compliance
Lightning Source LLC
LaVergne TN
LVHW061203120826
845149LV00011B/1884
9798995077503